Advanced Introduction to U.S. Environmental Law

Elgar Advanced Introductions are stimulating and thoughtful introductions to major fields in the social sciences, business and law, expertly written by the world's leading scholars. Designed to be accessible yet rigorous, they offer concise and lucid surveys of the substantive and policy issues associated with discrete subject areas.

The aims of the series are two-fold: to pinpoint essential principles of a particular field, and to offer insights that stimulate critical thinking. By distilling the vast and often technical corpus of information on the subject into a concise and meaningful form, the books serve as accessible introductions for undergraduate and graduate students coming to the subject for the first time. Importantly, they also develop well-informed, nuanced critiques of the field that will challenge and extend the understanding of advanced students, scholars and policy-makers.

For a full list of titles in the series please see the back of the book. Recent titles in the series include:

Maritime Law
Paul Todd

American Foreign Policy
Loch K. Johnson

Water Politics
Ken Conca

Business Ethics
John Hooker

Employee Engagement
Alan M. Saks and Jamie A. Gruman

Governance
Jon Pierre and B. Guy Peters

Demography
Wolfgang Lutz

Environmental Compliance and Enforcement
LeRoy C. Paddock

Migration Studies
Ronald Skeldon

Landmark Criminal Cases
George P. Fletcher

Comparative Legal Methods
Pier Giuseppe Monateri

U.S. Environmental Law
E. Donald Elliott and Daniel C. Esty

Advanced Introduction to

U.S. Environmental Law

E. DONALD ELLIOTT

Professor of law, Yale Law School, 1981–2020 and Distinguished Adjunct Professor, Antonin Scalia Law School, George Mason University, USA

DANIEL C. ESTY

Hillhouse Professor of Environmental Law and Policy, Yale School of the Environment and the Yale Law School, USA

Elgar Advanced Introductions

 Edward Elgar
PUBLISHING

Cheltenham, UK • Northampton, MA, USA

Published by
Edward Elgar Publishing Limited
The Lypiatts
15 Lansdown Road
Cheltenham
Glos GL50 2JA
UK

Edward Elgar Publishing, Inc.
William Pratt House
9 Dewey Court
Northampton
Massachusetts 01060
USA

A catalogue record for this book
is available from the British Library

Library of Congress Control Number: 2021945181

This book is available electronically on *Elgar Advanced Introductions: Law*
www.advancedintros.com

Printed on elemental chlorine free (ECF)
recycled paper containing 30% Post-Consumer Waste

ISBN 978 1 80037 489 8 (cased)
ISBN 978 1 80037 491 1 (paperback)
ISBN 978 1 80037 490 4 (eBook)

Typeset by Cheshire Typesetting Ltd, Cuddington, Cheshire

Printed and bound in the USA

Contents

Acknowledgments

No book like this one can be written without a team behind the scenes. We are grateful for the support we have received, but of course, we are solely responsible for the opinions and errors that remain.

We are especially appreciative of the support provided by the Yale Law School and the Yale School of the Environment—with special thanks to Law School Dean Heather Gerken and Environment School Dean Indy Burke. We have benefitted from the give-and-take with our faculty colleagues and students over many years, but most especially Bruce Ackerman, Carol Rose, Doug Kysar, and Gerald Torres.

For her substantive contributions to this volume, we wish to make special mention of Linda Abbott. We also want to thank a number of other friends and colleagues who read parts or all of the draft manuscript: Eric Biber, Sanne Knudsen, Linda Fisher, Rob Klee, Rita Schoeny and Jim Salzman.

This *Advanced Introduction to U.S. Environmental Law* is intended to introduce the reader to key concepts and controversies in the text, but also to provide references in the footnotes where the reader might go for further information on a wide variety of environmental topics. Tracking down the underlying materials entailed a great deal of editorial support by an outstanding team of student research assistants at Yale led by Gillian Cowley and including Alisa White, Liam Gunn, Sam Peltz, Mack Ramsden, Benjamin Santhouse-James (of Imperial College London), Isabella Soparkar, and Brent Mobbs—all of whom worked under the guidance of Tyler Yeargain, the Associate Director of the Yale Center for Environmental Law and Policy. We cannot thank them enough for their long hours and diligent efforts. All websites to which we refer in the text were live as of March 2021.

We also wish to express our appreciation to Stephen Harries, our editor at Edward Elgar Publishing, who invited us to write this book and guided the project from its first days to the appearance of the volume you now are reading. And we extend our thanks to others on the Elgar team who moved the manuscript through to publication and into the marketplace, including Beatrice McCartney and Caroline Cornish.

As with any book that summarizes a dynamic and growing field of law, the materials covered will continue to evolve. Policies will change, new regulations will be promulgated, cases decided, agency guidance and interpretations announced, private initiatives launched, and—perhaps someday—new laws passed. We invite you to help us keep the material fresh and accurate by posting updates on the *Advanced Introduction to U.S. Environmental Law* website at: envirolawbook.com. And for our readers, please check the website for updates.

E. Donald Elliott
Daniel C. Esty
New Haven, Connecticut
2021

Acronyms

ACC	American Chemistry Council
ACE	Affordable Clean Energy
ADR	Alternative Dispute Resolution
ANSI	American National Standards Institute
ANWR	Arctic National Wildlife Refuge
APA	Administrative Procedure Act
API	American Petroleum Institute
B2B	Business-to-Business
BACT	Best Available Control Technology
BAT	Best Available Technology
BMP	Best Management Practice
BOD	Biochemical Oxygen Demand
BOEMRE	Bureau of Ocean Energy Management, Regulation and Enforcement (at the Department of the Interior)
CAA	Clean Air Act
CAFE	Corporate Average Fuel Economy Standards
CASAC	Clean Air Science Advisory Committee (at EPA)
CBD	Convention on Biological Diversity
CBDR	Common but Differentiated Responsibility
CDC	Center for Disease Control
CE	Categorical Exclusion
CEQ	Council on Environmental Quality (at the White House)
CEQA	California Environmental Quality Act
CERCLA	Comprehensive Environmental Response Compensation and Liability Act
CFC	Chlorofluorocarbon
CITES	Convention in International Trade in Endangered Species
COP	Conference of the Parties
CPP	Clean Power Plan
CSR	Corporate Social Responsibility
CWA	Clean Water Act
CWSRF	Clean Water State Revolving Fund

CZMA   Coastal Zone Management Act
DEP   Department of Environmental Protection
DMR   Discharge Monitoring Report
EA   Environmental Assessment
EAB   Environmental Appeals Board (at EPA)
ECHA   European Chemicals Agency
EDF   Environmental Defense Fund
EIR   Environmental Impact Report
EIS   Environmental Impact Statement
EPA   Environmental Protection Agency
EPCRA   Emergency Planning and Community Right to Know Act
ESA   Endangered Species Act
ESG   Environmental, Social, and Governance
FDA   Food and Drug Administration
FIFRA   Federal Insecticide Fungicide Rodenticide Act
FIP   Federal Implementation Plan
FONSI   Finding of No Significant Impact
FQPA   Food Quality Protection Act
FWS   U.S. Fish and Wildlife Service
GHG   Greenhouse Gas
GWP   Global Warming Platform
HFC   Hydrofluorocarbon
IARC   International Agency for Research on Cancer
IPCC   Intergovernmental Panel on Climate Change (at the UN)
IPCS   International Programme on Chemical Safety
ISO   International Standards Organization
ITC   Investment Tax Credit
IUCN   International Union for Conservation of Nature
LAER   Lowest Achievable Emission Rate
LEP   Licensed Environmental Professional
LULUs   Locally Undesired Land Use
MACT   Maximum Achievable Control Technology
MATS   Mercury and Air Toxics Standard
MCL   Maximum Contaminant Level
MCLG   Maximum Contaminant Level Goal
MMS   Minerals Management Service (at the Department of
            Interior)
NAAQS   National Ambient Air Quality Standard
NAFTA   North American Free Trade Agreement
NASA   National Aeronautics and Space Administration
NCP   National Contingency Plan
NDC   Nationally Determined Contribution

NEPA	National Environmental Policy Act
NESHAPs	National Emission Standards for Hazardous Air Pollutants
NGO	Non-Governmental Organization
NIOSH	National Institute for Occupational Safety and Health (at CDC)
NMFS	National Marine Fisheries Service (at NOAA)
NOAA	National Oceanic and Atmospheric Administration (in the Department of Commerce)
NPDES	National Pollution Discharge Elimination System
NPDWRs	National Primary Drinking Water Regulations
NPL	National Priority List
NPRM	Notice of Proposed Rulemaking
NPS	National Park Service
NRDC	Natural Resources Defense Council
NSPS	New Source Performance Standard
NSR	New Source Review
OAR	Office of Air and Radiation (at EPA)
OECD	Organization for Economic Cooperation and Development
OEHHA	California Office of Health Hazard Assessment
OIRA	Office of Information and Regulatory Affairs (at the White House)
OMB	Office of Management and Budget (at the White House)
OPA90	Oil Pollution Act of 1990
ORD	Office of Research and Development (at EPA)
OSHA	Occupational Safety and Health Act
OSHA	Occupational Safety and Health Administration (at the Department of Labor)
PEL	Permissible Exposure Limit
PFAS	Per- and Poly-Fluoroalkyl Substances
POTW	Publicly Owned Treatment Work
PPE	Personal Protective Equipment
PSD	Prevention of Significant Deterioration
PTC	Production Tax Credit
RCRA	Resource Conservation and Recovery Act
REACH	Registration, Evaluation, Authorization, and Restriction of Chemicals
RGGI	Regional Greenhouse Gas Initiative
RIA	Regulatory Impact Analysis
RIF	Remedial Investigation and Feasibility Study
ROD	Record of Decision

RTR	Risks and Technology Review
SARA	Superfund Amendments and Reauthorization Act
SDWA	Safe Drinking Water Act
SEC	Securities and Exchange Commission
SEP	Supplemental Environmental Project
SIP	State Implementation Plan
SNUR	Significant New Use Rule
TMDL	Total Maximum Daily Loads
TNC	The Nature Conservancy
TRI	Toxic Release Inventory
TSCA	Toxic Substances Control Act
TSDF	Treatment Storage and Disposal Facility
TTIP	Transatlantic Trade and Investment Partnership
UAO	Unilateral Administrative Order
UHC	Underlying Hazardous Constituents
UIC	Underground Injection Control
UNFCCC	UN Framework Convention on Climate Change
WHO	World Health Organization
WOTUS	Waters of The United States Rule

To our many students at the Yale Law School and
the Yale School of the Environment,
who have taught us at least as much over the years
as we have taught them.

1   How U.S. environmental law is *really* made

The concept that those who like sausage and legislation should never see how they are made is a line often attributed to Bismarck.[1] On the contrary, those who wish to understand U.S. environmental law must first understand how it is really made.

Some people might try to tell you that courts and legislatures make environmental law,[2] but they would be wrong—at least for the United States. The overwhelming majority of environmental law in the United States is made by administrative agencies, primarily the national Environmental Protection Agency (EPA), but also similar agencies at the state level. Legislatures delegate power to administrative agencies to make law,[3] and courts sometimes rein them in by ruling that they have gone too far, but the vast majority of the content of U.S. environmental law is elaborated by agency rules and interpretations, as we will detail in the pages that follow.

Many features of U.S. environmental law are attributable to these distinctive aspects of how regulatory law is actually made in the United States.

Most environmental law is made through agency rulemaking and guidance

If we think of legislatures, administrative agencies, and courts as the hardware that makes environmental law, then substantive environmental statutes are like the programs of instructions that tell a

---

1 Robert Pear, *If Only Laws Were Like Sausages*, N.Y. TIMES (Dec. 4, 2010), https://www.nytimes.com/2010/12/05/weekinreview/05pear.html.

2 JONATHAN Z. CANNON, ENVIRONMENT IN THE BALANCE: THE GREEN MOVEMENT AND THE SUPREME COURT (2015).

3 DAVID SCHOENBROD, POWER WITHOUT RESPONSIBILITY: HOW CONGRESS ABUSES THE PEOPLE THROUGH DELEGATION (1993).

computer what to do, and administrative law is like the operating system that mediates between the two. As we describe below, administrative law, the law that governs actions of government officials, has changed remarkably over the last two generations, which was the formative period in which environmental law developed at the national level in the United States. The evolving form and function of administrative law has many implications for how U.S. environmental law has developed.

Note that environmental law in the United States exists at the state level as well, but we do not talk about state environmental law much in this book because the laws are different in 50 states, plus in territories and for Native American tribes, but it is generally similar to what occurs at the national level. Anyone making environmental decisions should be consulting state level legal obligations (and sometimes local ordinances) as well as federal law, regulations, and interpretations.

Environmental federalism

In parallel with the roles of the Congress and President, state legislatures adopt environmental statutes that Governors sign into law and state courts interpret. As we discuss below, America's longstanding commitment to *federalism* means that regulatory authority is shared by national and state authorities on many issues. Thus, just as EPA implements federal pollution control law, most states have a Department of Environmental Protection (DEP) that manages state environmental programs—although the name of this agency and precise scope of responsibilities vary from state to state. In many states, local authorities (at the county, city, or town level) exercise control over some environmental activities, particularly land use regulation including wetlands protection, as well as garbage collection and thus some aspects of waste management. The federal government has several Cabinet-level land management departments: notably, the Department of Interior, which includes the National Park Service and the Fish and Wildlife Service, and the Department of Agriculture, which includes the Forest Service. Their roles are discussed later, primarily in Chapters 12 and 13. Many states also have parks, forests, and wildlife areas managed by their DEP or a separate natural resource agency. Public health activities related to the environment, including drinking water regulation, may also fall within the jurisdiction of the DEP or be lodged in a separate Department of Public Health.

Structures from administrative law

In sketching out the legal framework of national environmental protection and sustainability policy more broadly, a number of structural features derived from administrative law deserve special attention as they have profoundly shaped U.S. environmental law:

1. Broad delegations of power from Congress to administrative agencies comprised of thousands of permanent officials with limited political supervision;
2. Expansion of informal rulemaking—also called *notice and comment rulemaking*—that allows agencies to promulgate detailed regulations that have the force of law by publishing the text and taking written comments;[4]
3. Expansive review in court by judges of general jurisdiction at the behest of any person adversely affected by these administrative rules;
4. Courts defer to agency interpretations of both statutes and regulations. *Deference* can be defined as a court upholding an agency's interpretation even if the court would disagree with it if the court were deciding the question in the first instance. The courts have struggled with the question of how much *deference* to give to an agency's interpretation of its own regulations.[5]
5. Extended reach of the authority of the federal (i.e., national) government to direct actions by the states by threatening to withhold federal funding;
6. Broad use of *guidance*, agency statements of policy and interpretations which, while not technically legally binding,[6] are nonetheless influential because regulated parties ignore the agency's position on what the statute and their regulations require at their peril, and may face expensive enforcement

---

4 Administrative Procedure Act, 5 U.S.C. § 553, https://www.law.cornell.edu/uscode/text/5/553.

5 *Compare* Auer v. Robbins, 519 U.S. 452 (1997) (agency interpretations of their own regulations get deference from the courts unless "inconsistent with the language" of the rule) *with* Kisor v. Wilkie, 139 S. Ct. 2400 (2019) (holding 5-4 that agency interpretations only receive deference from a court if after applying traditional tools of interpretation the court determines two possible interpretations are "in equipoise."). These cases are discussed further below in the text at note 33.

6 Administrative Conference of the United States, Agency Guidance Through Interpretive Rules (Recommendation number: 2019-1), https://www.acus.gov/recommendation/agency-guidance-through-interpretive-rules.

proceedings which also result in adverse publicity if they do not comply.[7]

7. Increasing use of enforcement to advance broad interpretations of existing legal provisions, a process sometimes called *regulation by litigation*. In some instances, this happens because an informal norm has developed that political appointees do not interfere in enforcement, though they do have greater authority over changes to regulations. In addition, agencies sometimes wish to avoid the expense and delay of revising a regulation through notice and comment rulemaking;[8]

8. Development of *administrative adjudicatory systems* within agencies. Agency adjudicatory hearings are held by *administrative law judges* who are agency employees, rather than federal judges. Decisions by these bodies such as EPA's *Environmental Appeals Board* (EAB)[9] are subject to review in court, but under deferential standards such as "unsupported by substantial evidence on the record as a whole" or "capricious and arbitrary, or an abuse of discretion" depending upon the nature of the administrative proceeding;[10] and

9. Extensive policymaking through *Executive Orders*, particularly with regard to how to balance environmental protection goals with economic costs and other competing policy goals. (Executive Orders are commands from the President to departments and agencies in the executive branch. They typically do not go through notice and comment or create judicially enforceable rights for persons outside the executive branch, but they can be invalidated by courts if they go beyond the President's powers under the Constitution and statutes.[11] The less-than-supreme status of Executive Orders represents an important feature of U.S. law, as in some other countries, executive edicts are the highest form of lawmaking.)

---

7 United States v. Mead Corp., 533 U.S. 218 (2001) (agency interpretations of statutes by officials other than the head of an agency are entitled to lesser *Skidmore* deference based on their "power to persuade" rather than *Chevron* deference).

8 *See* REGULATION THROUGH LITIGATION (W. Kip Viscusi ed., 2002).

9 For a description of the EAB's jurisdiction and role, see Environmental Appeals Board, EPA, https://yosemite.epa.gov/oa/EAB_Web_Docket.nsf.

10 APA, 5 U.S.C. § 706, https://www.law.cornell.edu/uscode/text/5/706.

11 *Heritage Explains: Executive Orders*, HERITAGE FOUNDATION, https://www.heritage.org/politi cal-process/heritage-explains/executive-orders.

These administrative procedures have enabled environmental law to become the most pervasive and detailed body of regulatory law in the United States. Taken as a whole, this framework amounts to a revolution of constitutional dimensions in how law is made in the United States, which is sometimes called *the rise of the administrative state*.[12] This term has taken on pejorative connotations in some contexts, especially among critics, of the degree of authority that has been delegated to regulatory agencies (and the unelected *bureaucrats* within them). They worry that these officials have *captured* the government and elected representatives are no longer in control.[13] Others reject this view and vigorously defend the administrative state and the career *civil servants* serving within it.[14]

In the 1970s, when most of our national environmental laws were passed, the center of gravity of policymaking in the United States was shifting into a process called *informal* or *notice and comment* rulemaking. The 1946 Administrative Procedure Act (APA) created this device for making law. In informal rulemaking, a government agency announces its intention to promulgate regulations via a daily publication called the *Federal Register*.[15] This *notice of proposed rulemaking* (NPRM) is supposed to contain either the terms of the proposed new rule or a summary of the subjects.[16]

Unlike formal rulemaking or adjudication, which are other ways that administrative agencies in the United States make binding law,

---

12 *See, e.g.*, E. Donald Elliott, *How James Comey's Revenge Is Changing Our Constitution: The battle over who runs the federal government*, AMERICAN SPECTATOR (Oct. 28, 2019, 1:13 PM), https://spectator.org/how-james-comeys-revenge-is-changing-our-constitution.

13 Gary Lawson, *The Rise and Rise of the Administrative State*, 107 HARV. L. REV. 1231 (1994); Richard A. Epstein, *Why the Modern Administrative State is Inconsistent with the Rule of Law*, 3 NYU J.L. & LIBERTY 491 (2008); Steven G. Calabresi & Gary Lawson, *The Depravity of the 1930s and the Modern Administrative State*, 49 NOTRE DAME L. REV. 821 (2019); Charles J. Cooper, *Confronting the Administrative State*, 46 NAT'L AFFS. (Fall, 2015), http://www.nationalaffairs.com/publications/detail/confronting-the-administrative-state.

14 Perhaps the most eloquent version of the arguments in favor of the administrative state can be found in Justice Elena Kagan's dissent in Seila Law LLC v. Consumer Fin. Prot. Bureau, 140 S. Ct. 2183 (2020); Jon D. Michaels, *A Constitutional Defense of the Administrative State*, REGUL. REV. (Dec. 17, 2019), https://www.theregreview.org/2019/12/17/michaels-constitutional-defense-administrative-state; Matt Ford, *Elena Kagan's Fiery Defense of the Administrative State*, NEW REPUBLIC (July 2, 2020), https://newrepublic.com/article/158348/elena-kagans-fiery-defense-administrative-state.

15 The product of this process is interchangeably referred to as *rules* or *regulations*.

16 APA, 5 U.S.C. § 553(a).

informal rulemaking requires no oral hearing or cross-examination of witnesses. Rather, after considering the comments submitted in response to the NPRM, the agency publishes the text of the rule it proposes to adopt in the Federal Register and invites interested parties to submit written comments on the proposal. While not mandatory, in some cases, agencies also hold oral hearings to get further feedback on their draft regulations. The agency then responds to the comments by publishing an explanation of why it either adopted or rejected them along with the text of the final rule, which immediately becomes effective unless the agency decides to adopt a later effective date or a court issues a *stay*, a court order that prohibits the rule from going into effect during judicial review.

The proposal, the comments, and the agency's responses to the concerns raised become the *record for judicial review* if anyone challenges the rule as beyond the agency's legal authority or as an abuse of its discretion.[17] Most environmental statutes provide that *any person* may challenge a rule in court, but judicial decisions have narrowed this *standing* to sue to only those who are, or are threatened to be, actually and personally affected by the rule. Most environmental statutes provide a very short statute of limitations within which a new or amended rule may be challenged, such as 60 days. This approach is called *pre-enforcement review* because legal challenges to the substance of the rule must be brought immediately after rule is promulgated and cannot be raised later when the rule is actually enforced against someone—unless "the petition is based solely on grounds arising after" the 60-day period.[18]

This system allows agencies to promulgate thousands of pages per year of very detailed legally-binding rules that would take hundreds of years to evolve through a common law process of case-by-case adjudication. Moreover, the fact that agencies can fill in the details allows the Congress to legislate in generalities, such as "protect the public health

---

17 APA, 5 U.S.C. § 706.
18 Clean Air Act § 307(b)(1), 42 U.S. § 7607(b)(1):

   Any petition for review under this subsection shall be filed within sixty days from the date notice of such promulgation, approval, or action appears in the Federal Register, except that if such petition is based solely on grounds arising after such sixtieth day, then any petition for review under this subsection shall be filed within sixty days after such grounds arise.

with an adequate margin of safety," and leave it to agencies, such as EPA, to define what vague statutory terms actually mean in practice.[19]

Informal rulemaking greatly expanded the capacity of the national government to promulgate legally-binding norms beyond what courts and legislatures had been able to do prior to the 1970s. Perhaps that is an example of what the legal historian, Sir Henry Maine meant, when he wrote that "substantive law has at first the look of being gradually secreted in the interstices of procedure."[20] In any case, the structure and form of substantive environmental law in the United States is clearly shaped by the processes that make it.[21] As a result of all these features, but particularly of informal rulemaking and judicial deference to agency interpretations of statutes and rules, decisions by courts are less important in shaping U.S. environmental law than in many other areas of our law.

Cooperative federalism

The capacity of the federal government to regulate activities affecting the environment was further expanded by the theory of *cooperative federalism*. Developed by the Nixon Administration in the late 1960s and early 1970s, cooperative federalism enables the federal government to set mandatory minimums but leaves implementing these goals up to the states. Many U.S. environmental laws, including the Clean Air and Clean Water Acts, use this system, as several of the chapters that follow discuss in more detail. This structure of shared responsibilities across levels of government provides flexibility to the states to implement national programs consistent with local circumstances and preferences. But critics decry federal dictates that come without financial support as *unfunded mandates*.

---

19 For a critique that argues the elected Congress should go back to making rules, rather than merely declaring goals, see David Schoenbrod, *Goal Statutes or Rules Statutes: The Case of the Clean Air Act*, 30 UCLA L. REV. 740 (1982); *See also* DAVID SCHOENBROD, POWER WITHOUT RESPONSIBILITY: HOW CONGRESS ABUSES THE PEOPLE THROUGH DELEGATION (1993).

20 HENRY MAINE, DISSERTATIONS ON EARLY LAW AND CUSTOM 389 (1883) ("substantive law is secreted in the interstices of procedure"), *quoted in* Frederic Maitland, *The Forms of Action at Common Law*, in EQUITY AND THE FORMS OF ACTION AT COMMON LAW 295 (1932).

21 "Substantive law is shaped and articulated by procedural possibilities." Geoffrey Hazard, *The Effect of the Class Action Device on the Substantive Law*, 58 F.R.D. 299, 307 (1973).

Early on, a few Supreme Court cases declared that the states could not be turned into regional offices to implement federal policy.[22] However, the Supreme Court has also held that the federal government may condition substantial funding that it provides to the states from a combination of federal income taxes and federal borrowings on state implementation of federal mandates that are logically related to the purposes for which the federal funding is provided.[23] As a practical matter, this means that the federal government, including administrative agencies such as EPA, may dictate environmental policy to the states. The usual form of environmental law is for the federal government to adopt minimum standards via informal rulemaking that states must follow, but to leave states' discretion to be more, but not less, protective of the environment if they choose.

Guidance

However, even this multi-layered system does not fully capture all the detailed rules of environmental law that the federal government prescribes. Notably, in addition to making rules, federal agencies such as EPA also interpret their rules through *guidance documents*. Administrative law does not require that these memoranda, written by subsidiary agency officials, go through the public notice and comment rulemaking procedure. Technically, guidance documents are not legally binding,[24] but merely announce the position that the agency intends to take as to what its rules mean. Indeed, in an earlier era, they were called *advance advice*. How much deference, if any, courts should give to agency interpretations that did not go through rulemaking has been a continuing controversy in the courts.[25] As a practical matter, however, a regulated party or a state agency that does not follow EPA's guidance acts at its peril because it faces the threat of sanctions in an

---

22 Printz v. United States, 521 U.S. 898 (1997); New York v. United States, 505 U.S. 144 (1992) (under the 10th Amendment, federal legislation may not "commandeer state governments into the service of federal regulatory purposes").

23 South Dakota v. Dole, 483 U.S. 203 (1987) (upholding conditioning of federal highway funding upon state adoption of drinking age of 21 despite states' "virtually complete control" of alcoholic beverages under 21st Amendment).

24 McLouth Steel Products Co. v. EPA, 838 F.2d 1317 (D.C. Cir. 1988).

25 Kisor v. Wilkie, 139 S. Ct. 2400 (2019); United States v. Mead Corp., 533 U.S. 218 (2001); *compare* David Hasen, *The Ambiguous Basis of Judicial Deference to Administrative Rules*, 17 YALE J. ON REG. 327 (2000), *with* Connor Raso, *The Supreme Court curtails but retains agency rule deference – How much will it matter?*, BROOKINGS (Sept. 24, 2019), https://www.brookings.edu/research/the-supreme-court-curtails-but-retains-agency-rule-deference-how-much-will-it-matter.

enforcement case. In 2019, the Trump Administration attempted to impose greater transparency and political control over agency guidance documents through two Executive Orders dictating *good guidance procedures*, including making all guidance documents available to the public on the Internet and stating that guidance alone could not be the basis for an enforcement action.[26] However, on the first day of President Biden's tenure in office, he revoked both rules.[27]

Regulatory swings

Another important feature of agency lawmaking through rulemaking is that incoming administrations are free to revoke or change the rules of the prior administration without legislation, provided that the changes go through another round of notice and comment and that justification is provided that passes muster in the courts as reasonable.[28] This means that policies only survive over the long run if successive administrations find them acceptable. For example, the conservative Trump Administration changed many of the environmental rules that had been promulgated by its predecessors, the more liberal Obama and Clinton Administrations, and now the Biden Administration has pledged to change many of them back.[29]

Taking effective action against climate change has been difficult because Democratic administrations generally favor regulatory measures to address climate change and Republican administrations generally oppose them, although there are a few exceptions on both sides.[30] Similar problems have occurred in developing a policy that is stable over time with regard to federal as opposed to local control over wetlands.[31]

---

26 Exec. Order No. 13,891 on Promoting the Rule of Law Through Improved Agency Guidance Documents, 84 Fed. Reg. 55, 235 (Oct. 15, 2019); Exec. Order No. 13,892 on Promoting the Rule of Law Through Transparency and Fairness in Civil Administrative Enforcement and Adjudication, 84 Fed. Reg. 55, 239 (Oct. 19, 2019).

27 Exec. Order No. 13,992, 86 Fed. Reg. 7049 (Jan. 20, 2021) (repealing Trump Administration Executive Orders 13771, 13777, 13875, 13891, 13892, and 13893).

28 Motor Vehicle Mfrs. Ass'n v. State Farm Mut. Auto Ins. Co., 463 U.S. 29 (1983).

29 *See* Coral Davenport, *Restoring Environmental Rules Rolled Back by Trump Could Take Years: President Biden has promised to reinstate more than 100 rules and regulations aimed at environmental protection that his predecessor rolled back. It won't happen overnight.* N.Y. Times (Jan. 22, 2021, Updated Jan. 27, 2021), https://www.nytimes.com/2021/01/22/climate/biden-environment.html.

30 *See* discussion of U.S. Climate Change Law and Policy in Chapter 5.

31 *See* discussion of Scope of National Government Clean Water Act Authority in Chapter 4.

Agency deference

In recent years, however, a partisan logjam in Congress[32] has made it more difficult to pass environmental laws than in the 1970s and 1980s. The courts have adapted by developing a legal principle, the *Chevron doctrine*, after the case in which it first appeared,[33] that gives administrative agencies, and most pertinently to our subject, EPA, wide latitude to interpret existing legislation creatively to address problems that Congress did not resolve one way or the other.[34] Some legal commentators have condemned the degree of deference to agency judgments on statutory interpretations that the *Chevron* doctrine mandates, but others argue that agencies with expertise in the area are better-suited than courts of general jurisdiction to decide questions that Congress never actually decided.[35]

A similar issue of the scope of judicial review arises when agencies' interpretations of their own regulations face court challenges. The Supreme Court's 1997 *Auer* decision suggested that courts should give deference to agencies' interpretations of their own ambiguous regulations unless their proposed interpretation was *inconsistent* with the underlying regulatory language, a standard even more deferential than *Chevron* deference to agency interpretations of statutes which have to be *reasonable*. In its 2019 *Kisor* decision, the Supreme Court narrowed *Auer deference* by saying that courts should defer to agency interpretations of their own regulations only when: (1) the regulation is "genuinely ambiguous;" (2) the agency's interpretation is "reasonable;" and (3) the foundation for agency's interpretation merits deference

---

32 DAVID SCHOENBROD, RICHARD B. STEWART, AND KATRINA M. WYMAN, BREAKING THE LOGJAM: ENVIRONMENTAL PROTECTION THAT WILL WORK (2010); E. Donald Elliott, *Politics Failed, Not Ideas*, ENV'T FORUM (Sept./Oct., 2011).

33 Chevron v. NRDC, 467 U.S. 837 (1984).

34 There is an extensive literature on the *Chevron* doctrine and its implications. *See, e.g.*, Cass R. Sunstein, *Law and Administration After* Chevron, 90 COLUM. L. REV. 2071 (1990); E. Donald Elliott, *Chevron Matters: How the Chevron Doctrine Re-Defined the Roles of Congress, Courts and Agencies in Environmental Law*, 16 VILL. ENVTL. L.J. 1 (2005).

35 Nat'l Cable & Telecomms. Ass'n v. Brand X Internet Servs., 545 U.S. 967, 982 (2005):

> In *Chevron*, this Court held that ambiguities in statutes within an agency's jurisdiction to administer are delegations of authority to the agency to fill the statutory gap in reasonable fashion. Filling these gaps, the Court explained, involves difficult policy choices that agencies are better equipped to make than courts. If a statute is ambiguous, and if the implementing agency's construction is reasonable, *Chevron* requires a federal court to accept the agency's construction of the statute, even if the agency's reading differs from what the court believes is the best statutory interpretation (citations omitted).

because it is (a) "authoritative and official," (b) based on the agency's "substantive expertise," and (c) "fair and considered."[36]

Regulatory power sharing

Unlike some countries where courts or legislation are the primary makers of environmental law, in the United States, legislators, administrative agencies, and courts engage in a *three-cornered conversation* to develop environmental law through an on-going dialogue of reacting to one another and jointly making the law.[37] As we will illustrate, Congress often fails to anticipate all the issues that may emerge during agency implementation. While agencies often are the first to address an issue, sometimes the issue first emerges in the courts and then Congress amends the statute against the backdrop of agency and judicial interpretations. You will see that story play out over and over in the pages that follow.

A wise 19th-century Englishman, Walter Bagehot, who some say is the founder of political science, wrote that this sharing of lawmaking power among multiple institutions was the distinctive feature of the American Constitution.[38] This principle of powersharing plays out particularly vividly in the realm of U.S. environmental law—both *horizontally*, with all three branches of government playing important roles, and *vertically*, with authority spread across the federal, state, and local levels. As legal responsibilities often overlap, multiple agencies and officials sometimes contend for control but in other circumstances work collaboratively in a framework one of us has called *regulatory co-opetition*.[39]

---

36 Kisor v. Wilkie, 139 S. Ct. 2400, 2416–18 (2019); *see also* Shamita Etienne-Cummings and David M. Tennant, *Kisor Deference: The New Judicially-Driven Auer Deference*, WHITE & CASE (July 17, 2019), https://www.whitecase.com/publications/alert/kisor-deference-new-judicially-driven-auer-deference#:~:text=Pursuant%20to%20Kisor%2C%20a%20federal,interpretation%20meets%20minimum%20thresholds%20to.

37 E. Donald Elliott, *Review of* MELNICK, REGULATION AND THE COURTS, 23 J. ECON. LIT. 654, 654 (1985) (describing "interactive lawmaking, in which legislatures, agencies and courts work together to shape the law").

38 "The English constitution, in a word, is framed on the principle of choosing a single sovereign authority, and making it good; the American, upon the principle of having many sovereign authorities, and hoping that their multitude will atone for their inferiority." WALTER BAGEHOT, THE ENGLISH CONSTITUTION AND OTHER POLITICAL ESSAYS 296 (rev. ed., 1901).

39 Daniel C. Esty and Damien Geradin, *Regulatory Co-opetition*, 3 J. INT'L ECON. L. 235 (2000).

Additional resources

Andrews, Richard N.L. (2020). *Managing the Environment, Managing Ourselves: A History of American Environmental Policy.* 3rd edition. New Haven: Yale University Press.

Barnes, A. James, Graham, John D. and Konisky, David M. (eds.) (2021). *Fifty Years at the US Environmental Protection Agency: Progress, Retrenchment, and Opportunities.* New York: Rowman & Littlefield.

Cannon, Jonathan Z. (2015). *Environment in the Balance: The Green Movement and the Supreme Court.* Cambridge: Harvard University Press.

Esty, Daniel C. and Geradin, Damien (eds.) (2001). *Regulatory Competition and Economic Integration: Comparative Perspectives.* Oxford: Oxford University Press.

Lazarus, Richard J. (2004). *The Making Of Environmental Law.* Chicago: University of Chicago Press.

2 Recurrent themes in U.S. environmental law

Much of what is distinctive about U.S. environmental law cuts across various regulatory schemes. In this chapter, we review several recurrent themes in the U.S. approach to environmental law.

The role of science/risk assessment

U.S. environmental law prides itself on being *science-based*, but also on integrating scientific considerations with social values, including economics, which is discussed in the next section. As a result, most environmental regulation in the United States balances competing goals. With a few exceptions, U.S. law does not ban substances or practices but strives instead to regulate them by setting safe levels of exposure or limiting releases of pollution. The basic method for integrating science into the policy mix is called *risk assessment*.

A combination of career civil servants and political appointees nominated by the President and confirmed by the Senate who serve at the pleasure of the President (and whose tenure is often just two to four years) make most decisions. EPA, for example, has an Office of Research and Development (ORD), with a staff of several hundred scientists, engineers, and other technical experts. An EPA Assistant Administrator (nominated by the President and confirmed by the Senate) leads the Office and is replaced (along with a Deputy Assistant Administrator and a few other ORD officials) when a new Administration takes over. As a result, policy changes at the margins and sometimes more dramatically as different presidential administrations come and go.[1] EPA and other agencies also use outside scientists,

---

1 As political parties in the United States shift further apart, Presidents tend to express more divergent views on policy, resulting in dramatic, but often temporary shifts in government policy. For example, the Trump Administration changed many Obama environmental policies, which the Biden Administration will probably change back to a position closer to the Obama Administration.

including some science advisory boards and panels made up of outside experts.

Congress evokes risk reduction and prevention when writing environmental statutes but has not generally crafted legislation requiring agencies to integrate risk assessment into their regulatory processes or agenda setting. Rather, a series of executive orders has added a focus on risk assessment on a largely bipartisan basis over the last eight presidential administrations.[2] The job of reviewing proposed rules with a significant impact (generally defined as more than $100 million a year in compliance costs) belongs to a small but powerful office, the Office of Information and Regulatory Affairs (OIRA) within the White House Office of Management and Budget (OMB).[3] OIRA issues guidance to the agencies on how to conduct regulatory analyses, including benefit-cost analyses and risk assessments, and then reviews proposed new rules at both the proposal and final stages before they may appear in the *Federal Register*. Benefit-cost analysis and risk assessment are linked, as the risk reductions quantified through risk assessment are monetized and counted as benefits and compared to the costs in benefit-cost analyses. How much power OIRA actually wields varies from Administration to Administration depending upon the sitting President's priorities and the internal politics of the White House.

Our capacity as human beings to judge risks intuitively is often poor and quickly overwhelmed when presented with multiple different kinds of risks. Risk perception is influenced by attributes of the risk, such as whether it is voluntary or involuntary; natural or anthropogenic; familiar or novel; or instills a sense of dread.[4] The public and experts

---

See Coral Davenport, *Restoring 100 rules and regulations aimed at environmental protection that his predecessor rolled back. It won't happen overnight*, N.Y. TIMES (Jan. 27, 2021), https://www.nytimes.com/2021/01/22/climate/biden-environment.html.

2   For an official summary of OIRA's role and the sources of its legal authority, see *Information and Regulatory Affairs*, THE WHITE HOUSE OFFICE OF MANAGEMENT AND BUDGET, https://www.whitehouse.gov/omb/information-regulatory-affairs/.

3   During the George W. Bush administration, the Office of Information and Regulatory Affairs proposed to standardize risk assessment across the federal government. This proposal was rejected by the National Academy of Sciences on grounds that risk assessments should differ from agency to agency. *See* Press Release, The Nat'l Academies of Scis., Eng'g., and Med., Report Recommends Withdrawal of OMB Risk Assessment Bulletin (Jan. 11, 2007), https://www8.nationalacademies.org/onpinews/newsitem.aspx?RecordID=11811.

4   Baruch Fischoff and Granger Morgan, *The Science and Practice of Risk Ranking*, 3 HORIZONS 40 (2008), https://www.cmu.edu/epp/people/faculty/research/Fischhoff-SciencePracticeRiskRanking.pdf. The process may also permit countervailing risks to be tracked and risk balancing to be

have different perceptions of risk.[5] *Risk ranking* is a tool for ordering risks by their importance and can be useful in setting priorities. In some cases, however, even big risks will be hard to address. For example, for many years EPA recognized mercury pollution from coal-fired powerplants as a serious public health issue, but it delayed regulating for over a decade because of a perceived lack of a cost-effective control technology.

Risk assessment

Risk assessment permits decisionmakers to evaluate potential risks and risk mitigation strategies systematically.[6] It provides a transparent framework for organizing science while also acknowledging the data gaps and uncertainties inherent in estimating the likelihood of harm. Filling the data gaps demands assumptions, which often root from policy judgments and which stakeholders and the public rigorously debate. Agencies develop perceived worst-case assumptions to err on the side of not underestimating risks. If this crude, conservative, screening-risk assessment fails to identify a substantial risk, it is deemed unnecessary to spend the time required to refine the analysis.

Risk assessments facilitate decisionmaking under uncertainty but may not be capable of making precise predictions accurately. Like a weather report, they indicate general trends but may also be inaccurate when applied at a fine scale. As with benefit-cost assessments, some argue that risk assessments are too imprecise to use for *fine-tuning* regulations.[7] Sources of uncertainty in risk assessment include the practice of extrapolation, which entails using a limited set of data

---

undertaken. RISK VS. RISK: TRADEOFFS IN PROTECTING HEALTH AND THE ENVIRONMENT (John D. Graham and Jonathan B. Wiener eds., 2009).

5 Stephen Breyer argued in his past life as a professor prior to his becoming a judge and then a Supreme Court Justice that EPA and other agencies would benefit from having more risk experts on which to rely ensuring more *rational* regulatory choices detached from the pressures of politics. STEPHEN BREYER, BREAKING THE VICIOUS CIRCLE: TOWARD EFFECTIVE RISK REGULATION (1993).

6 The risk assessment process is often broken down into distinct stages. *See* NATIONAL RESEARCH COUNCIL, SCIENCE AND DECISIONS: ADVANCING RISK ASSESSMENT (2009), https://www.nap.edu/catalog/12209/science-and-decisions-advancing-risk-assessment.

7 *See* E. Donald Elliott, *Only a Poor Workman Blames His Tools: On Uses and Abuses of Benefit-Cost Analysis in Regulatory Decision Making About the Environment*, 157 U. PA. L. REV. PENNUMBRA 178 (2009), https://digitalcommons.law.yale.edu/cgi/viewcontent.cgi?article=6111&context=fss_papers; *see also* DOUGLAS A. KYSAR, REGULATING FROM NOWHERE: ENVIRONMENTAL LAW AND

to make assumptions about a related area where data are unavailable. Often, this involves using data from one end of a curve to estimate the other end of the curve. Two commonly debated forms are extrapolating the response to toxicants from one species to another (usually humans) and extrapolating responses to low levels of toxicants from responses to high levels. EPA typically uses tenfold *safety factors* (also called *uncertainty factors*) to adjust for these uncertainties.

Scientific measurement, modeling, and scale issues

Physical, chemical, and biological phenomena occur over specific temporal and spatial scales. Mismatches of scale between scientific data and policy actions can distort the analysis of whether policy goals have been achieved. Policy evaluation demands scientific studies conducted at spatial (local, regional, or global) and temporal scales consistent with the policy's goals. In addition, the data used for policy development and analysis may sometimes be empirical measurements, but those are often difficult to obtain, and usually only provide a small sample, which can be misleading. As a result, environmental standard-setting often relies on modeled estimates which are intentionally conservative so as not to under-estimate risks. Empirical data such as monitoring provides actual measurements, but only for a limited number of stations. Extrapolating monitoring data to the policy-relevant spatial, temporal, or ecological scales creates uncertainty. Modeling readily generates estimates over spatial and temporal scales unattainable through monitoring, but those estimates are subject to the biases and uncertainties inherent in the underlying model.[8] Peer review improves the quality and credibility of scientific studies and is a requirement for influential and highly influential scientific data the federal government disseminates.[9]

THE SEARCH FOR OBJECTIVITY (2010); Frank Ackerman and Lisa Heinzerling, *Pricing the Priceless: Cost-Benefit Analysis of Environmental Protection*, 150 PENN L. REV. 1553 (2002).

8 *See* NATIONAL RESEARCH COUNCIL, MODELS IN ENVIRONMENTAL REGULATORY DECISION MAKING (2007), https://www.nap.edu/catalog/11972/models-in-environmental-regulatory-decision-making.

9 Memorandum from the Office of Mgmt. and Budget to the Heads of Dep't and Agencies (Dec. 16, 2004), https://www.cio.noaa.gov/services_programs/pdfs/OMB_Peer_Review_Bulletin_m05-03.pdf.

Economics and benefit-cost analysis

No issue in U.S. environmental law has been more perennially controversial than the tradeoff between economic considerations and environmental goals. Unlike many other nations, the United States does not have a constitutional provision guaranteeing a right to a clean environment at the national level. Therefore, Congress decides *how clean is clean*—what level of environmental risk is acceptable—in individual statutes. Some statutory language is clear that "costs" must be considered,[10] and other provisions are equally clear that economic costs may *not* be.[11] However, in order to obtain the majorities necessary for passage, Congress often writes evocative but ambiguous language that delegates to administrative agencies, courts, and states how much weight to give to economics and benefit-cost analysis.

The U.S. Supreme Court has ruled on whether economics may be weighed in the balance under numerous different statutory schemes, and even different sections of the same statute. The current legal standard is that unless Congress has decided the issue clearly one way or the other in the legislation, administrative agencies have discretion to interpret ambiguous statutory provisions and courts will defer to their interpretations if "reasonable."[12] Some analysts (who, incidentally, are former OIRA officials) have plausibly interpreted *dicta* in the most recent Supreme Court decisions as creating a general presumption in favor of considering costs and benefits.[13]

Regardless of whether the law permits an agency to weigh the health and economic benefits of risk reduction versus the costs of compliance in deciding on an appropriate level of regulation, under a series of executive orders issued over a generation, most agencies, including environmental agencies, must prepare a *regulatory impact analysis* (RIA) identifying and quantifying to the extent possible the costs and

---

10 *See* Chapters 3 and 8 for the contrast in whether balancing of costs and environmental gains is forbidden or must be considered.

11 *See* discussion of Clean Air Act § 109 in Chapter 3.

12 Michigan v. EPA, 576 U.S. 743 (2015), https://www.supremecourt.gov/opinions/14pdf/14-46_bqmc.pdf. For an extended discussion, see Michigan v. EPA, 129 HARV. L. REV. 311 (2015), https://harvardlawreview.org/2015/11/michigan-v-epa/.

13 Paul R. Noe and John D. Graham, *The Ascendancy of the Cost-Benefit State?*, 5 ADMIN. L. REV. ACCORD 85 (2020), http://www.administrativelawreview.org/wp-content/uploads/2020/01/Ascendancy-of-the-Cost-Benefit-State_Accord-5.3_Final.pdf. But note that *dicta* are generally considered non-binding.

benefits of proposed regulations. The justification is that, even if costs and benefits may not be considered under current law, they should be identified for the public and Congress, which might consider changing the law.

The RIA is submitted to OIRA which reviews and circulates it to other federal agencies for *interagency review*. OIRA must sign off on both proposed and final regulations and requires agencies to make significant changes in about one-third of rules—often to ensure their conformity with executive orders and other Administration policy preferences.[14] Note, however, that compliance with executive orders is not something third parties can raise in judicial review of rules.

In the U.S. legal system, presidential edicts, such as the executive orders establishing OIRA review, may not override statutes passed by Congress and signed by the President or passed by two-thirds super-majorities over the President's veto. Thus, agencies are required to adopt OIRA's suggestions only to "the extent permitted by [statutory] law."[15] Despite this check, OIRA's reach and influence should not be underestimated. Similarly, if Congress has set a statutory deadline for issuing a rule, an agency may not delay past the deadline in order to accommodate OIRA.

The 1981 version of the executive order creating OIRA review required that agencies determine that their rules produce *net social benefits*. However, a 1993 amendment, which is still in effect with only minor changes, broadened the standard to include distributional considerations such as effects on particularly sensitive or historically disadvantaged subpopulations.[16] OIRA has promulgated detailed guidance that agencies must following in preparing RIAs.[17] However, some critics have argued persuasively that benefit-cost analysis has been

---

14 *See generally* U.S. Gov't Accountability Office, OMB's Role in Reviews of Agencies' Draft Rules and the Transparency of Those Reviews (2003), https://www.gao.gov/new.items/do3929.pdf.

15 Exec. Order No. 12866, § 1(b), 3 C.F.R. § 638 (1994), *reprinted in* 5 U.S.C. § 601 app. at 557–61 (1994), https://www.archives.gov/files/federal-register/executive-orders/pdf/12866.pdf.

16 *Id.* For an elaboration of OIRA's roles and legal authority, see *Information and Regulatory Affairs*, The White House Office of Management and Budget, https://www.whitehouse.gov/omb/information-regulatory-affairs/.

17 Office of Information and Regulatory Affairs, Regulatory Impact Analysis: A Primer, https://www.reginfo.gov/public/jsp/Utilities/circular-a-4_regulatory-impact-analysis-a-primer.pdf.

applied inconsistently and can be manipulated by making different assumptions.[18]

Enforcement

One of the best, and most unusual, features of U.S. environmental law is its approach to enforcing environmental rules and regulations.[19] The key design principal is *redundancy*: most statutes provide a combination of criminal, civil, and administrative penalties. In addition, many environmental laws also provide for enforcement not only by national and state governments but also through *citizens suits* by "any person," including environmental groups, that can show they have a concern that violations may adversely affect them—thus authorizing them to act as a *private attorney general.*[20]

Another strength of the U.S. system is the ability to translate high-level statutory provisions such as *reasonable certainty of no harm* into transparent, facility-specific, quantitative limits. This approach to operationalizing legal requirements comes at the price of extended administrative proceedings at both the national and state levels, but the end result is that every major polluting facility in the United States is subject to legally-binding, quantitative restrictions on the types and amounts of regulated pollution that it may emit. Both the permit limits and periodic reports of emissions are transparent and available to the public. Admittedly, some pollutants, including greenhouse gases, are not currently regulated, as is discussed in a subsequent chapter,[21] but for those pollutants that are covered, this system achieves high levels of compliance and significant emissions reductions.[22]

---

18 *See, e.g.,* Richard L. Revesz and Michael A. Livermore, Reviving Rationality: Saving Cost-Benefit Analysis for the Sake of the Environment and Our Health (2020); Doug Kysar, Regulating from Nowhere: Environmental Law and the Search for Objectivity (2010); Frank Ackerman and Lisa Heinzerling, Priceless: On Knowing the Price of Everything and the Value of Nothing (2004).

19 E. Donald Elliott, *U.S. Environmental Law in Global Perspective: Five Do's and Five Don'ts from Our Experience,* 5 Nat'l Taiwan U. L. Rev. 144 (2010), http://digitalcommons.law.yale.edu/fss_papers/2717/.

20 Friends of the Earth, Inc. v. Laidlaw Environmental Services, Inc., 528 U.S. 167 (2000), https://supreme.justia.com/cases/federal/us/528/167/.

21 *See* Chapter 4.

22 *See* data and discussion Chapters 3 and 5.

The most effectively enforced statutes, such as the Clean Air Act and the Clean Water Act, also require detailed self-monitoring and public reporting of emissions by polluters as well as verification via government inspections. This process deputizes the private sector to report on itself and produces more compliance monitoring information than government inspections alone. However, some regulated entities have been known to misrepresent their emissions, a fraud that carries multi-billion dollar civil and criminal penalties if detected.[23]

Some states permit private *licensed environmental professionals* (LEPs) to certify corporate compliance with the state's environmental clean-up standards at toxic waste sites but the state retains the right to audit and take over if necessary. Some environmental advocates have criticized this partial *privatization* of clean-up as an inappropriate delegation of an inherently governmental activity. Some observers have even suggested that the use of LEPs amounts to having the fox guard the chicken coop. On the other hand, scholars have examined the role LEPs and other *gatekeepers* play and concluded that their need to maintain their credibility and reputation with the government regulators keeps them honest.[24] As states faced serious budget crises over the past several decades and pressure mounted to trim the headcount in state agencies, the opportunity to shift compliance costs to the private sector (as the corporations being inspected pay for the work of the LEPs) proved to be irresistible.

Another important feature of the U.S. regulatory system is that compliance with the modern environmental law system generally does *not* immunize a polluter against liability in civil lawsuits for damages under the older common law system of nuisance and tort law. Rather, most regulatory statutes supplement rather than replace pre-existing remedies. This system of remedies (remedies are available in court as well as through administrative regulation) means that even if one type of regulation is ineffective, others back it up.[25]

---

23 EPA, Volkswagen Clean Air Act Civil Settlement, https://www.epa.gov/enforcement/volkswagen-clean-air-act-civil-settlement.

24 Reinier H. Kraakman, *Gatekeepers: The Anatomy of a Third-Party Enforcement Strategy*, 2 J.L. Econ. & Org. 53 (1986), http://jleo.oxfordjournals.org/content/2/1/53.full.pdf.

25 E. Donald Elliott and Jacques Pelkmans, *Greater TTIP Ambition in Chemicals: Why and How*, in Rule Makers or Rule Takers? Exploring the Transatlantic Trade and Investment Partnership 423 (Daniel S. Hamilton and Jaques Pelkmans eds., 2015). Elliott and Pelkmans argue that despite the failure of the 1976 Toxic Substances Control Act to regulate existing

But there are limits to the principle that common law liability rein-
forces statutory enforcement. Specifically, the Supreme Court ruled
in *American Electric Power v. Connecticut* that a comprehensive
federal statutory structure pre-empts federal common law claims[26]—
specifically declaring in this 2011 case that public nuisance claims
based on a powerplant's greenhouse gas emissions cannot be heard in
federal court. The Court's unanimous decision turned on the theory
that Congress had delegated exclusive regulatory control over air pollution to EPA under the Clean Air Act. Whether the same exclusion
applies to state common law claims has not yet been decided—but
likely will be in the coming years as environmental advocates seek to
litigate responsibility for climate change in state courts.[27]

Most environmental laws provide large maximum daily penalties
(currently up to $99,681 a day, a figure that is periodically adjusted
for inflation), with each day counting as a separate violation.[28] This
can potentially result in multi-million, or even billion, dollar financial
penalties for violations. EPA has developed a system to reduce these
civil penalties, which would go into the U.S. Treasury, in exchange for
the defendant agreeing to fund *Supplemental Environmental Projects*
(SEPs), which are environmentally beneficial projects that have some
logical relationship to the harm caused by excess pollution.[29] For example, an electric utility that violates pollution standards might pay to
convert school buses from fossil fuels to electricity to reduce pollution.
A 2020 memorandum from the Trump Department of Justice have
questioned the legal authority for SEPs[30]—though this memorandum

---

chemicals effectively, the level of chemical safety in the United States and the European Union is
comparable due to the threat of private suits for damages.

26 American Electric Power Corp. v. Connecticut, 564 U.S. 410, 429 (2011), https://supreme.justia.
com/cases/federal/us/564/410/.

27 *See* Chapter 4.

28 EHS Daily Advisor Staff, *Higher EPA Penalties for Noncompliance Are in Effect*, EHS DAILY
ADVISOR (Feb. 6,, 2019), https://ehsdailyadvisor.blr.com/2019/02/higher-epa-penalties-for-non-
compliance-are-in-effect/.

29 Memorandum from Cynthia Giles, Assistant Administrator of EPA to the Regional
Administrators, Issuance of the 2015 Update to the 1998 U.S. Environmental Protection Agency
Supplemental Environmental Projects Policy (Mar. 10, 2015), https://www.epa.gov/sites/produc
tion/files/2015-04/documents/sepupdatedpolicy15.pdf.

30 Memorandum from Jeffrey Bossert Clark, Assistant Attorney General, to Environment and
Natural Resources Division Deputy Assistant Attorney Generals and Section Chiefs, Supplemental
Environmental Projects ("SEPs") in Civil Settlements with Private Defendants (Mar. 12, 2020),
https://digitalcommons.law.yale.edu/cgi/viewcontent.cgi?article=6111&context=fss_papers.

was withdrawn several weeks into the Biden Administration[31]—and their future is uncertain.

Regulatory approaches: command-and-control vs. market mechanisms

Environmental regulation in the United States falls into two broad categories: (1) government-mandated actions (often called *command-and-control* regulation) or (2) price signals that incentivize polluters to reduce emissions (often called *market mechanisms* or sometimes *economic incentive based regulations*).

In the first phase of U.S. environmental law in the 1970s and 1980s, most of the regulations adopted were of the command-and-control variety. Led by EPA, the federal government often specified as a practical matter what particular pollution control equipment factories had to install, and a great deal of effort went into identifying *best available control technology* (BACT or BAT) requirements on an industry-by-industry basis.[32] In other situations, as we will discuss in the chapters that follow, EPA or state regulators set emissions limits on how much air pollution could go up a smokestack or the amount of liquid that could flow out of a pipe into a river. Other requirements include: plans for responding to spills or accidents; insurance or bonding to ensure that funds are available to respond to pollution problems; design standards for production processes or products (e.g., liners for landfills to reduce groundwater contamination); product use limitations or bans (for example, how pesticides can be applied); and information disclosure about product contents or risks.

In recent years, the command-and-control approach to environmental regulation has been criticized as bureaucratic, inflexible, costly, and inefficient. Critics have further noted that the existing system of setting BAT standards or emissions limits also has produced a great deal of litigation that slows the adoption of regulations and adds significant

---

31 Memorandum from Jean E. Williams, Deputy Assistant Attorney General, to Environmental and Natural Resources Division Section Chiefs and Deputy Section Chiefs, Withdrawal of Memoranda and Policy Documents (Feb. 4, 2021), https://www.justice.gov/enrd/page/file/1364716/download.

32 As a technical matter, most U.S. pollution limits are *performance standards* which in theory can be met with any technology that is able to achieve a specified level of control. However, requirements were often set based on the existing technology that achieved the lowest level of pollution and thus could only be met with a particular technology, such as a flue gas scrubber.

transaction costs to the regulatory process. Critics of this approach to regulation observe that command-and-control mandates do not create incentives to reduce pollution below regulatory requirements: once standards have been set and the regulated industry has installed whatever pollution control equipment the government has specified, polluters have no incentive to innovate to produce new and better pollution control strategies and technologies.[33]

As a result, more recent environmental protection efforts have focused on implementing what is sometimes called the *Polluter Pays Principle*. This regulatory strategy puts a price on emissions, thus creating an incentive to cut the level of pollution and spur both the regulated entity and others to think creatively about how to further reduce emissions. In the language of economists, making polluters pay for their emissions *internalizes externalities*—and ensures that companies cannot benefit by imposing spillovers of pollution onto the community at large. *Price signals* generally offer more flexibility than government mandates, minimizing regulatory compliance costs and encouraging innovation.

These price signals can take a number of forms, including a tax or charge that rises with the level of pollution, such as a carbon charge on each ton of greenhouse gas emissions. Such *harm charges* are sometimes called a *Pigouvian tax* after the economist Arthur Cecil Pigou who first theorized that government could neutralize the effect of negative externalities by imposing a countervailing tax on the spillover.[34] Alternatively, the government can set up an emissions allowance trading system that sets an overall cap on emissions and requires emitters to acquire an allowance for each ton of pollution they release. Under such a *cap and trade program*, polluters that are able to reduce their pollution cheaply can sell their extra allowances to other enterprises that are having trouble cutting their emissions cost-effectively. Provided that the regulated entities have different marginal costs to control pollution and relatively low transaction costs, trading allows the overall level of emissions to be reduced at a lower cost than having

---

33 Daniel C. Esty, *Red Lights to Green Lights: From 20th Century Environmental Regulation to 21st Century Sustainability*, 47 ENVTL. L. 1 (2017), https://digitalcommons.law.yale.edu/cgi/viewcontent.cgi?article=6186&context=fss_papers.

34 ARTHUR C. PIGOU, THE ECONOMICS OF WELFARE (1932). For a good summary, see ARTHUR CECIL PIGOU, THE LIBRARY OF ECONOMICS AND LIBERTY, https://www.econlib.org/library/Enc/bios/Pigou.html.

every polluter meet a specified emissions target.[35] Because the government generally lacks the ability to pick the optimal level of control for each regulated entity, trading systems that allow private bargaining to rearrange the initial assignment of control obligations by government can be more economically efficient and cost effective than inflexible government mandates.

Price signals can also come in the form of grants or subsidies to companies or individuals who improve their environmental performance. Such monetary benefits, such as bonus payments for clean power production or tax subsidies for purchasers of electric vehicles, may be easier to put in place than making polluters pay for the harm they cause, which often leads to political pushback.

Taking private property for public use without just compensation

The Fifth Amendment to the U.S. Constitution provides "nor shall private property be taken for public use, without just compensation."[36] This restriction applies to both the federal government and the states through the Due Process Clause of the Fourteenth Amendment. In addition, all fifty states also have provisions in their state constitutions protecting private property against governmental actions, but often in words that differ slightly from the national *Takings Clause* structure.[37]

The national constitutional provision does not prohibit any action by government. Instead, it requires that if government *takes* private property for a public use, the government must pay the owner fair market value as determined by a court. Some states interpret the *public use* requirement in their state constitution to be a significant limitation on the purposes for which government may take private property, but, at the federal level, courts generally defer to the judgment of the legislature on what is a "public use."[38]

---

35 Ronald H. Coase, *The Problem of Social Cost*, 3 J.L. ECON. 1 (1960), https://www.law.uchicago.edu/files/file/coase-problem.pdf.

36 U.S. CONST. art 5.

37 *Current State Constitutional Provisions About Eminent Domain*, CASTLE COALITION, http://castlecoalition.org/current-state-constitutional-provisions-about-eminent-domain.

38 Kelo v. City of New London, 545 U.S. 469 (2005), https://supreme.justia.com/cases/federal/us/545/469/ (upholding taking of private residences to construct a privately-owned shopping center).

The *just compensation* provision could have become a significant limitation on environmental law by setting a boundary between what the government could do by regulation with costs to be borne by the owner and when government had to pay owners for restrictions imposed on their use of their property.[39] Early Supreme Court cases suggested that takings law might develop to protect individual owners against bearing more than their "just share" of measures that benefit the public generally[40] by requiring the costs of regulatory burdens that "went too far"[41] to be shared with the larger community through the tax system.

Modern cases, however, restrict the concept of *regulatory takings* to situations in which there was either a physical invasion of property[42] or the property was rendered entirely valueless.[43] Depriving an owner of the most lucrative uses of property is not a Fifth Amendment taking for which just compensation is due, provided that other uses are still available. Some courts construing state constitutions reach a different result, however. Even a total ban is permitted if the type of harm emanating from the property would have constituted a nuisance at common law.[44] This result is justified by the legal fiction that when the owner acquired the property, the government retained a *reserved power* to regulate nuisances. This doctrine immunizes most types of pollution control statutes against takings claims, although regulatory

---

39 For an excellent summary of how takings law has changed over time, see ROBERT MELTZ, CONGRESSIONAL RESEARCH SERVICE, TAKINGS DECISIONS OF THE U.S. SUPREME COURT: A CHRONOLOGY (2015), https://fas.org/sgp/crs/misc/97-122.pdf.

40 Monongahela Navigation Co. v. U.S. 148 U.S. 312, 325 (1893), https://supreme.justia.com/cases/federal/us/148/312/ (the just compensation requirement is designed to prevent "the public from loading upon one individual more than his just share of the burdens of government . . ."); *see also* Nollan v. California Coastal Comm'n, 483 U.S. 825, 835 n. 4 (1987), https://supreme.justia.com/cases/federal/us/483/825/ ("One of the principal purposes of the Takings Clause is 'to bar Government from forcing some people alone to bear public burdens which, in all fairness and justice, should be borne by the public as a whole.'" (quoting Armstrong v. U.S., 364 U.S. 40, 49 (1960), https://supreme.justia.com/cases/federal/us/364/40/)).

41 Pennsylvania Coal Co. v. Mahon, 260 U.S. 393 (1922), https://supreme.justia.com/cases/federal/us/260/393/. .

42 Loretto v. Teleprompter Manhattan CATV Corp., 458 U.S. 419 (1982), https://supreme.justia.com/cases/federal/us/458/419/.

43 Lucas v. South Carolina Coastal Council, 505 U.S. 1003 (1992), https://supreme.justia.com/cases/federal/us/505/1003/.

44 *Id.*

requirements must be "proportional" and must have a logical "nexus" to the harms being addressed.[45]

In assessing whether property is *taken*, the effect on the property as a whole is considered, rather than the effect on a particular property right. Consequently, a *partial taking* such as prohibiting building in the air rights above an historic landmark[46] or restricting construction or farming in wetlands does not require just compensation, provided that beneficial use of other portions of the parcel remain available.[47] These doctrines have been applied in environmental law to prohibit a lumber company from harvesting timber on land that it owns because the trees constitute *critical habitat* for an endangered species,[48] and to uphold a ban on the sale of eagle feathers, on the theory that other uses such as collecting or leaving them to one's heirs remain permissible.[49]

Most environmentalists applaud this modern narrowing of takings law. They had feared that there would be less protection of the environment if the government had to pay for adverse effects on property owners. However, a few academics argue that there might be less political resistance to environmental protection if those who suffer were compensated, or partially compensated, as in some other countries such as Australia.[50] Some U.S. environmental programs do provide partial compensation to losers through preferential tax deductions or transitional assistance for workers, but these are matters of legislative grace not constitutional requirement. Economic incentives such as subsidies that provide positive benefits have sometimes proved effective and are often more attractive politically than regulatory prohibitions that impose costs, as is discussed in the water and climate change chapters.[51]

---

45 Nollan v. California Coastal Comm'n, 483 U.S. 825 (1987), https://supreme.justia.com/cases/fed eral/us/483/825/; Dolan v. City of Tigard, 512 U.S. 374 (1994), https://supreme.justia.com/cases/ federal/us/512/374/.

46 Penn Central Transportation Co. v. New York City, 438 U.S. 104 (1978), https://supreme.justia. com/cases/federal/us/438/104/.

47 Palazzolo v. Rhode Island, 533 U.S. 606 (2001), https://supreme.justia.com/cases/federal/ us/533/606/.

48 Babbitt, Secretary of the Interior v. Sweet Home Chapter of Communities for a Great Oregon, 515 U.S. 687 (1995), https://supreme.justia.com/cases/federal/us/515/687/.

49 Andrus v. Allard, 444 U.S. 51 (1979), https://supreme.justia.com/cases/federal/us/444/51/.

50 *See* E. Donald Elliott, *How Takings Legislation Could Improve Environmental Regulation*, 38 WM. & MARY L. REV. 1177 (1997), http://digitalcommons.law.yale.edu/fss_papers/2215/.

51 *See* Chapter 4 and Chapter 5.

Environmental justice

In 1987, the United Church of Christ published a now famous study concluding that hazardous waste disposal sites were more frequently located in postal codes inhabited predominately by minority populations. This analysis led to broader charges of *environmental racism* regarding exposure to pollution and other *locally unwanted land uses* (LULUs). While the United Church of Christ study has been criticized on methodological grounds,[52] subsequent studies have borne out its basic conclusions—and concern about *environmental justice*, or "EJ" as it has come to be called, has thus become a major issue in the environmental policy arena.[53]

Indeed, EPA has created a variety of environmental justice offices and programs that act as internal watchdogs to make sure that EJ concerns are considered in agency actions.[54] But taking account of such equity considerations has proven to be challenging. In fact, a 2011 report by the Government Accountability Office concluded that EPA had made some progress on taking account of EJ burdens but needed to take additional actions.[55]

Ironically, some environmental justice problems may be an unintended consequence of the extensive opportunities for public participation and litigation provided by U.S. law. These entry points into policymaking increase the relative power of wealthy communities that can afford to

---

52 Vicki Been, *What's Fairness Got to Do With It? Environmental Justice and the Siting of Locally Undesirable Land Uses*, 78 CORNELL L. REV. 1001 (1993), https://scholarship.law.cornell.edu/clr/vol78/iss6/1/.

53 For a good summary of the critiques, subsequent studies, and the environmental justice movement generally, see Alan Ramo, *Book Review: The Promise and Peril of Environmental Justice* 40 SANTA CLARA L. REV. 941 (2000) (reviewing CHRISTOPHER H. FOREMAN, JR., THE PROMISE AND PERIL OF ENVIRONMENTAL JUSTICE (1998)), http://digitalcommons.law.ggu.edu/cgi/viewcontent.cgi?article=1133&context=pubs.

54 *See, e.g.*, EPA, Environmental Justice, https://www.epa.gov/environmentaljustice; EPA, Summary of Executive Order 12898 - Federal Actions to Address Environmental Justice in Minority Populations and Low-Income Populations, https://www.epa.gov/laws-regulations/summary-executive-order-12898-federal-actions-address-environmental-justice; EPA, National Environmental Justice Advisory Council, https://www.epa.gov/environmentaljustice/national-environmental-justice-advisory-council; EPA, EJ 2020 Action Agenda: EPA's Environmental Justice Strategy, https://www.epa.gov/environmentaljustice/ej-2020-action-agenda.

55 U.S. GOVERNMENT ACCOUNTABILITY OFFICE, ENVIRONMENTAL JUSTICE: EPA NEEDS TO TAKE ADDITIONAL ACTIONS TO HELP ENSURE EFFECTIVE IMPLEMENTATION (2011), https://www.gao.gov/assets/590/585654.pdf.

use them to resist LULUs. While some communities lack voice, others have the resources to engage effectively in political debates or legal processes and thus block waste sites, incinerators, and other undesirable activities—often called the *NIMBY syndrome*—as the politically organized declare: "Not In My Back Yard."

As environmental justice becomes a central lens through which we evaluate efforts to promote sustainability, multiple dimensions of the concern about *equity* that underpins the EJ concept must be recognized. First, while some questions of fairness center on who pays for pollution control, who pays for inaction in the face of environmental harms represents an equally important issue. Specifically, we must ask: who ends up breathing polluted air, drinking contaminated water, or facing the consequences of unabated climate change? Second, in addition to domestic issues of equity, environmental justice must also reflect international aspects of fairness, particularly for inescapably transboundary issues such as climate change. Finally, with regard to problems that extend into the future (sometimes called issues with a *long tail*), questions of intergenerational fairness must be answered. Specifically, are we leaving our children, grandchildren, and generations beyond that with environmental problems of our creation for which they will have to pay?

Competitiveness concerns

Whenever Congress, a state legislature, or an administrative agency debates how stringent to be in setting environmental standards, the most significant pushback often comes from those who worry about the impact of new and potentially expensive standards on the competitiveness of individual companies and the economy as a whole. The fear will often be expressed in terms of burdening local enterprises as they try to sell into a marketplace where competitors have a structural advantage based on lower costs of production that derive in part from lower expenses on pollution control and other environmental obligations.

How material the differences in environmental compliance costs are varies depending upon their relative weight compared to other factors such as labor costs and proximity to markets. Those who take competitiveness impacts seriously often speak of the risk of a *race to the bottom* in environmental controls that may result in strategic behavior by various jurisdictions that seek to maintain the competitiveness of their industries and their broader economic vitality by adopting lax standards.[56] Others see a range of regulatory requirements as a natural result of a diversity of economic circumstances, risk preferences, and geographic factors, viewing the resulting competition as beneficial.[57] In coming to this conclusion, they often cite the influential work of the economist Charles Tiebout, who theorized that regulatory competition across jurisdictions helps to deliver the optimal provision of public goods (including regulation) and thus should be regarded as welfare enhancing.[58] Harvard Business School professor and competitiveness guru Michael Porter makes an interesting alternative claim. He argues that high environmental standards can drive corporate innovation and enhance competitiveness.[59]

Whether to mitigate competitiveness concerns and harmonize environmental laws across the United States, or even across international boundaries, has been vigorously debated for years.[60] This question has recently reemerged with new force in the context of a broader pushback against globalization and the impacts of international trade.[61] Thus, while the economic case for worrying about environmentally derived competitive disadvantage remains contested, the political reality of these concerns cannot be denied.

56 Daniel C. Esty, *Revitalizing Environmental Federalism*, 95 MICH. L. REV. 570 (1996), https://digitalcommons.law.yale.edu/cgi/viewcontent.cgi?article=1449&context=fss_papers. *See also* Scott Barrett, *Strategy and Environment*, 27 COLUM. J. WORLD BUS. (1993).

57 Richard Revesz, *Rehabilitating Interstate Competition: Rethinking the 'Race-to-the-Bottom' Rationale for Federal Environmental Regulation*, 67 N.Y.U. L. REV. 1210 (1992), https://heinonline.org/HOL/LandingPage?handle=hein.journals/nylr67&div=43&id=&page=.

58 Charles Tiebout, *A Pure Theory of Local Expenditures*, 64 J. POL. ECON. 416 (1956), https://www.jstor.org/stable/1826343.

59 Michael E. Porter and Claas van der Linde, *Toward a New Conception of the Environment-Competitiveness Relationship* 9 J. ECON. PERSP. 97 (1995), https://www.aeaweb.org/articles?id=10.1257/jep.9.4.97.

60 E. Donald Elliott et al., *Toward a Theory or Statutory Evolution, The Federalization of Environmental Law*, 2 J. L. ECON. & ORG. 313, 326–27 (1985), https://digitalcommons.law.yale.edu/fss_papers/2668/; DANIEL C. ESTY, GREENING THE GATT 157–63 (1994).

61 Daniel C. Esty, *Free Trade and Environmental Protection*, in THE GLOBAL ENVIRONMENT: INSTITUTIONS, LAW AND POLICY (Regina S. Axelrod & Stacy D. Vandeveer eds., 5th ed. 2020).

Additional resources

Elliott, E. Donald and Esty, Daniel C. (2021). The End Environmental Externalities Manifesto: A Rights-Based Foundation for Environmental Law. *New York University Environmental Law Journal*, 29(3), forthcoming.

Fischoff, Baruch (2011). *Communicating Risks and Benefits: An Evidence-Based User's Guide*. Food and Drug Administration. https://www.fda.gov/files/about%20ofda/pub lished/Communicating-Risk-and-Benefits---An-Evidence-Based-User%27s-Guide-%28Printer-Friendly%29.pdf.

Graham, John D. and Wiener, Jonathan B. (2009). *Risk vs. Risk: Tradeoffs in Protecting Health and the Environment.* Harvard University Press.

National Research Council (2009). *Science and Decisions: Advancing Risk Assessment.* https://www.nap.edu/catalog/12209/science-and-decisions-advancing-risk-assessment.

Nordhaus, William D. (2021). *The Spirit of Green: The Economics of Collisions and Contagions in a Crowded World.* Princeton University Press.

Rodricks, Joseph V. (2007). *Calculated Risks: The Toxicity and Human Health Risks of Chemicals in Our Environment* (2nd ed.). Cambridge University Press.

Society for Risk Analysis (2018). *Core Subjects of Risk Analysis.* https://www.sra.org/wp-content/uploads/2020/04/SRA-Core-Subjects-R2.pdf.

3   The Clean Air Act: successful but slow

In an era in which many people perceive most U.S. government programs as failing,[1] the Clean Air Act (CAA) stands out as a notable success. It has achieved measurable progress in reducing every pollutant that it regulates.[2] Most of the benefits to human health achieved by U.S. environmental law are attributable to reductions in air pollution. In addition, many of the innovations in U.S. environmental law, such as offsets and tradeable pollution rights, were pioneered by Environmental Protection Agency's (EPA) air program, the Office of Air and Radiation (OAR).

Nevertheless, 137 million people, about one-third of the U.S. population, live in counties that violate one or more of the health-based *National Ambient Air Quality Standards* (NAAQS).[3] As of the date of this writing, EPA has not developed a successful program to address climate change that will withstand judicial and political review.[4] In addition, some have criticized EPA's air pollution control programs as slow, bureaucratic, and too expensive.[5]

What we call the *Clean Air Act* is technically the *Clean Air Act Amendments of 1970*, which built on top of various pieces of national clean air legislation that go back as far as 1955. The 1970 Amendments were the first to move primary responsibility for regulating air

---

1 PETER H. SCHUCK, WHY GOVERNMENT FAILS SO OFTEN: AND HOW IT CAN DO BETTER (2014).

2 *National Air Quality: Status and Trends of Key Air Pollutants*, EPA (Aug. 20, 2020), https://www. epa.gov/air-trends. EPA sets NAAQS for six "ubiquitous" pollutants: (1) ground-level ozone (VOCs), (2) particulate matter, (3) carbon monoxide (CO), (4) lead, (5) sulfur dioxide (SO2), and (6) nitrogen dioxide (NOx). Pollutants that only create localized problems—as opposed to those that are found everywhere—are regulated separately under § 112 of the CAA. *Id.*

3 *Air Quality – National Summary*, EPA (Nov. 23, 2020), https://www.epa.gov/air-trends/air-quality-national-summary.

4 *See* Chapter 4 on climate change.

5 For a balanced assessment of pros and cons, see E. Donald Elliott, *A Critical Assessment of EPA's Air Program at 50 and a Suggestion for How It Might Do Even Better*, 70 CASE WESTERN L. REV. 895 (2020), https://scholarlycommons.law.case.edu/caselrev/vol70/iss4/6/.

pollution, which previously had been left to states and localities, to the national level. The 1970 Amendments established the main contours of the air pollution control system that applies today, but significant amendments in 1977 and 1990 added important features.

The 1977 Clean Air Act Amendments made mid-course corrections to address unintended consequences that developed under the 1970 law. The 1990 Amendments modernized the statute by creating an acid rain emissions allowance trading program, repairing ineffective air toxics provisions, and copying successful permitting and enforcement systems from the Clean Water Act. They also implemented the Montreal Protocol to phase out chlorofluorocarbons (CFCs) that had been identified as an anthropogenic cause of the breakdown of the Earth's protective ozone layer.[6] Most experts consider this international treaty to phase out ozone-depleting substances to be the most successful international environmental agreement to date.[7]

Overview of lawmaking under the Clean Air Act

The drafters of the 1970 Clean Air Act Amendments realized that they did not know how to accomplish the gargantuan task of regulating millions of individual sources of air pollution. Instead, they created a toolbox that would give EPA multiple tools to address air pollution, as shown in Table 3.1 below.

This toolbox strategy allowed for agency experimentation to determine which techniques were most successful. Some elements, such as the *Imminent and Substantial Endangerment* provision, which has emerged as an important tool for controlling toxic waste under the Resource Conservation and Recovery Act (RCRA), have hardly ever been used under the CAA. Other provisions, such as the *Prevention of Significant Deterioration* (PSD) of air quality and *non-attainment* requirements, were first developed by administrative interpretation and then codified and elaborated by legislation. This structure of regulatory evolution is a pattern that we will see repeated over and over in U.S. environmental law, as legislatures, administrative agencies, and

---

6 *See* Chapter 4 for a summary of the Montreal Protocol.

7 *International Day for the Preservation of the Ozone Layer*, UNITED NATIONS, https://www.un.org/en/events/ozoneday.

Table 3.1 Key sections of the Clean Air Act

Section	Topic	Full Text
§ 108	Criteria Documents	https://www.law.cornell.edu/uscode/text/42/7408
§ 109	National Ambient Air Quality Standards (NAAQS)	https://www.law.cornell.edu/uscode/text/42/7409
§ 110	State Implementation Plans (SIPs)	https://www.law.cornell.edu/uscode/text/42/7410
§ 111	New Source Performance Standards (NSPS)	https://www.law.cornell.edu/uscode/text/42/7411
§ 112	National Emissions Standards for Especially Hazardous Air Pollutants (NESHAPs aka MACT standards)	https://www.law.cornell.edu/uscode/text/42/7412
§ 113	Enforcement	https://www.law.cornell.edu/uscode/text/42/7413
§ 116	"Savings Clause" (states may regulate more stringently except autos)	https://www.law.cornell.edu/uscode/text/42/7416
§§ 160-199	Prevention of Significant Deterioration (PSD)	https://www.law.cornell.edu/uscode/text/42/7470 to https://www.law.cornell.edu/uscode/text/42/7479
§§ 170-193	Non-Attainment	https://www.law.cornell.edu/uscode/text/42/7501 to https://www.law.cornell.edu/uscode/text/42/7515
§ 303	Imminent and Substantial Endangerment	https://www.law.cornell.edu/uscode/text/42/7603
§ 304	Citizens Suits	https://www.law.cornell.edu/uscode/text/42/7704
§ 307	Public Participation and Procedure	https://www.law.cornell.edu/uscode/text/42/7707
§ 201-250	Regulation of Mobile Sources	https://www.epa.gov/clean-air-act-overview/clean-air-act-title-ii-emission-standards-moving-sources-parts-through-c

Table 3.1   (continued)

Section	Topic	Full Text
§ 211	Regulation of Fuels	https://www.law.cornell.edu/uscode/text/42/7545
§§ 401–416	Acid Rain	https://www.law.cornell.edu/uscode/text/42/7651 to https://www.law.cornell.edu/uscode/text/42/7651f
§§ 501–507	Permits	https://www.law.cornell.edu/uscode/text/42/7661 to https://www.law.cornell.edu/uscode/text/42/7661f
§§ 601–618	Stratospheric Ozone	https://www.law.cornell.edu/uscode/text/42/7671 to https://www.law.cornell.edu/uscode/text/42/7671q

Source: *The Clean Air Act in a Nutshell: How It Works*, EPA (Mar. 22, 2013), https://www.epa.gov/sites/production/files/2015-05/documents/caa_nutshell.pdf.

courts engage in a *three-cornered conversation*[8] that develops policy interactively in the light of experience. In what follows, we discuss the most important features of this complex statute and EPA's extensive administrative rules and interpretations implementing it.

Cooperative federalism: NAAQS and SIPs

Initially, the mainstay of regulation of air pollution under the CAA was a system of *cooperative federalism*, in which the national government identified mandatory minimum air quality targets based on expert evaluation of science but delegated implementation to the states.[9]

---

8 E. Donald Elliott, *Book Review*, 23 J. ECON. LITERATURE 654 (1985) (reviewing R. SHEP MELNICK, REGULATION AND THE COURTS: THE CASE OF THE CLEAN AIR ACT (1983)).

9 Union Elec. Co. v. EPA, 427 U.S. 246 (1976), https://supreme.justia.com/cases/federal/us/427/246/.

The first step is developing criteria documents under section 108 for a core set of various types of air pollution, sometimes called *criteria air pollutants*.[10] These documents are literature reviews of the science regarding the adverse effects of pervasive air pollutants, such as those from burning fossil fuels, which outside experts, the Clean Air Science Advisory Committee (CASAC), review and comment upon. Next, EPA proposes and adopts NAAQS via notice and comment rulemaking under section 109 for ubiquitous pollutants. The NAAQS are minimum[11] standards of air quality that are necessary to protect human health with an adequate margin of safety and to eliminate non-health adverse *welfare* effects of air pollution, such as reduced visibility. EPA then directs states to prepare *state implementation plans* (SIPs) to meet the standards that have been set. *Plans* is a misnomer because SIPs are a collection of state laws and regulations to limit pollution from stationary sources of air pollution such as factories and powerplants. States submit their SIPs for approval by EPA and, once approved, SIPs become enforceable under federal as well as state law. Every SIP is supposed to add up to achieving *attainment and maintenance* of compliance with the NAAQS. If a SIP is inadequate, EPA may issue a *SIP call* directing the state to revise it, and if it fails to do so, EPA may issue its own *federal implementation plan* (FIP). EPA sometimes develops a draft FIP to signal to a recalcitrant state what sort of regulatory provisions it should anticipate if it does not produce an adequate SIP—with the hope that the threat of federal intervention will prod the state into action.

Fixing unintended consequences Part I: PSD

EPA initially established NAAQS on a uniform basis nationally. The unintended consequence was that a company could no longer build a new factory in an already polluted area, but it could build the same factory without any add-on pollution controls in a pristine area where there was enough room left under the emissions limits of the national standards. If nothing were done to right the situation, the incentives created by the uniform national pollution limits would have resulted in a homogenized level of pollution just below the national standards

---

10 The CAA *criteria air pollutants* are: carbon monoxide (CO), lead, ground-level ozone (O_3), particulate matter (PM), nitrogen oxides (NOx), and sulfur dioxide (SO_2).

11 Clean Air Act § 116, 42 U.S.C. § 7416, https://www.law.cornell.edu/uscode/text/42/7416.

throughout the country—with new industry moving to pristine places with low levels of air pollution.

The Sierra Club sued, basing its argument on the introductory statement of purpose that Congress intended the 1970 law to "protect and enhance the quality" of the air rather than to make it uniformly dirty. Unlike courts in Europe, courts in the United States do not normally place much credence on the precatory statements of purpose in legislation, but in this case, a single federal district judge in Washington, D.C., Judge John Pratt, accepted the Sierra Club's argument. Judge Pratt issued a handwritten injunction prohibiting EPA from approving any state SIPs that allowed "significant deterioration" of air quality in clean air areas that were already meeting their NAAQS.[12] Thus, was born the requirement for *prevention of significant deterioration* or PSD, a term that at the time was not defined either in the statute or in Judge Pratt's opinion. Judge Pratt's opinion was affirmed without opinion on appeal, which handed the problem back to EPA to figure out how to prevent the air in areas meeting the national standards from getting significantly dirtier.

EPA promulgated regulations in November 1974, inventing the concept of *PSD increments*, quantitative limits on how much dirtier the air is allowed become in clean areas.[13] These were set at 10 percent of the NAAQS. States would be permitted to authorize new or modified sources of pollution to increase their pollution in relatively clean areas, provided that they installed *best available control technology* (BACT) and that the remaining pollution that was emitted did not consume more than the PSD increment remaining available. EPA also invented the concept of particularly sensitive Class I areas such as national parks or wilderness areas that get even more stringent protection. In short, states were allowed discretion to make their air a little dirtier but not by too much. Eventually Congress ratified and strengthened EPA's approach in the 1977 Amendments.

Today PSD is one of the most complicated, and most litigated, parts of America's clean air program. The definition of a *physical or*

---

12 Sierra Club v. Ruckelshaus, 344 F. Supp. 253 (D.D.C. 1972), *aff'd*, (D.C. Cir. 1972), *aff'd by an equally divided court sub nom*; Fri v. Sierra Club, 412 U.S. 541 (1973), https://law.justia.com/cases/federal/district-courts/FSupp/344/253/2303400/.

13 Press Release, EPA, EPA Issues "Significant Deterioration" Regulations (Nov. 27, 1974), https://archive.epa.gov/epa/aboutepa/epa-issues-significant-deterioration-regulations.html.

operational change triggering PSD review is several pages long in the Code of Federal Regulations[14] and PSD is the subject of hundreds of court decisions, rulemakings and guidance documents.

Fixing unintended consequences Part II: non-attainment

The 1970 Clean Air Act Amendment's unrealistic goal to clean up the air nationwide in just five years, by 1975, was a product of a political competition to out-promise one another between then-President Richard Nixon and his likely political opponent in the 1972 election, Senator Edmund Muskie of Maine, the primary congressional drafter of both the Clean Air and Clean Water Acts.[15] This unrealistic deadline came and went, leading to the need for measures to deal with *non-attainment areas* which continued to have pollution levels above the national standards.[16] When the deadline passed, EPA had to figure out what to do in areas that were violating the mandatory air quality standards. Would the government stop issuing permits to build new factories because additional sources of pollution would exacerbate non-compliance with air quality standards? Paul DeFalco, EPA's Regional Administrator for Region 9, which includes California, came up with a clever solution: issue permits for new factories or other major sources of air pollution in non-attainment areas but on two conditions:

(1) that they must install on the proposed new source the most stringent air pollution controls anywhere in the world; and
(2) that they also obtain compensating reductions (called *offsets*) within the same airshed to make up for the additional air pollution that would be emitted despite controls.

That way, construction of a new source would not make air pollution in the non-attainment area any worse (although it was not being made any better either). The head of EPA's air program in Washington

---

14 40 C.F.R. § 52.21 (2020), https://www.law.cornell.edu/cfr/text/40/52.21. For a general overview, see Art Fraas et al., *EPA's New Source Review Program: Time for Reform?*, 47 ENVTL. L. REP. 10026 (2017).
15 The story of the political competition between Nixon and Muskie that shaped the Clean Air Act is told in E. Donald Elliott et al., *Toward a Theory of Statutory Evolution: The Federalization of Environmental Law*, 1 J.L. ECON. & ORG. 313 (1985), https://core.ac.uk/download/pdf/72829994.pdf.
16 Roger Strelow, *Reviewing the Clean Air Act*, 4 ECOLOGY L. Q. 583 (1975), https://www.jstor.org/stable/24112495?seq=1#metadata_info_tab_contents.

at that time, Roger Strelow, recognized this good idea and adopted Region 9's approach as national policy. Eventually, Congress incorporated this approach into the 1977 Amendments, which mandated that areas out of compliance with the national ambient air quality standards could continue to build provided:

(1)   the state adopted a revised plan to make *reasonable further progress* to get into compliance;
(2)   new sources installed pollution control technology with the *lowest achievable emission rate* (LAER) of any plant of that type operating anywhere in the world, or even lower if EPA's engineering projections concluded that a plant of that type could do better; and
(3)   that the new pollution source obtained offsets to make up for the remaining pollution.

Offsets could be generated by buying a facility that emitted pollution of the same type and reducing its pollution either by shutting it down or installing better pollution controls. Eventually, *offset banks* were set up where companies that wanted to build in a non-attainment area could buy the required offsets from third parties, and a market developed for facilities that could be shut down or else have additional pollution controls installed. Congress contemplated none of this when it originally passed the law in 1970, but creative interpretations by EPA developed it over time. Today, marketable offsets are widely used under several programs to provide additional compliance options. Congress strengthened the law regarding non-attainment areas in 1990, adding a requirement that in the most heavily polluted areas, new sources had to supply offsets up to 150 percent of their added pollution, thereby making the situation better rather than merely no worse.

The biggest problem with both the PSD and *New Source Review* (NSR) programs was that they only applied initially to new or modified sources of air pollution but exempted existing sources. This approach is called *grandfathering*, and it created incentives to keep older dirtier plants online longer.[17] Eventually EPA fixed that by bringing hundreds of enforcement cases against individual sources, claiming that physical

---

17   *See* Richard Revesz and Jack Lienke, Struggling for Air: Power Plants and the "War on Coal" (2016).

or operational changes triggered PSD or non-attainment requirements. The Supreme Court eventually accepted EPA's creative legal theories.[18]

Direct federal regulation: NSPS and NESHAPs

The system of NAAQS and SIPs has been criticized as requiring multiple steps, which makes it cumbersome and slow.[19] In retrospect, it appears to be a transitional strategy from state to federal regulation, although it remains in effect today.

The health and welfare-based NAAQS, sometimes called *media quality-based standards*, are supplemented by a series of *technology-based standards* set at the national level that apply directly to categories of industry that cause or contribute to air pollution; both require polluters to install variations of *best available control technology* (BACT) regardless of whether they are creating a health issue in the immediate vicinity. These are *new source performance standards* (NSPS), which apply to over 140 categories of industries,[20] and *national emissions for especially hazardous air pollutants* (NESHAPs), which apply to emitters of carcinogens and other air toxics that are not ubiquitous but may create health risks in a local area.[21]

One advantage of setting standards based on technology, rather than media quality, is that the engineering issues are usually less difficult than the scientific ones of establishing a safe level of air pollution. By many measures, the NSPS program is one of EPA's most successful. It provides a modest role for economics and other values such as energy in setting standards. NSPS levels generally work out to be about 90 to 95 percent reductions from uncontrolled levels of pollution; these limits tend to be less controversial and easier to adopt politically than more stringent requirements under other sections of the statute. Sometimes pushing for less in the short run ends up accomplishing more in the long run.

18 Envtl. Def. v. Duke Energy Corp., 549 U.S. 561 (2007), https://supreme.justia.com/cases/federal/us/549/561/.
19 National Research Council, AIR QUALITY MANAGEMENT IN THE UNITED STATES (2004), https://doi.org/10.17226/10728; *see also* RICHARD REVESZ AND JACK LIENKE, STRUGGLING FOR AIR: POWER PLANTS AND THE "WAR ON COAL" (2016).
20 40 C.F.R. § 60 (2020), https://www.law.cornell.edu/cfr/text/40/part-60.
21 40 C.F.R. § 63 (2020), https://www.law.cornell.edu/cfr/text/40/part-63.

The NESHAPs program as originally enacted in 1970 required EPA to prove that the emissions of specific chemical compounds would be hazardous to health. This requirement proved difficult to implement and resulted in extensive litigation. In twenty years, EPA had only set seven air toxics standards, and several of them were still tied up in litigation. The 1990 Amendments revised the NESHAPs program along the lines of the more successful NSPS program. In the first round of regulation, EPA sets technology-based *maximum achievable control technology* (MACT) requirements, which are based on the best existing controls for plants of similar types. Then in a second round of regulation, EPA goes back to assess whether the *residual risks* remaining after the application of MACT are unacceptable through *risks and technology reviews* (RTRs) every eight years.[22] In addition, in 1990, Congress directed EPA to regulate 189 specific substances identified by name in the statute unless they were proven not to be hazardous (called *delisting*), thereby reversing the burden of proof.[23] This system has proven more successful, and today NESHAPS regulate over 150 categories of industry, comprising thousands of individual sources of pollution.[24]

Mobile sources and *technology forcing*

By most measures, Title II of the CAA, which regulates *mobile sources* such as automobiles, trucks, trains, and airplanes, has been a great success. A car sold in the United States today produces less than 10 percent of the air pollution than one did in 1970.[25] The mainstay of these reductions has been *technology forcing* regulations that set mandatory pollution limits per vehicle mile traveled, even in advance of the invention of technology capable of meeting them, thereby creating incentives for industry to develop the necessary technology.[26] Despite

---

22 *Risk and Technology Review of the National Emissions Standards for Hazardous Air Pollutants*, EPA (Mar. 24, 2020), https://www.epa.gov/stationary-sources-air-pollution/risk-and-technology-review-national-emissions-standards-hazardous.

23 For a general argument that placing the burden to prove safety on polluters, rather than the burden on government to prove harm reduces incentives for delay, see David Roe, *Barking Up the Right Tree: Recent Progress in Focusing the Toxics Issue*, 13 COLUM. J. ENVTL L. 275 (1988).

24 40 C.F.R. § 63 (2020), https://www.law.cornell.edu/cfr/text/40/part-63.

25 *History of Reducing Air Pollution from Transportation in the United States* (Nov. 4, 2020), EPA, https://www.epa.gov/transportation-air-pollution-and-climate-change/accomplishments-and-success-air-pollution-transportation.

26 Thomas O. McGarity, *Radical Technology-Forcing in Environmental Regulation*, 27 LOY. L.A. L. REV. 943 (1994), https://digitalcommons.lmu.edu/llr/vol27/iss3/11/.

these dramatic reductions in the pollution from each individual car, increasing vehicle-miles-traveled have eaten up about half the gains (an example of a phenomenon called the *Jevons effect* or *rebound effect* by which some of the benefits of technological improvements are lost due to changes in behavior[27]). Today, Americans drive about twice as far every day as Europeans do because our cities are more spread out and many lack good public transportation.[28] This regulatory focus reflects a general trend in U.S. environmental law which tends to rely more on technology and less on incentives to change consumer behavior than in Europe.

1990 CAA Amendments: regional approaches and technology-based regulation

One harsh critic of the air program, New York Law School professor David Schoenbrod, has taken Congress to task for supposedly not realizing when it enacted the 1970 law that many air pollution problems are regional because emissions do not stop at states lines.[29] By 1990, that had become obvious in the form of acid rain, which affected New York, Connecticut, and other Northeastern states as well as several Canadian provinces but was caused largely by coal-burning powerplants in the Midwest. Led by President George Herbert Walker Bush, Congress responded by enacting the Acid Rain Trading Program in the 1990 Amendments. This economic incentive-based regulatory strategy was the first large-scale experiment with tradeable air pollution rights, an idea that economists had been suggesting since 1968.[30] Under an emissions allowance trading approach, sometimes called a *cap and trade* program, rather than the government specifying a mandatory level of control for each plant, the law provides allowances to each

27 WILLIAM STANLEY JEVONS, THE COAL QUESTION; AN INQUIRY CONCERNING THE PROGRESS OF THE NATION, AND THE PROBABLE EXHAUSTION OF OUR COAL MINES (1866).

28 E. Donald Elliott, *Why the United States Does Not Have a Renewable Energy Policy*, 43 ENVTL. L. REP. 10095 (2013), https://digitalcommons.law.yale.edu/fss_papers/5114/.

29 David Schoenbrod, *The Clean Air Act Is in No Shape to Be Celebrated*, HUFFINGTON POST (Sept. 3, 2010, 12:44 PM), https://www.huffpost.com/entry/the-clean-air-act-is-in-n_b_704631.

30 JOHN H. DALES, POLLUTION, PROPERTY AND PRICES: AN ESSAY IN POLICY-MAKING AND ECONOMICS (1968); W. David Montgomery, *Markets in Licenses and Efficient Pollution Control Programs*, 5 J. ECON. THEORY 395 (1972), https://www.sciencedirect.com/science/article/abs/pii/0022053172900049X; BRUCE A. ACKERMAN ET AL., THE UNCERTAIN SEARCH FOR ENVIRONMENTAL QUALITY (1974); Hugh S. Gorman and Barry D. Solomon, *The Origins and Practice of Emissions Trading*, 14 J. POL'Y HIST. 293 (2002).

plant to emit a specified amount of pollution, but allows the polluters to trade allowances with others.

As a result, plants that can reduce their pollution efficiently, and thus reduce their emissions below their allowance allocation, can sell their unused pollution allotments to other plants which are having trouble reducing their emissions cost-effectively. Thus, some plants overperform, which allows others to control less pollution, but in the aggregate the total level of pollution will be the same. By most accounts, the acid rain cap and trade program has been a remarkable success, "reduc[ing] more pollution in the last decade than all other Clean Air Act command-and-control programs combined, and . . . at two-thirds of the cost to accomplish those reductions using a 'command-and-control' system."[31] Some feared that *hot spots* would develop as trading concentrated emissions in local areas, a plausible fear but one that did not materialize.[32]

However, the acid rain cap and trade program only applied to a single pollutant, sulfur dioxide. Attempts to pass legislation authorizing EPA to create similar cap and trade systems for other pollutants failed in Congress in 1990 and again in 2002 to 2003 and 2009. Once again, EPA stepped in to correct Congress's shortcomings by interpretation. EPA used its existing authority to require states to revise their SIPs if they were creating NAAQS violations in other states and to allow efficient regional pollution trading modeled on the acid rain program as a compliance method. It took 20 years, but finally the Supreme Court upheld EPA's creative interpretation to allow regional trading of other pollutants.[33] However, when EPA tried to use its interpretive authority under a different section of the law to create a trading system for greenhouse gases, the Supreme Court issued an unusual stay

---

31 Press Release, The White House, Executive Summary – The Clear Skies Initiative, https:// georgewbush-whitehouse.archives.gov/news/releases/2002/02/clearskies.html.

32 Byron Swift, *Allowance Trading and SO2 Hot Spots—Good News from the Acid Rain Program*, 31 ENVTL REP. 954 (2000), https://www.eli.org/research-report/allowance-trading-and-so2-hot-spots-good-news-acid-rain-program.

33 EPA v. EME Homer City Generation, L.P., 572 U.S. 489 (2014), https://supreme.justia.com/cases/ federal/us/572/489/#:~:text=EME%20Homer%20City%20Generation%2C%20L.%20P.%2C%20 572%20U.S.%20489%20(2014)&text=The%20Clean%20Air%20Act%20(CAA,protect%20pub lic%20health%2C%2042%20U.S.C. The full story is told in E. Donald Elliott, *A Critical Assessment of EPA's Air Program at 50 and a Suggestion for How It Might Do Even Better*, 70 CASE WESTERN L. REV. 895 (2020), which criticizes the system as having "too many moving parts" and therefore taking almost 50 years to address interstate air pollution.

preventing the Obama Administration's Clean Power Plan from going into effect by a five-to-four vote,[34] and it was later revoked by the Trump Administration.[35] On January 19, 2021—the day before Joe Biden was sworn into office as President—a panel of the D.C. Circuit invalidated the Trump Administration's rule replacing and revoking the Obama Administration's Clean Power Plan by a two-to-one vote, holding that Section 111(d) of the Clean Air Act does not unambiguously prohibit consideration of shifting load to cleaner generating sources as the Trump Administration had contended.[36] Unless overturned by the court *en banc* or the Supreme Court, which seems unlikely as of this writing, this decision wipes the slate clean and means the Biden Administration is likely to try again, either through new legislation or new regulations issued under EPA's existing statutory authority.

The 1990 Amendments also expanded a system of operating permits to all major sources, which was modeled on the successful permit program under the Clean Water Act. However, under the air act, unlike the water act, permits may not impose or change pollution control requirements, but merely codify in a single document the requirements that come from SIPs, NSPSs and NESHAPs, as well as specify testing and other administrative requirements.[37] Most permits are issued by states pursuant to EPA requirements,[38] but some are issued by EPA's regional offices where no approved state permitting program exists.

In conclusion, the CAA has been one of the most successful environmental programs ever adopted in the United States. It has dramatically improved air quality across the nation for those pollutants that it regulates, as shown in Figure 3.1 below. Critics might argue that some of these accomplishments have taken a generation or more. And

34 West Virginia v. EPA, 136 S.Ct. 1000 (2016); *see also* Countney Scobie, *Supreme Court Stays EPA's Clean Power Plan*, ABA (Feb. 17, 2016), https://www.americanbar.org/groups/litigation/committees/environmental-energy/practice/2016/021716-energy-supreme-court-stays-epas-clean-power-plan/.

35 Repeal of the Clean Power Plan; Emission Guidelines for Greenhouse Gas Emissions From Existing Electric Utility Generating Units; Revisions to Emission Guidelines Implementing Regulations, 84 Fed. Reg. 32520 (July 8, 2019) (to be codified at 40 C.F.R. pt. 60).

36 American Lung Association et al. v. EPA, No. 19-1140 (D.C. Cir. Jan 19, 2021), https://www.cadc.uscourts.gov/internet/opinions.nsf/6356486C5963F49185258662005677F6/$file/19-1140.correctedopinion.pdf.

37 For more details, see *Permitting Under the Clean Air Act*, EPA, (Nov. 5, 2020), https://www.epa.gov/caa-permitting.

38 40 C.F.R. § 70 (2020), https://www.law.cornell.edu/cfr/text/40/part-70.

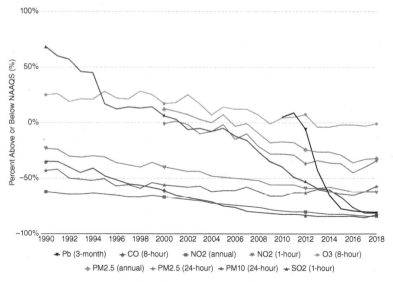

Source: *Our Nation's Air*, EPA (2019), https://gispub.epa.gov/air/trendsreport/2019/.

Figure 3.1   Declining national air pollutant concentration averages

others would suggest that the CAA approach has entailed unnecessary costs and inefficiencies. But the bottom line is a record of significant accomplishment.

The CAA's main drawbacks are its failure to date to address greenhouse gas (GHG) pollution despite an official 2009 endangerment finding that GHGs are contributing to climate change,[39] and the claims by some critics that the successes of the air program took too long and cost too much.[40]

---

39 Endangerment and Cause or Contribute Findings for Greenhouse Gases under the Section 202(a) of the Clean Air Act, 74 Fed. Reg. 66495, 66496 (Dec. 15, 2009) (to be codified at 40 C.F.R.).

40 For a summary, see E. Donald Elliott, *A Critical Assessment of EPA's Air Program at 50 and a Suggestion for How It Might Do Even Better*, 70 Case Western L. Rev. 895 (2020), https://scholarlycommons.law.case.edu/caselrev/vol70/iss4/6/.

Additional resources

Ackerman, Bruce A. and Hassler, William T. (1981). *Clean Coal/Dirty Air: or, How the Clean Air Act Became a Multibillion-dollar Bailout for High Sulphur Coal Producers and What Should Be Done About It.* Yale University Press.

Elliott, E. Donald (2020). A Critical Assessment of EPA's Air Program at 50 and a Suggestion for How It Might Do Even Better. *Case Western Law Review, 70*(4) 895–972.

National Research Council (2004). Air Quality Management in the United States. https://doi.org/10.17226/10728.

Revesz, Richard and Lienke, Jack (2016). *Struggling for Air: Power Plants and the "War on Coal".* Oxford University Press.

Schoenbrod, David (2010, September 3). The Clean Air Act Is in No Shape to Be Celebrated. *Huffington Post.* https://www.huffpost.com/entry/the-clean-air-act-is-in-n_b_704631.

4   Climate change: an "existential threat"[1] not yet addressed

Climate change is *the* environmental issue of over-arching importance for many people.[2] It also poses fundamental challenges for law and policy, for reasons we explain below.

According to leading climate scientists, the build-up of greenhouse gases (GHGs) in the atmosphere threatens to produce not only global warming but also more intense hurricanes, sea level rise that could inundate coastal communities or require expensive dike systems, and changed rainfall patterns that might disrupt farming and ranching and leave us with more floods, droughts, and uncontrolled forest fires.[3] Warming temperatures also risk unleashing new pests, such as the pine bark beetle that has devastated forests across the American West,[4] and wider geographical distributions, new vectors, and increased prevalence for diseases that might threaten public health.[5]

---

1 UN Secretary General António Guterres calls climate change an "existential threat" to humanity in a Keynote Address to R20 Austrian World Summit. *Climate change: An "existential threat" to humanity, UN chief warns*, UN NEWS (May 18, 2018), https://news.un.org/en/story/2018/05/1009782.

2 For example, Robert Post, the former dean of the Yale Law School opines, "Global warming is perhaps the single most significant threat facing the future of humanity on this planet." Robert Post, *Exxon-Mobil is abusing the first amendment*, WASH. POST (June 24, 2016), https://www.washingtonpost.com/opinions/exxonmobils-climate-change-smoke-screen/2016/06/24/2df8b29c-38c4-11e6-9ccd-d6005beac8b3_story.html.

3 *Sixth Assessment Report Climate Change 2021: Impacts, Adaptation, and Vulnerability*, Intergovernmental Panel on Climate Change (forthcoming 2021), https://www.ipcc.ch/report/sixth-assessment-report-working-group-ii/.

4 Daniel Strain, *Climate Change Sends Beetles into Overdrive*, SCIENCE (Mar. 16, 2012), https://www.sciencemag.org/news/2012/03/climate-change-sends-beetles-overdrive.

5 "Climate is one of the factors that influence the distribution of diseases borne by vectors (such as fleas, ticks, and mosquitoes, which spread pathogens that cause illness)." *Diseases Carried by Vectors*, CENTER FOR DISEASE CONTROL (June 18, 2020), https://www.cdc.gov/climateandhealth/effects/vectors.htm; *see also* John S. Brownstein et al., *Effect of Climate Change on Lyme Disease Risk in North America*, 2 ECOHEALTH 38 (2015), https://doi.org/10.1007/s10393-004-0139-x.

Climate change science and the Intergovernmental Panel on Climate Change

We know all of this—to the extent that humans can ever *know* the future on a subject as complex as how the mixture of gases in the atmosphere affects climate worldwide—due to the efforts of a unique institution that has not received sufficient attention, the Intergovernmental Panel on Climate Change (IPCC).[6] Established in 1988 by the World Meteorological Organization and the United Nations Environment Programme, the IPCC presents to policymakers the consensus of "thousands of experts from around the world [synthesizing] the most recent developments in climate science, adaptation, vulnerability, and mitigation every five to seven years."[7] Other scientific consensus panels also provide advice to policymakers on environmental issues including climate change—for example, those convened by the U.S. National Academy of Sciences and other national scientific societies—but none have been as influential worldwide as the IPCC, which shared the 2007 Nobel Peace Prize with Al Gore. Within the United States, many agencies undertake important climate science including the National Oceanic and Atmospheric Administration (NOAA) and the National Aeronautics and Space Administration (NASA), the national labs of the Department of Energy, and the Environmental Protection Agency (EPA), as well as many universities, often with grant support from the government.

The legal framework for addressing climate change involves multiple tiers of law, from global to national to state and local. It is also multi-dimensional as it must address a range of greenhouse gases including: (1) carbon dioxide (CO_2) from fossil fuel burning, (2) methane released during natural gas production and distribution as well as from landfills and various agricultural activities, and (3) a set of industrial chemicals such as sulfur hexafluoride (SF_6) used in various manufacturing processes. Moreover, it encompasses the laws that shape energy markets including electricity generation and distribution, incentives for energy efficiency, and public utility regulation.

---

6 *See* IPCC, https://www.ipcc.ch/.

7 *The IPCC: Who Are They and Why Do Their Climate Reports Matter?* Union of Concerned Scientists (Oct. 11, 2018), https://www.ucsusa.org/resources/ipcc-who-are-they#:~:text=The%20 Intergovernmental%20Panel%20on%20Climate%20Change%20(IPCC)%20was%20established%20 in,of%20the%20risk%20of%20human%2D.

Fashioning an effective response to climate change represents a particularly difficult policy challenge because GHG emissions blanket the Earth, making the problem inescapably global in scope and meaning that no nation can address the harm effectively on its own. These emissions, furthermore, have different atmospheric effects. Methane, for example, is about 30 times more potent (i.e., has a much larger *global warming potential*)[8] than carbon dioxide. But GHGs also vary considerably in their atmospheric lifetimes. Though more potent, methane only lasts about ten years in the atmosphere, while carbon dioxide lasts hundreds of years but with a *long tail*, meaning some emissions persist for 500 to 1000 years.[9] These factors, combined with the actual quantity of pollution emitted, lead to the calculation of *radiative forcing*, a measure of how much extra energy the Earth's surface has absorbed.[10]

This distribution across space and time makes climate change a particularly vexing problem with some commentators calling it a "super-externality."[11] Others describe climate change as a "super wicked" issue[12] and bemoan the mismatch between the transboundary scale of the problem and the national limits of regulatory authority. In

---

8 Global warming potential (GWP) is the heat absorbed by a mass of methane in the atmosphere compared to the same mass of carbon dioxide over a hundred-year timeframe. For further explanation and a quantitative summary of the GWP, lifetimes, and impacts of GHGs, see Flora Mactavish and Simon Buckle, *Climate change, greenhouse gases and radiative forcing* (Grantham Briefing Note 6) (2013), https://www.imperial.ac.uk/media/imperial-college/grantham-institute/public/publications/grantham-notes/Climate-change,-greenhouse-gases-and-radiative-forcing---Grantham-Note-6.pdf.

9 For a non-technical overview, see Moore, L. (2008, February 26). Greenhouse Gases: How Long Will They Last? http://blogs.edf.org/climate411/2008/02/26/ghg_lifetimes/; this also provides a counter-consideration to GWP for policymakers. See Shoemaker, J. K., and Schrag, D. P. (2013). The danger of overvaluing methane's influence on future climate change. *Climatic Change, 120*, 903–14. https://scholar.harvard.edu/files/dschrag/files/138._the-danger-of-overvaluing-methanes-influence-2013.pdf.

10 A brief yet comprehensive overview of radiative forcing can be found in Section C: Drivers of Climate Change of the Summary for Policymakers in IPCC, in *Climate Change 2013: The Physical Science Basis. Contribution of Working Group I to the Fifth Assessment Report of the Intergovernmental Panel on Climate Change*, IPCC (2013), https://www.ipcc.ch/site/assets/uploads/2018/02/WG1AR5_all_final.pdf.

11 DANIEL C. ESTY AND ANDREA DUA, SUSTAINING THE ASIA PACIFIC MIRACLE: ENVIRONMENTAL PROTECTION AND ECONOMIC INTEGRATION 7–8, 59–60 (1997).

12 Richard J. Lazarus, *Super Wicked Problems and Climate Change: Restraining the Present to Liberate the Future*, 94 CORNELL L. REV. 1153 (2009), https://www.lawschool.cornell.edu/research/cornell-law-review/upload/Lazarus.pdf; Kelly Levin et al., *Overcoming the Tragedy of Super Wicked Problems: Constraining Our Future Selves to Ameliorate Global Climate Change*, 45 POLICY SCIENCES 123 (2012), https://link.springer.com/article/10.1007/s11077-012-9151-0.

addition, since 1992,[13] the two main political parties in the United States have adopted different attitudes toward climate change, with Democrats generally favoring aggressive regulatory strategies and many, but not all, Republicans opposing ambitious policies to combat climate change.[14] While the Biden Administration has pledged to move forward decisively to fight climate change, as of 2021, it has only narrow majorities in the House and Senate and it remains to be seen whether it can get legislation passed on this subject. Despite this political constraint, federal agencies already possess a degree of statutory authority to address climate change without new legislative action.[15] For example, Professor Elliott has argued that EPA has existing statutory authority to impose a *user fee* on releases of GHGs and other pollutants into the atmosphere.[16]

Global policy framework

Because the atmosphere is an Earth systems resource shared worldwide, climate change is sometimes called a problem of the *global commons*, meaning that a successful response demands international collaboration.[17] In light of this reality, the countries of the world have come together and adopted a series of international agreements in which they commit to mutual action to address GHG emissions. But international law is not like domestic law. There is no legislature to pass statutes nor any police to enforce rules. As a result, the response to the problem has been halting.[18]

---

13 For a general description of the realignment of U.S. political parties on environmental issues following the 1992 elections, see E. Donald Elliott, *Politics Failed, Not Ideas*, 28 ENVTL FORUM 42 (2011), https://digitalcommons.law.yale.edu/fss_papers/5110/.

14 Drew Hudson, *RNC platform goes off the deep end of Climate Denial*, ENVTL ACTION, https://environmental-action.org/blog/rnc-platform-goes-off-the-deep-end-of-climate-denial/.

15 *See, e.g.,* Sierra D. McClain, *USDA May Use $30B Fund to Create Carbon Bank: Under a Biden administration, USDA may use Commodity Credit Corporation dollars to fight climate change*, CAPITAL PRESS (Feb. 1, 2021), https://www.capitalpress.com/nation_world/agriculture/usda-may-use-30b-fund-to-create-carbon-bank/article_7073db42-64cf-11eb-9391-db3b42e455ff.html.

16 E. Donald Elliott, *EPA's Existing Authority to Impose a Carbon "Tax"*, 49 ELR 10919 (2019), https://digitalcommons.law.yale.edu/cgi/viewcontent.cgi?article=6379&context=fss_papers.

17 For further reading on the theory of the atmosphere as a global commons, see Ottmar Edenhofer et al., *The Atmosphere as a Global Commons – Challenges for International Cooperation and Governance*, Harvard Project on Climate Agreements (2013), https://www.belfercenter.org/sites/default/files/files/publication/hpcadp58_edenhofer-flachsland-jakob-lessmann.pdf.

18 Daniel C. Esty and Anthony Moffa, *Why Climate Change Collective Action has Failed and What Needs to be Done Within and Without the Trade Regime*, 15 J. INT'L. ECON. L. 777 (2012).

Building on the first IPCC scientific assessment in 1990, negotiators established the United Nations Framework Convention on Climate Change (UNFCCC), an international agreement that was *signed* by Presidents and Prime Ministers at the 1992 Rio Earth Summit and ratified by 197 nations in the months and years that followed.[19] This treaty set an objective of stabilizing GHG concentrations in the atmosphere "at a level that would prevent dangerous anthropogenic interference with the climate system."[20] To avoid climate change, the UNFCCC called on a core set of 43 developed nations (called the *Annex I* nations) to "aim to reduce their emissions in the year 2000 to 1990 levels."[21] In adopting a principle of *common but differentiated responsibilities*, the 1992 agreement imposed no substantive obligations on the other nations of the world including major economies (and significant GHG emitters) such as China, India, and Brazil.[22]

Under U.S. law, treaties become binding domestic law once *ratified*, which requires the advice and consent of the U.S. Senate by a two-thirds majority vote. The Senate overwhelmingly approved the UN Framework Convention (by a voice vote with no roll call) just four months after President George H.W. Bush signed it at the Rio Earth Summit in June 1992. But the limited participation and non-binding structure of the 1992 agreement quickly proved to be insufficient to the task of addressing climate change. Far from reducing GHG emissions in the year 2000 to 1990 levels, U.S. emissions rose 13 percent.[23] Many other *Annex I* countries also failed to hit their emissions control targets. Even more significantly, emissions across the fast-growing nations of the developing world, most notably China, skyrocketed.

Kyoto Protocol

As the limitations of the 1992 Framework Convention became evident, the nations of the world came together again in 1997 and concluded a new international agreement that came to be called the Kyoto Protocol,

---

19 Ultimately, 192 nations ratified the Framework Convention on Climate Change and this agreement remains the foundation for international cooperation on the issue. United Nations Framework Convention on Climate Change, May 9, 1992, S. Treaty Doc. No. 102-38, 1771 U.N.T.S. 107.

20 *Id.*

21 *Id.*

22 *Id.*

23 *Time Series – Annex I*, UNFCCC (2015), https://di.unfccc.int/time_series.

after the city in Japan where the final round of negotiations took place. This Protocol[24] defined specific GHG targets and timetables for emissions reductions by the Annex I countries. The Kyoto Protocol called for the United States to reduce its emissions by 7 percent below 1990 levels by 2012. But the politics of climate change had become more contentious by the late 1990s, and the Clinton Administration never submitted the Protocol to Congress for approval. In fact, in 1997, the U.S. Senate adopted a resolution rejecting any new climate change commitments unless developing countries took on parallel obligations by a vote of 95–0.[25] And in 2001, the George W. Bush Administration renounced the Kyoto Protocol, leaving the global framework of response to climate change in tatters.

2015 Paris Agreement

Each year, the nations that have ratified the 1992 Framework Convention gather for a Conference of the Parties (or *COP*) at which they assess progress, discuss implementation of the treaty, and consider possible further emissions control commitments. In 2009, a number of countries and NGOs made an effort to strengthen the global response to climate change at COP 15 in Copenhagen. But this effort to conclude a new agreement with more ambitious commitments fell flat as a result of disorganization on the part of the host nation Denmark, division within the U.S. government, and the unwillingness of critical developing nations, notably China and India, to accept emissions control obligations.[26]

At COP 21, hosted in 2015 by the French government in Paris, a new accord was reached that restructured the global response to climate change in several important respects. The 2015 Paris Agreement established a target of net zero GHG emissions by the end of the century with a goal of keeping global warming to under 2 degrees Celsius—and a further aspiration to limit warming to 1.5 degrees Celsius, reflecting the insistence on greater ambition by the island nations most

24 In international law, a *protocol* is an addition to or refinement of a prior treaty, in this case the Framework Convention on Climate Change.
25 Known as the "Byrd-Hagel" Resolution. S. Res. 98, 105th Cong. (1997), https://www.congress.gov/bill/105th-congress/senate-resolution/98/text.
26 Note that the Copenhagen COP did produce the foundation on which the later Paris Agreement would be built. Copenhagen Accord, 2/CP.15, U.N. Doc. FCCC/CP/2009/11/Add.1, (Dec. 19, 2009), https://unfccc.int/resource/docs/2009/cop15/eng/11a01.pdf.

immediately threatened by a changing climate.[27] Alongside *mitigation* efforts that aim to reduce GHG emissions, the Paris Agreement also highlights the importance of *adaptation* to the reality that some degree of climate change is already upon us and will continue for many years whatever we do, a reality that makes investing in hardened infrastructure and *resilience* a priority.[28]

Perhaps more notably, the parties recast the principle of *common but differentiated responsibilities* with new emphasis on the idea of *shared responsibility* and adopted a framework that asked every nation to define its own *nationally determined contribution* (NDC) to global GHG emissions control. This more flexible approach meant that developing nations felt comfortable making substantive commitments. As a result, 196 nations have now ratified the Agreement, and 188 have put forward their climate change action plans. On the other hand, under the Paris Agreement, each nation selects its own targets and timetables, and meeting them is only subject to peer pressure as the targets and timetables are not legally binding and there are no sanctions for missing the self-defined goals.[29]

The negotiators of the 2015 Agreement recognized that the original vision of a top-down climate change response led by national governments and framed in terms of mandatory targets and timetables had not worked.[30] Thus, the Paris Agreement highlights the need for bottom-up implementation of emissions control efforts not just at

---

27 Paris Agreement to the United Nations Framework Convention on Climate Change, Dec. 12, 2015, T.I.A.S. No. 16-1104, https://unfccc.int/process-and-meetings/the-paris-agreement/the-paris-agreement.

28 For a discussion on climate adaption policies, see *Climate Adaptation Policies are Needed More Than Ever*, ECONOMIST (May 30, 2020), https://www.economist.com/schools-brief/2020/05/30/climate-adaptation-policies-are-needed-more-than-ever. For a general argument that environmental policy should rely on *resilience*, the ability to recover from harm, as well as attempting to anticipate and prevent harm, see AARON WILDAVSKY, SEARCHING FOR SAFETY (1988).

29 Sue Biniaz, the State Department's lead climate change lawyer, argues that the flexibility provided was essential to getting developing nations to sign on to the Paris Agreement and that any threat of sanctions would have unraveled the broader non-binding commitment to action that the 2015 negotiations achieved. *See* Sue Biniaz, *The Who, What, and When of "Flexibility" in the Paris Agreement's Transparency Framework*, SABIN CENT. CLIMATE CHANGE L. BLOG (Dec. 28, 2018), http://blogs.law.columbia.edu/climatechange/2018/12/20/the-who-what-and-when-of-flexibility-in-the-paris-agreements-transparency-framework/.

30 Daniel Bodansky and Lavanya Rajamani, *The Evolution and Governance Architecture of the United Nations Climate Change Regime*, in GLOBAL CLIMATE POLICY: ACTORS, CONCEPTS, AND ENDURING CHALLENGES 13 (Detlef F. Sprinz and Urs Luterbacher eds., 2018).

the national level but also at the state and local levels as well as by the private sector.[31] In encouraging broader engagement, the Paris Agreement builds on the support that had emerged from Governors and Premiers across the world who were leading state and provincial efforts to reduce emissions, as well as from hundreds of Mayors who had put together city-scale climate change strategies.

U.S. climate change law and policy

President Obama *accepted* the Paris Agreement on behalf of the United States under his authority as President, which is a commonly used (but controversial) method for implementing international accords through what is called an *executive agreement.*[32] In doing so, he sidestepped the need for formal ratification by the Senate. But as a result, some consider the agreement only *politically* binding and not *legally* binding.

The Obama Administration committed the United States to emissions reductions of 26–28 percent by 2030 as part of the U.S. nationally determined contribution to the global action plan called for by the 2015 Paris Agreement. Some other nations offered more ambitious NDCs—the European Union, for example, set a target of at least a 40 percent GHG reduction by 2030. Other countries put forward more modest goals—China, for instance, committed to have its GHG emissions peak in 2030 and to lower the GHG intensity of its economy by 60–65 percent by 2030.[33] The fact that the Paris Agreement allowed China (a nation now responsible for 28 percent of global GHG emissions compared to 15 percent for the United States)[34] to increase its emissions while the United States reduced its emissions significantly

---

31 For further reading on the bottom-up approach taken in the Paris Agreement, see Daniel C. Esty and Dena P. Adler, *Changing International Law for a Changing Climate*, 112 AM. J. INT'L L. 279 (2018), https://doi.org/10.1017/aju.2018.76; Yann Robiou du Pont and Malte Meinshausen, *Warming Assessment of the Bottom-up Paris Agreement Emissions Pledges*, 9 NATURE COMMC'N 4810 (2018), https://doi.org/10.1038/s41467-018-07223-9.

32 Daniel Bodansky and Peter Spiro, *Executive Agreements Plus*, 49 VANDERBILT J. OF TRANSNAT'L L. 885 (2016); *but see* John C. Yoo, *Laws as Treaties?: The Constitutionality of Congressional-Executive Agreements*, 99 MICHIGAN L. REV. 757 (2009), https://repository.law.umich.edu/mlr/vol99/iss4/3.

33 Climate Action Tracker's website provides details on the NDCs of all nations. CLIMATE ACTION TRACKER, https://climateactiontracker.org.

34 The Union of Concerned Scientists' website offers a range of perspectives on GHG emissions. *Each Country's Share of CO2 Emissions*, UNION OF CONCERNED SCIENTISTS (Aug. 12, 2020), https://www.ucsusa.org/resources/each-countrys-share-co2-emissions.

BOX 4.1 MONTREAL PROTOCOL: A GLOBAL COOPERATION SUCCESS STORY

While global-scale environmental law faces special challenges, especially related to enforcement, international agreements can be effective. In particular, agreed-upon guidelines (often called *soft law*) may harden over time and become more binding, with ever more nations adhering to the standards ever more completely. For example, the 1987 Montreal Protocol—an extension of the 1985 Vienna Convention for the Protection of the Ozone Layer—set nations on a path to phasedown and then eliminate by the year 2000 a broad class of industrial chemicals known as chlorofluorocarbons (or CFCs) that were identified in the 1970s as causing the Earth's protective ozone layer to thin, particularly over the Antarctic. This ozone hole resulted in more harmful ultraviolet radiation from the sun striking the Earth's surface, creating a risk of higher levels of skin cancer and cataracts, not to mention sunburns. Note that, while CFCs are greenhouse gases and thus part of the climate change problem, their impact on the ozone layer is an entirely distinct concern.

Originally signed by just 46 nations, the agreement now has 197 countries and the European Union committed to its requirements—and has broadly succeeded. Despite some cheating (by China and Russia in particular), the use of CFCs has fallen dramatically, and in 2019, scientists found that the Antarctic ozone hole had been reduced to its smallest size since tracking began in the early 1980s. On the current trajectory, the ozone hole is expected to close by the middle of the century. Adherence to the Protocol has been encouraged by both carrots and sticks. Developing nations were given access to a fund to subsidize their purchase of CFC substitutes. But the Protocol also authorizes trade restrictions on goods made in violation of the CFC ban.

The phaseout of CFCs pushed those using these products in refrigerators, air conditioners, and in other applications to switch to substitute chemicals—often hydrofluorocarbons (or HFCs). But HFCs were later identified as potent greenhouse gases, so the world community came together in 2016 to adopt the Kigali Amendment, which requires a reduction of HFCs by 80 percent and seeks to push companies to move toward climate-friendly alternatives.

led Republican critics to denounce the Paris Agreement for failing to hold China "accountable."[35]

To fulfill America's Paris commitment, the Obama Administration developed a regulatory emissions control program called the Clean Power Plan (CPP), which imposed emissions limits on a state-by-state basis with each Governor having the responsibility of determining how best to meet the designated GHG target. This regulatory framework was done entirely through the agency rulemaking process under authority the Obama Administration believed was delegated to such agencies under existing provisions of the Clean Air Act (CAA). However, the Supreme Court disagreed, and by a narrow five-to-four vote along party lines issued a *stay*, an unusual court order preventing the CPP from going into effect based on a ruling that those challenging the plan as beyond the agency's legal authority had a "probability of success" on the merits of their challenge.[36]

President Trump announced in 2017 that the United States would withdraw from the Paris Agreement and it did so in November 2020. However, on his first day in office, President Biden announced that the United States would rejoin the Paris Agreement—and thus the United States is once again a part of the global response to climate change.

The Trump Administration also pulled back Obama's CPP rule claiming that it went beyond EPA's legal authority by requiring states to regulate other sources of greenhouse gases "outside the fenceline" of the coal-fired powerplants it purported to regulate. This position drew some legal support from the Supreme Court's *stay* on implementation of the CPP, as noted above. The Trump Administration replaced the Obama-era CPP with a more limited GHG emissions control regulatory package called the Affordable Clean Energy (ACE) rule, which proposed to more narrowly regulate the coal-fired powerplants that

---

35 *See* Senator Rick Scott's statement. *Senator Rick Scott: The Paris Climate Agreement is a Bad Deal for Americans*, SENATOR RICK SCOTT (Jan. 20, 2021), https://www.rickscott.senate.gov/senator-rick-scott-paris-climate-agreement-bad-deal-americans.

36 Order in Pending Case, West Virginia v. EPA, U.S. No. 15A773 (Feb. 9, 2016); *see also* Courtney Scobie, *Supreme Court Stays EPA's Clean Power Plan*, ABA (Feb. 17, 2016), https://www.americanbar.org/groups/litigation/committees/environmental-energy/practice/2016/021716-energy-supreme-court-stays-epas-clean-power-plan/.

were the subject of the statutory section in question—described by Trump EPA as more "legally defensible."[37]

Note that in 2007, the Supreme Court held in *Massachusetts v. EPA* that EPA has the authority under the Clean Air Act to regulate vehicle GHG emissions, rejecting arguments that carbon dioxide was beyond the scope of the statute.[38] The Court went on to say that while EPA does not have to regulate such emissions, if the Agency finds that GHGs meet the *endangerment test*, then EPA must take regulatory action to address the pollutants in question.[39] In putting forward the new ACE rule, the Trump Administration never revoked the Obama Administration's *endangerment finding* under Section 202(a) of the Clean Air Act, which formally declared that greenhouse gases "threaten the public health and welfare of current and future generations."[40]

As we noted in the chapter 3 CAA discussion, the D.C. Circuit Court of Appeals invalidated the Trump Administration's ACE rule and its revocation of the Obama Administration's Clean Power Plan by a two-to-one vote, holding that Section 111(d) of the Clean Air Act does not unambiguously limit the "best system of emission reduction" to only "inside the fenceline" controls at coal-fired powerplants as the Trump Administration had contended.[41] Unless overturned by the D.C. Circuit Court *en banc* or by the Supreme Court, which seems unlikely as of this writing, this decision wipes the slate clean and gives the Biden Administration an opportunity to put forward new regulations issued under EPA's existing statutory authority—or to propose new climate change legislation.

---

37 Repeal of the Clean Power Plan; Emission Guidelines for Greenhouse Gas Emissions from Existing Electric Utility Generating Units; Revisions to Emission Guidelines Implementing Regulations, 40 C.F.R. § 60 (2019), https://www.federalregister.gov/documents/2019/07/08/2019-13507/repeal-of-the-clean-power-plan-emission-guidelines-for-greenhouse-gas-emissions-from-existing.

38 Massachusetts v. EPA, 549 U.S. 497 (2007).

39 Clean Air Act, 42 U.S.C. § 7521(a)(1), https://www.law.cornell.edu/uscode/text/42/chapter-85/subchapter-II ("The [EPA] Administrator shall by regulation prescribe . . . standards applicable to the emission of any air pollutant . . . which may reasonably be anticipated to endanger public health or welfare . . .").

40 Endangerment and Cause or Contribute Findings for Greenhouse Gases Under Section 202(a) of the Clean Air Act; Final Rule, 74 Fed. Reg. 66,496 (Dec. 15, 2009) (to be codified at 40 C.F.R. chpt. undef.), https://www.federalregister.gov/documents/2009/12/15/E9-29537/endangerment-and-cause-or-contribute-findings-for-greenhouse-gases-under-section-202a-of-the-clean.

41 American Lung Association et al. v. EPA, No. 19-1140 (D.C.Cir. Jan 19, 2021), https://www.cadc.uscourts.gov/internet/opinions.nsf/6356486C5963F49185258662005677F6/$file/19-1140.correctedopinion.pdf.

The new Administration has backed away from a number of the Trump rules and regulatory rollbacks —and has now indicated to courts across the country that EPA will redo the contested regulations. Most notably from a climate change perspective, the Biden team has signaled its intention to require that the *social cost of carbon* be factored into regulatory decisions and restore the scheduled rise in vehicle fuel economy (or "CAFE") standards that the Obama Administration had negotiated with the auto industry that would have required cars and light-duty trucks to average 54.5 miles per gallon by 2025—but which the Trump team had abandoned.

The Obama Administration's decision to address climate change in 2014 through existing CAA regulatory authority reflected the political difficulty of getting any climate change action plan through a divided Congress. In fact, comprehensive climate change legislation, known as the Waxman-Markey bill, was introduced in 2009. This legislation would have created an emissions allowance trading system for GHGs modeled on the successful acid rain emissions trading program. While it passed the House by a vote of 219 to 212 in June 2009,[42] the legislation was never brought up for a vote in the Senate even though Democrats were in the majority at the time.[43]

In addition to the CPP, the Obama Administration undertook several other lines of attack on climate change. Perhaps most notably, EPA's 2015 *Mercury and Air Toxics Standards* (MATS) caused hundreds of coal-fired electric generating units to cease operations, dramatically reducing mercury emissions but also cutting millions of tons of CO_2 from the power sector. The Obama Administration also used federal subsidies to help expand renewable power projects with a 30 percent *investment tax credit* (ITC) for solar installations and a *production tax credit* (PTC) of one to two cents per kilowatt hour for wind energy.[44] President Biden has indicated that he intends to pursue a "whole of government" approach to climate change that will entail actions by every department to help move the nation toward a clean-energy

---

42 For a good summary of the provisions of Waxman-Markey, see Waxman-Markey Short Summary, CENTER FOR CLIMATE AND ENERGY SOLUTIONS (June 2009), https://www.c2es.org/document/waxman-markey-short-summary/.

43 For the political history of its demise, see generally John M. Broder, *'Cap and Trade' Loses Its Standing as Energy Policy of Choice*, N.Y. TIMES (Mar. 25, 2010), https://www.nytimes.com/2010/03/26/science/earth/26climate.html.

44 *Production Tax Credit and Investment Tax Credit for Wind*, WINDEXCHANGE, https://windexchange.energy.gov/projects/tax-credits.

future[45]—with leadership from EPA and the Department of Energy as well as a *Climate Czar* in the White House and a high-profile climate change envoy in charge of ensuring that the United States returns to a leadership posture on the international stage. President Biden has further declared that he wants the United States to match other nations in committing to net zero greenhouse gas emissions by 2050. Debate has thus begun on what *deep decarbonization*[46] would require both domestically[47] and internationally.[48]

Climate change leadership at the state, local, and corporate levels

While federal action to address climate change has been limited, several Governors, mayors, and corporate leaders have advanced significant programs to reduce greenhouse gas emissions.[49] Ten northeastern states set up a *cap and invest* system to limit greenhouse gas emissions from powerplants in 2009. This Regional Greenhouse Gas Initiative (RGGI) requires powerplants to buy allowances at twice per year auctions for every ton of CO_2 they emit.

45 Press Release, White House, FACT SHEET: President Biden Takes Executive Actions to Tackle the Climate Crisis at Home and Abroad, Create Jobs, and Restore Scientific Integrity Across Federal Government (Jan. 27, 2021) https://www.whitehouse.gov/briefing-room/ statements-releases/2021/01/27/fact-sheet-president-biden-takes-executive-actions-to-tackle-the-climate-crisis-at-home-and-abroad-create-jobs-and-restore-scientific-integrity-across-federal-government/ (announcing that President Biden's *Tackling the Climate Crisis at Home and Abroad* executive order "establishes the National Climate Task Force, assembling leaders . . . to enable a whole-of-government approach to combatting the climate crisis.").

46 Deep decarbonization refers to the level of GHG emissions control required to meet the agreed-upon international target of limiting global warming to 2.0 degrees Celsius (or more ambitiously 1.5 degrees), which most analysts see as requiring net zero emissions by 2050. *America's Zero Carbon Action Plan*, ZERO CARBON CONSORTIUM (2020), https://www.unsdsn.org/Zero-Carbon-Action-Plan; *see also* MACHAEL B. GERRARD AND JOHN C. DERNBACH, LEGAL PATHWAYS TO DEEP DECARBONIZATION IN THE UNITED STATES (2019).

47 *See America's Zero Carbon Action Plan*, SUSTAINABLE DEVELOPMENT SOLUTIONS NETWORK (2020), https://www.unsdsn.org/Zero-Carbon-Action-Plan; *Accelerating Decarbonization of the U.S. Energy System*, NATIONAL ACADEMY OF SCIENCES (2021), https://www.nap.edu/cata log/25932/accelerating-decarbonization-of-the-us-energy-system.

48 *What's the path to deep decarbonization?*, WORLD ECONOMIC FORUM (Dec. 2, 2015), https:// www.weforum.org/agenda/2015/12/whats-the-path-to-deep-decarbonization/; *Mission Possible: Reaching Net-Zero Carbon Emissions From Harder-to-Abate Sectors by Mid-Century*, SYSTEMIQ (Nov. 19, 2018), https://www.systemiq.earth/resource-category/mission-possible/.

49 Robert J. Klee, *Searching for a New Deal on Climate? Look to the States*. YALE CLEAN ENERGY FORUM (Oct. 1, 2019), https://www.cleanenergyfinanceforum.com/series/searching-for-new-deal-on-climate-look-to-the-states.

RGGI put a price on GHG emissions (currently about $6/ton). Although this *carbon price* is well below the federal government's estimate of the *social cost of carbon*,[50] studies show that RGGI has spurred emissions reductions and investments in energy efficiency. Across the RGGI region, power sector emissions fell by almost half in the period from 2009 to 2019—exceeding the national rate of emissions control by 90 percent.[51] The allowance auction proceeds generate more than $300 million per year, which funds energy efficiency and renewable power investments across the region.[52] This flow of funds has allowed both Connecticut and New York to set up Green Banks—an innovative funding mechanism that uses limited public money to leverage private capital investments in clean energy. This model is now being replicated across the world.[53]

California has also emerged as a leader on climate change with its own *cap and trade* emissions control structure covering not just power plants but any entity that emits over 25 000 tons of CO_2 per year.[54] California's carbon price, which averaged about $17 per ton in 2019,[55] generates over $1 billion per year.[56] The California Air Resources Board has further implemented a series of regulatory actions designed to drive greenhouse gas emissions down 40 percent by 2030 from the 1990 level. These state-level regulations include a low-carbon fuel

---

50 "The social cost of carbon (SCC) is an estimate, in dollars, of the economic damages that would result from emitting one additional ton of greenhouse gases into the atmosphere." Keven Rennert and Cora Kingdon, *Social Cost of Carbon 101*, RESOURCES FOR THE FUTURE (Aug. 1, 2019), https://www.rff.org/publications/explainers/social-cost-carbon-101/.

51 *The Regional Greenhouse Gas Initiative: Ten Years in Review*, ACADIA CENTER (Sept. 17, 2019), https://acadiacenter.org/wp-content/uploads/2019/09/Acadia-Center_RGGI_10-Years-in-Review_2019-09-17.pdf.

52 *Investment of RGGI Proceeds in 2017*, REGIONAL GREENHOUSE GAS INITIATIVE (Oct. 2019), https://www.rggi.org/sites/default/files/Uploads/Proceeds/RGGI_Proceeds_Report_2017.pdf.

53 *See* CT GREEN BANK, https://www.ctgreenbank.com. On the broader push to set up Green Banks, see THE COALITION FOR GREEN CAPITAL, https://www.coalitionforgreencapital.com; *see also* Whitney A. Leonard, *Clean is the New Green: Clean Energy Finance and Deployment Through Green Banks*, 33 YALE L. & POL. REV. (2014).

54 *California's cap-and-trade program step by step*, EDF (Sept. 2018), https://www.edf.org/sites/default/files/californias-cap-and-trade-program-step-by-step.pdf.

55 *USA-California Cap-and-Trade Program*, ICAP (Feb. 18, 2021), https://icapcarbonaction.com/en/?option=com_etsmap&task=export&format=pdf&layout=list&systems%5B%5D=45.

56 Nathanael Johnson, *California makes big money from its carbon pricing program. Who gets it?*, GRIST (Jan. 31, 2018), https://grist.org/article/california-makes-big-money-from-its-carbon-pricing-program-who-gets-it/.

standard, building efficiency standards, and rules requiring a transition to zero-emissions electric trucks.[57]

Mayors are also driving progress on climate change. Under the banner of *C40* (Cities Climate Leadership Group),[58] a dozen big-city mayors are collaborating with colleagues from across the world to draft emissions control plans, build sustainable cities, and meet the emissions reduction targets of the 2015 Paris Agreement. Similarly, under the auspices of groups such as *America's Pledge*,[59] *U.S. Climate Alliance*,[60] and the *We Are Still In*[61] coalition, dozens of Governors, more than 400 mayors, and thousands of CEOs have committed to implement climate change action plans within their jurisdiction or corporation.

Though the federal government has been largely paralyzed on climate change for years, considerable progress continues to be made at other levels of government and in other sectors of society.[62] In fact, despite the lack of strong national policy, U.S. emissions of GHGs have actually declined in recent years, largely as a result of cheap natural gas from fracking replacing coal in many powerplants as well as the other initiatives described above.[63] This capacity for *bottom-up* leadership[64]—and policy innovations from subnational levels of government, the private sector, and NGOs[65]—represents one of the great strengths of American federalism.[66]

---

57 The California Air Resources Board website provides further information on the regulatory actions. CALIFORNIA AIR RESOURCES BOARD, https://ww2.arb.ca.gov/.

58 C40 CITIES, https://www.c40.org/.

59 AMERICA'S PLEDGE, https://www.americaspledgeonclimate.com/.

60 U.S. CLIMATE ALLIANCE, http://www.usclimatealliance.org/.

61 WE ARE STILL IN, https://www.wearestillin.com/.

62 For an overview of the United States's reliance on a decentralized approach of state, local and private actions as well as government to address environmental issues, see E. Donald Elliott, *Why the United States Does Not Have a Renewable Energy Policy*, 43 ENVTL L. REP. 10,095 (2013), http://dx.doi.org/10.2139/ssrn.1878616; *see also* Chapter 15 for further examples.

63 Zeke Hausfather, *Analysis: Why US carbon emissions have fallen 14% since 2005*, CARBON BRIEF (Aug. 15, 2017), https://www.carbonbrief.org/analysis-why-us-carbon-emissions-have-fallen-14-since-2005.

64 Daniel C. Esty, *Bottom-Up Climate Fix*, N.Y. TIMES (Sept. 21, 2014), http://www.nytimes.com/2014/09/22/opinion/bottom-up-climate-fix.html.

65 *See* discussion of the Nature Conservancy's private initiative to preserve millions of acres of land in an undeveloped state in Chapter 13.

66 For a discussion of the vertical and horizontal *co-opetition* in U.S. policymaking, see Daniel C. Esty and Geradin Damien, *Regulatory Co-opetition. in* REGULATORY COMPETITION AND ECONOMIC INTEGRATION (Daniel C. Esty and Damien Geradin eds., 2001); *see also* MICHAEL

Climate change litigation against private parties

A number of lawsuits have been brought by plaintiffs who seek redress for the effects of climate change, for which they hold fossil fuel producers accountable. But U.S. courts have repeatedly rejected such claims. In *Connecticut v. AEP*,[67] the Supreme Court dismissed public nuisance claims brought by eight states against fossil-fuel burning utilities, concluding that the CAA displaces federal common law claims and thus precludes the plaintiffs from bringing their legal action. Likewise, a case brought by an Alaskan Native tribe against a number of oil companies and utilities seeking redress for the erosion of their village, due to melting permafrost and other changes that they attributed to fossil fuel burning causing climate change, was dismissed in *Village of Kivalina v. ExxonMobil Corp.*[68] The court ruled that the presence of a pervasive federal statute (in this case the CAA) displaces federal common law and thus pre-empts the claims of the native community.

A new series of nuisance-based legal challenges to fossil fuel companies has been launched in state courts under state law (rather than federal common law). In most cases, the defendant energy companies have challenged the litigation by seeking *removal* of the matter to federal court where the pre-emption principle discussed above might result in dismissal of the case. But these climate change state law tort claims have so far survived removal challenges and are now proceeding in state courts.[69]

Climate change litigation looks likely to continue to expand in the coming years with new legal theories being tested against not only private defendants associated with fossil fuel sale and extraction but also governments, encouraged perhaps by courts that appear to be frustrated by the lack of systematic action to respond to the threats

---

P. VANDENBERG AND JONATHAN GILLIGAN, BEYOND POLITICS: THE PRIVATE GOVERNANCE RESPONSE TO CLIMATE CHANGE (2017).

67 Connecticut v. AEP, 564 U.S. 410 (2011).

68 Village of Kivalina v. ExxonMobil Corp., 696 F.3d 849 (9th Cir. 2012).

69 Among the cases are: Baltimore v. BP, No. 24-C-18-004219, (Cir. Ct. Baltimore 2020) and Rhode Island v. Chevron Corp., No. PC-2018-4716 (Providence Sup. Ct. 2020), City. of San Mateo v. Chevron Corp., No. 18-15499, 2020 WL 2703701 (9th Cir. May 26, 2020), and City of Oakland v. BP PLC, No. 18-16663, 2020 WL 2702680 (9th Cir. May 26, 2020).

of irreversible harm that plaintiffs have been able to demonstrate.[70] Notably in this regard, a set of young plaintiffs brought a case in Oregon against the federal government claiming that they faced injury from climate change and that the federal government had acted with deliberate indifference to this threat. The *Juliana* plaintiffs survived a motion for *summary judgment*[71] which would have ended their case immediately in the trial court. But the 9th Circuit Court of Appeals later dismissed the lawsuit for lack of *standing*,[72] concluding that the judicial branch of government was not positioned to provide the requested remedy.[73]

International climate change litigation

While U.S. courts have been hesitant to take up climate change legal claims, courts in other countries have begun to do so with some regularity. In the 2015 *Urgenda* case in the Netherlands, a court held that the Dutch government had breached its duty of care to society under Dutch tort law and ordered the government to adopt a more ambitious climate change mitigation plan.[74] Likewise, in Pakistan, the Lahore High Court ruled in the *Ashgar Leghari* case that the government's modest climate change policy framework constituted a breach of the country's human rights obligations.[75] In an especially sweeping 2019 ruling, the French

---

70 Daniel C. Esty et al., (2019, October). *Litigating Climate Change.* Working Paper presented at the Yale Law School 2019 Global Constitutionalism Seminar: Fragile Futures and Resiliency, New Haven, CT, https://documents.law.yale.edu/sites/default/files/gcs2019.pdf.

71 Summary judgment motions offer defendants an early-stage opportunity to challenge the basic legal foundations of a lawsuit. If successful, the suit is dismissed.

72 Standing refers to the question of whether the plaintiffs meet the basic procedural requirements to bring a lawsuit. To establish the "irreducible constitutional minimum of standing" under Art III, § 2 of the U.S. Constitution, a plaintiff must (1) demonstrate an "injury in fact" that is both (a) concrete and particularized and (b) actual or imminent, not conjectural or hypothetical, (2) prove a causal connection between the injury and the defendant's alleged actions, and (3) establish redressability. Lujan v. Defenders of Wildlife, 504 U.S. 555, 560–61 (1992); Friends of the Earth, Inc. v. Laidlaw Envtl. Servs (TOC), Inc, 528 U.S. 167, 180–81 (2000).

73 Juliana v. United States, 339 F. Supp. 3d 1062 (D. Or. 2018), *rev'd and remanded*, 947 F.3d 1159 (9th Cir. 2020).

74 Urgenda Foundation v. The State of the Netherlands, District Court of The Hague Case No. C/09/456689 (2015); for an overview of the case and its implications, see Joana Setzer and Dennis van Berkel, *Urgenda v State of the Netherlands: Lessons for international law and climate change litigants*, GRANTHAM RSCH. INST. LSE (Dec. 10, 2019), http://www.lse.ac.uk/granthaminstitute/news/urgenda-v-state-of-the-netherlands-lessons-for-international-law-and-climate-change-litigants/.

75 Leghari v. Federation of Pakistan (2015), W.P. No. 25501/2015 (Lahore High Ct.).

Constitutional Council declared that "everyone has the right to live in a balanced and healthy environment."[76] In extending this principle in the 2020 *UIPP v. Prime Minister* case, the Council —the French equivalent of the Supreme Court—asserted in unequivocal terms that protection of the environment "constitutes an objective of constitutional value," potentially laying the foundation for future climate change litigation.[77] Similar claims are pending in a number of other countries, particularly ones where the national constitution has a provision related to environmental rights. Thus, while U.S. companies may not be subject to climate change litigation damages within the United States in federal court, those operating internationally may well face legal jeopardy in foreign courts as well as state courts in the coming years.

Additional resources

Elliott, E. Donald (2019). EPA's Existing Authority to Impose a Carbon "Tax." *Environmental Law Reporter*, 49(10), 10919–1094, https://digitalcommons.law.yale. edu/fss_papers/5368/.

Esty, Daniel C. (2008). Rethinking Global Environmental Governance to Deal with Climate Change: The Multiple Logics of Collective Action. *American Economic Review: Papers & Proceedings*, 98(2), https://www.aeaweb.org/articles?id=10.1257/ aer.98.2.116.

Esty, Daniel C. et al. (2019). *Litigating Climate Change*. Working Paper presented at the Yale Law School 2019 Global Constitutionalism Seminar: Fragile Futures and Resiliency, New Haven, CT, https://documents.law.yale.edu/sites/default/files/ gcs2019.pdf.

Ganguly, Geetanjali et al. (2018). If at First You Don't Succeed: Suing Corporations for Climate Change. *Oxford Journal of Legal Studies*, 38(4), 841–868, https://doi. org/10.1093/ojls/gqy029.

Garrard, Michael B. and Dernbach, John C. (2019). *Legal Pathways to Deep Decarbonization in the United States*. Washington, D.C.: Environmental Law Institute.

---

76 Conseil Constitutionnel [CC] [Constitutional Court] decision No. 2019-794 DC, Dec. 20, 2019 (Fr.).

77 Conseil Constitutionnel [CC] [Constitutional Court] decision No. 2019-823, Jan. 31, 2020 (Fr.). For a discussion of the potential foundation being laid for climate change litigation, see Daniel C. Esty, *Toward a Sustainable Future: Environmental Jurisprudence from France's Constitutional Council Breaks New Ground*, ANNUAL REVIEW OF THE FRENCH CONSTITUTIONAL COUNCIL (2020); *see also* Conseil d'Etat [CE] [Council of State] Grand-Synthe, No. 427301, Nov. 12, 2020 (Fr.).

Hilson, Chris (2013). It's All About Climate Change, Stupid! Exploring the Relationship Between Environmental Law and Climate Law. *Journal of Environmental Law*, 25(13), 359–370, https://doi.org/10.1093/jel/eqto19.

Lazarus, R.J. (2009). Super Wicked Problems and Climate Change: Restraining the Present to Liberate the Future. *Cornell Law Review, 94*(5), 1153–1233, https://www.lawschool.cornell.edu/research/cornell-law-review/upload/Lazarus.pdf.

5   Clean Water Act: major progress but persistent challenges

All life depends on water. The Federal Water Pollution Control Act of 1948[1] was the first major U.S. law to address water pollution.[2] However, the 1948 Act limited federal authority "to preparing pollution abatement plans and providing support to the states" and generally proved ineffective.[3]

Throughout the twentieth century, industry and agriculture expanded rapidly in the United States to meet the needs of a growing nation and dumping waste into rivers and streams was a convenient method of low-cost disposal. As a result, water quality in America's streams, rivers, lakes, and ponds deteriorated badly.

A sense of crisis grabbed the public's attention in June 1969, when Cleveland's Cuyahoga River caught fire just downriver from the Republic Steel mill, which had for decades dumped industrial waste into the adjacent water. Republic Steel was not the only polluter, and indeed the river had caught fire on several prior occasions. But the 1969 inferno generated public outrage, stoked in part by coverage in *Time* magazine[4] and a popular song.[5] The images of water on fire helped to fuel nationwide demonstrations in April 1970 against the degradation of the nation's water, land, and air. Roughly twenty million Americans participated in these protests and teach-ins (now recognized as the first Earth Day), which in turn helped to create momentum for federal pollution control legislation.

---

1 Federal Water Pollution Control Act of 1948, ch. 758, Pub. L. No. 845, 62 Stat. 1155.
2 Ann Powers, Federal Water Pollution Control Act (1948), ENCYCLOPEDIA.COM, https://www.encyclopedia.com/history/encyclopedias-almanacs-transcripts-and-maps/federal-water-pollution-control-act-1948.
3 *Id.*
4 Jennifer Latson, *The Burning River That Sparked a Revolution*, TIME (June 22, 2015, 10:30 AM), https://time.com/3921976/cuyahoga-fire/.
5 Randy Newman, *Burn On, on* SAIL AWAY (Reprise Records 1972), https://www.youtube.com/watch?v=VtW8RkI3-c4.

The Clean Water Act of 1972

In response, Congress enacted the 1972 Clean Water Act Amendments, which for the first time gave the national government regulatory authority over pollution of *navigable waters*. The new law declared an ambitious goal of "fishable and swimmable" rivers, lakes, and streams[6] that established a structure of state-by-state water quality standards and mandatory permits for "dischargers." Unlike the Clean Air Act, which focused on ambient air quality as the foundation of its regulatory framework, the Clean Water Act (CWA) regulates pollution flows into rivers, streams, and other waterbodies primarily through a structure of industry-specific technology-based mandates called *effluent limitations*, although states also retain authority to set Water Quality Standards. Drinking water is regulated separately under the Safe Drinking Water Act, which is discussed in Chapter 6.

The 1972 law established a multi-prong regulatory structure which reflected the fact that water pollution comes in many forms, including:

- organic contamination, often gauged by biochemical oxygen demand (or "BOD")
- elevated temperature from discharges of industrial cooling water
- bacteria, notably fecal coliform from human or animal waste
- suspended solids (or "turbidity")
- total dissolved solids from excess nitrogen or phosphorus
- toxic substances from industrial effluent
- heavy metals including mercury and cadmium from industrial activities

The sources of water pollution are equally wide-ranging, including not just *point sources*, such as factories, powerplants, and sewage treatment plants, but also *non-point sources*, such as runoff from farming, ranching, construction sites, mines, logging, and even backyards and streets.

The CWA imposed technology-based water pollution controls on point sources of pollutants along with a requirement that all such sources get a permit under the National Pollution Discharge Elimination System (NPDES) for any emissions into surface waters. States issue most

---

6 Clean Water Act § 402, 33 U.S.C. § 1318.

NPDES permits under authority delegated from the federal EPA.[7] To obtain a permit, a discharger must demonstrate that its discharges of pollution will comply with the federal technology-based "effluent limitations," as well as state water quality standards. The law also includes a unique *anti-backsliding* provision that provides that once a discharger has reduced its pollution, it may not go back to releasing more pollution except pursuant to certain narrowly-defined exceptions.[8] Even more stringent *best available technology* (or "BAT") standards were specified in section 306 for certain *new* sources of water pollution, while section 307 required EPA to set up a separate set of requirements for toxic substances.

For harder-to-control *non-point sources* of water pollution, such as runoff from farmers' fields that is not discharged through a defined outfall, the CWA provided a lighter framework of regulation based on a planning process and the adoption of *best management practices*. With an over-arching commitment to *zero discharge* by 1985, the law set out general effluent limitations for point source dischargers and spelled out special rules in section 301 for sewage treatment plants (known as *publicly owned treatment works*, or POTWs). Federal financial support to local communities to build sewage treatment plants has been one of the quiet success stories of the CWA, and illustrates that positive incentives (in this case, subsidies) can sometimes be a very effective technique for achieving environmental goals. From 1972 to 1987, the federal government handed out billions of dollars in grants to subsidize sewage treatment plant construction and upgrades.

This program was very popular politically because it allowed politicians to claim credit locally for "bringing home the bacon." However, in 1987, it was converted into a program of revolving loans that have to be paid back. Nonetheless, as of 2019, the federal government had provided $45.2 billion in aid to local communities to support water infrastructure programs.[9] As a result, waterborne diseases, which are one of the worst environmental problems worldwide and are estimated

---

7 CWA § 402(b), 33 U.S.C. § 1342(b).

8 Melissa A. Thorme, *Antibacksliding: Understanding One of the Most Misunderstood Provisions of the Clean Water Act*, 31 ENVTL. L. REP. 10322 (2001), https://www.waterboards.ca.gov/rwqcb8/water_issues/programs/stormwater/docs/sbpermit/2009/comments/SBCFCD_Att1-B--Thorme.pdf.

9 *Learn about the Clean Water State Revolving Fund (CWSRF)*, EPA, https://www.epa.gov/cwsrf/learn-about-clean-water-state-revolving-fund-cwsrf.

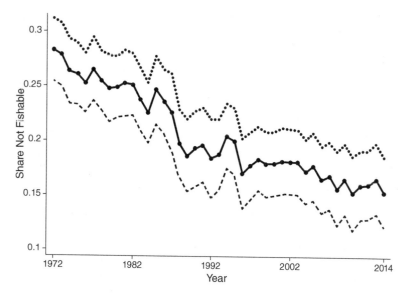

Source: David Keiser & Joseph S. Shapiro, The Clean Water Rule and Economic Research on U.S. Water Pollution Regulation, VOX EU (Oct. 5, 2019), https://voxeu.org/article/clean-water-rule-and-economic-research-us-water-pollution-regulation. Copyright American Economic Association; reproduced with permission of the Journal of Economic Perspectives.

Figure 5.1   Share of U.S. waters not fishable, 1972–2014

to account for an estimated 1.5 million deaths annually,[10] are virtually unknown in the United States.

The wide range of water quality problems and effluent sources has made implementation of the CWA goals rather difficult. Indeed, virtually every deadline established in the 1972 legislation and subsequent 1977 and 1987 amendments has been missed, although some of the targets were met at later dates. Moreover, both polluting industries and disappointed environmentalists have challenged in court many of the rules EPA laid out, resulting in years of delay and ongoing controversy. Thus, while water quality has improved in many places, persistent challenges remain – see Figure 5.1 above.

---

10 *Waterborne Diseases*, WORLD HEALTH ORGANIZATION, https://www.who.int/gho/publications/mdgs-sdgs/MDGs-SDGs2015_chapter5_snapshot_waterborne_diseases.pdf?ua=1.

Scope of national government Clean Water Act authority

One of the on-going legal battlegrounds in the water pollution arena concerns the scope of federal authority to regulate water pollution. On its face, the CWA applies to "navigable waters" of the United States, which section 502(7) goes on to define more broadly as "the waters of the United States."[11] This framing—highlighting waters as a pathway for commerce—provides a basis for the federal claim of *jurisdiction* and thus the legal authority to regulate. But this allusion to the Constitution's Commerce Clause does not resolve the issue. As a result, a number of cases have been brought challenging the regulatory decisions of EPA or the Army Corps of Engineers—a wing of the Pentagon with substantial domestic responsibilities for managing water flows, constructing dams and other elements of environmental infrastructure, and restoring ecosystems—with whom EPA shares responsibility for implementing certain CWA provisions.

In the 1985 *Riverside Bayview* case,[12] a unanimous Supreme Court concluded that wetlands adjacent to navigable waters are inseparably bound up with "the waters of the United States" and therefore a legitimate venue for federal regulation. But this functional approach to establishing the CWA's jurisdictional boundaries and its implied expansive view of the *waters* open to federal regulation has been regularly tested—and in several cases, trimmed back. In the 2001 *Solid Waste Agency of Northern Cook County* case[13] (often referred to as the *SWANCC* decision), the Supreme Court rejected the idea that isolated ponds used by migratory birds provided a sufficient basis for federal regulation. In narrowing the scope of the *Riverside Bayview* precedent, the Court majority declared that there must be a "significant nexus" between a waterbody or wetlands and navigable waters to establish federal jurisdiction.

And in the 2006 *Rapanos* case,[14] a divided Supreme Court (four-one-four) went even further when Justice Scalia authored a plurality opinion,

---

11 CWA § 502, 33 U.S.C. § 1362 (defining "discharge of a pollutant" as "any addition of any pollutant to navigable waters from any point source").

12 United States v. Riverside Bayview, 474 U.S. 121 (1985), https://supreme.justia.com/cases/federal/us/474/121/.

13 Solid Waste Agency of Northern Cook County v. United States Army Corps of Engineers, 531 U.S. 159 (2001), https://supreme.justia.com/cases/federal/us/531/159/.

14 Rapanos v. United States, 547 U.S. 715 (2006), https://supreme.justia.com/cases/federal/us/547/715/.

which declared that jurisdiction based on "waters of the United States" covers only relatively permanent or continuously flowing water bodies. Although the Scalia plurality (reluctantly) agreed that the waters of the United States covered more than what a boat could navigate, the plurality opinion would have required a continuous surface water connection to adjacent navigable waters. But Justice Kennedy, as the swing vote in the *Rapanos* case, rejected the Scalia plurality's legal framework. Instead, he offered his own, more sharply defined *significant nexus* test centered on the observation that wetlands that significantly affect the "chemical, physical, and biological integrity" of adjacent navigable waters provide a sufficient basis for federal jurisdiction and thus EPA or Army Corps regulation.

WOTUS rule

Substantial legal uncertainty in the wake of the Supreme Court's split *Rapanos* decision prompted EPA to launch in 2014 a rulemaking effort to define more clearly the *waters of the United States* (WOTUS). Based on an extensive survey undertaken by the Agency's Science Advisory Board of the scientific literature on the "connectivity of streams and wetlands to downstream waters,"[15] the proposed WOTUS rule (as it came to be known) triggered a great deal of debate with more than a million comments filed in the regulatory docket. The Obama Administration's final rule,[16] issued in 2015, largely codified Justice Kennedy's *significant nexus* test. But far from settling the dispute over the reach of federal water pollution authority, the WOTUS rule triggered a further flurry of lawsuits with competing claims in competing courts.

Before the legal morass that emerged could be disentangled, President Trump signed an executive order[17] directing the EPA and Army Corps to reconsider the WOTUS rule and adopt a new standard based on the narrower definition of "waters of the United States" Justice Scalia offered in the *Rapanos* case. Thus, in 2017, the Obama Administration's WOTUS rule was rescinded. In 2020, the Trump Administration

---

15 *Connectivity of Streams and Wetlands To Downstream Waters: A Review and Synthesis of the Scientific Evidence (Final Report)*, EPA (2015), https://cfpub.epa.gov/ncea/risk/recordisplay.cfm?deid=296414.

16 Clean Water Rule: "Definitions of Waters of the United States", 80 Fed. Reg. 37,053 (June 29, 2015) (to be codified at 33 C.F.R. pt. 328 and 40 C.F.R. pts. 110, 112, 116, 117, 122, 230, 232, 300, 302, & 401).

17 Exec. Order No. 13,778, 82 Fed. Reg. 12,497 (Feb. 28, 2017).

finalized a new definitional rule[18] that limited the reach of federal CWA jurisdiction in ways that it claimed would increase predictability and devolve more authority to regulate wetlands back to the states. But this new WOTUS rule has again drawn multiple legal challenges and its future is uncertain. On his first day in office, President Biden revoked the 2017 executive order directing the EPA and Army Corps to reconsider the WOTUS rule,[19] reflecting the fact that Democrats generally favor greater authority at the national level and Republicans generally favor more authority at the state level.

Wetlands protection

Many of the most controversial jurisdictional disputes center on wetlands regulation. Once considered unhealthy *swamps*, wetlands are today recognized as critical habitat for many species and the source of many ecosystem services such as flood control and pollution filtration. CWA section 404 regulates the discharge of dredged materials or fill into navigable waters—and by extension into adjacent wetlands as discussed above. As a result, those wishing to develop property that contains wetlands must get a permit from the Army Corps of Engineers under policy guidance developed jointly with EPA. EPA also provides enforcement of the permits the Army Corps issues and can veto permits under section 404(c) if it disagrees with the Army Corps' ecological assessment. Note that EPA only exercises this authority sparingly, having over-ridden Army Corps permit decisions in just 13 cases since 1972.

In practice, limited intrusions on wetlands are usually permitted so long as the developer of a parcel: (1) can show that the adverse impacts were minimized; and (2) undertakes *compensatory mitigation* including the restoration of other wetlands (sometimes through wetlands *mitigation banks*) or payment of fees to support wetlands protection. Most wetlands enforcement actions involve parties who failed to get an Army Corps permit or who violated the terms of their permit.

---

18 The Navigable Waters Protection Rule: Definition of "Waters of the United States", 85 Fed. Reg. 22,250 (Apr. 21, 2020) (to be codified at 33 C.F.R. pt. 328 and 40 C.F.R. pts. 110, 112, 116, 117, 120, 122, 230, 232, 300, 302, & 401).

19 Exec. Order No. 13,990, 86 Fed. Reg. 7,037 (Jan. 20, 2021).

It is important to bear in mind that over half the states also regulate wetlands,[20] so the absence of federal jurisdiction does not necessarily mean no regulation at all. Some have even argued that states are in a better position to regulate wetlands as they possess authority over the activities that can take place in adjoining uplands areas, which EPA does not.[21] In practice today in many areas, a permit is required from *both* the state authority that regulates wetlands and the federal permitting authority, the Army Corps of Engineers, because the two apply different standards.

Effluent limitations

Section 301 of the CWA limits the amount of pollution that can be discharged from an effluent pipe, outfall, or other conveyance. The effluent limitations reflect water quality standards established by each state subject to EPA approval.[22] The law requires existing polluters to deploy BAT, and after the 1977 CWA amendments, new sources must use the *best demonstrated control technology* for their industry category and class. Those discharging toxic substances into surface waters must meet BAT standards with even more strict requirements (set out in the 1987 amendments) for toxic *hotspots*. In addition, section 307 requires industrial dischargers to "pretreat" their effluent before releasing toxics into sewers. The CWA grants EPA significant discretion in determining what standards should apply to various industries, including the ability to take costs into account, but the law's implementation has still generated a great deal of dispute, litigation, and delay.

The CWA provides a separate set of standards for sewage treatment plants. Specifically, the CWA requires *secondary* wastewater treatment by which organic solid materials are physically separated and biological

---

20 John Kusler and Jeanne Christie, Common Questions: State Wetland Regulatory Programs (2020), https://www.aswm.org/pdf_lib/CQ_state_wetland_regulatory_6_26_06.pdf.

21 Brian F. Mannix, *The EPA at Fifty: Time to Give Bootleggers the Boot!*, 70 Case W. Res. L. Rev. 1081, 1083–84 (2020), https://scholarlycommons.law.case.edu/caselrev/vol70/iss4/12:

> Contrary to much of the press coverage, I think the recent rule narrowing the definition of "waters of the United States" is a step in the right direction. States have been protecting water quality for far longer than fifty years, and in many ways they are better equipped to carry out this task. They have the authority to regulate land use, for example, which can be one of the most important tools for protecting water quality.

22 Note that not all states have such *delegated authority*. In the absence of such a delegation, the EPA sets the standard.

processes are used to eliminate dissolved organic substances. The law also provides the basis for EPA regulation of *combined sewer overflows* in some 800 communities with older water infrastructure that channels street drains and other stormwater runoff into sewer pipes. After significant rainfall events, the combined flows of stormwater and sewage are often too much for the POTWs to process, resulting in untreated sewage going into major waterways. To help communities upgrade their POTWs or undertake other water quality infrastructure projects, the federal government manages a Clean Water State Revolving Fund (CWSRF) that provides low-cost matching financing. As of 2020, more than $100 billion worth of water infrastructure has been built with CWSRF support.

NPDES permits

To operationalize the effluent limitations, the CWA sets up a *National Pollution Discharge Elimination System* (NPDES), which requires all point sources of water pollution to get permits from EPA or state environmental authorities. NPDES permits specify the acceptable limits of what can be discharged, establish monitoring and reporting requirements (specifically mandating regular *discharge monitoring reports* (DMRs), which must be made available to the public), and may include other provisions designed to protect water quality. The program has proven difficult to administer as EPA has interpreted the law as requiring distinct rules for each industry class and category. This legal framework means that, in order to provide appropriate permits, EPA has had to master the production processes and pollution control technology opportunities across a wide range of industries, resulting in hundreds of lawsuits and further delay.

The DMRs required by NPDES permits create the foundation for a two-prong approach to enforcement of CWA requirements. As a general matter, EPA or a state department of environmental protection (DEP) can use the information provided to determine if a facility is in compliance with its permit. But CWA section 505 also provides for *citizen suits* to call out violations in the face of inaction by the government. Under this provision, environmental groups and other nongovernmental organizations (NGOs) are empowered to bring legal actions against factories or other dischargers they believe have violated their NPDES permit requirements based on the information in their DMRs. In acting as private attorneys general, such groups can obtain court orders requiring improved performance by deficient facilities and may be awarded costs including attorney fees for their efforts.

Regulation of non-point sources

Although agricultural runoff and other non-point sources of water pollution contribute significantly to degrading quality in many waterbodies, for decades EPA did little more than require states under CWA section 319 to identify potential non-point sources of harm and adopt *best management practices* (BMPs) to address the problematic activities. But by the 1990s, it became clear that fertilizer runoff was responsible for more than 80 percent of the nitrogen and phosphorous in lakes, ponds, rivers, and streams across the country—and these excessive nutrient *loadings* were causing serious eutrophication problems, where excessive algae blooms consumed the available oxygen in the water, leading to the death of animal life and creating biological *dead zones*.[23]

Thus, in 2000, EPA invoked its authority under CWA section 303 and required states to: (a) identify waterbodies where the effluent standards and regulation of point sources had proven to be insufficient; (b) establish *total maximum daily loads* (TMDLs) for these waters; and (c) tighten NPDES permits to meet the TMDLs. While the Bush Administration pulled back from these new rules in 2001, the Obama EPA reasserted the need for TMDL-based regulatory requirements.

EPA's use of its section 303 authority to require non-point sources of pollution to adhere to TMDL-based requirements was upheld in the 2002 *Pronsolino* case.[24] In this case, plaintiffs owning timberlands subject to new runoff controls and thus restrictions on logging roads argued that EPA had overstepped its CWA authority. The 9th Circuit rejected this argument, however, and reaffirmed EPA's use of TMDLs as a basis for regulating non-point sources of water pollution. TMDLs are now a foundational element of water pollution regulation across the nation, creating a watershed approach to water quality protection that scientists had long preferred to the original CWA emphasis on effluent limitations.

---

23 David Biello, *Fertilizer Runoff Overwhelms Streams and Rivers—Creating Vast "Dead Zones"*, Sci. Am. (Mar. 14, 2008), https://www.scientificamerican.com/article/fertilizer-runoff-overwhelms-streams/.

24 Pronsolino v. Nastri, 291 F.3d 1123 (9th Cir. 2002) (*cert. denied*, 539 U.S. 926 (2003)), https://casetext.com/case/pronsolino-v-nastri.

Coastal Zone Management Act

A separate law, the Coastal Zone Management Act (CZMA),[25] provides a second regulatory foundation for controlling non-point sources of water pollution along the nation's extensive coastline. Under the CZMA, states must develop Coastal Non-Point Pollution Control Programs, subject to EPA review and approval. They must also follow EPA guidance in implementing CZMA plans to qualify for federal funding. These requirements include siting of marinas, the use of pressure-treated lumber that might leach chemicals into the water, runoff control, and other best practices.

State land use controls

Many states have their own statutes protecting sensitive areas including waterbodies. Florida's Environmental Land and Water Management Act,[26] for example, sets limits on development including in areas that might affect aquatic ecosystems. Similarly, Maryland's Critical Areas Act[27] provides a 1000-foot buffer that prevents new development along the banks of Chesapeake Bay. In addition, most states have planning and zoning rules, often implemented at the city or town level, that require carefully designed project plans and permit applications when new construction might affect wetlands or other water resources.

Additional resources

Craig, Robin (2009). *Clean Water Act and the Constitution: Legal Structure and the Public's Right to a Clean and Healthy Environment* (2nd ed.). Washington, DC: Environmental Law Institute.

Dzurik, Andrew A. et al. (2018). *Water Resources Planning: Fundamentals for an Integrated Framework* (4th ed.). Lanham, Maryland: Rowman & Littlefield Publishers.

Houck, Oliver A. (2002). *The Clean Water Act TMDL Program*. Washington, DC: Environmental Law Institute.

Miller, Jeffrey G. et al. (2017). *Introduction to Environmental Law: Cases and Materials on Water Pollution Control* (2nd ed.). Washington, DC: Environmental Law Institute.

---

25 Coastal Zone Management Act, 16 U.S.C. §§ 1451–1465.

26 Fla. Stat. Ann. §§ 380.012–10 (Supp. 1973).

27 Md. Code Ann. Nat. Res. §§ 8-1803–06 (Supp. 1986).

Salzman, James (2012). *Drinking Water: A History*. New York: Overlook Duckworth Publishers.

Ryan, Mark A. (2018). *Clean Water Act Handbook* (4th ed.). Chicago, Illinois: American Bar Association Book Publishing.

6   Safe Drinking Water Act: once seen as a problem solved, but now new worries

As with so many of our environmental laws, the Safe Drinking Water Act of 1974 emerged from a perceived crisis. A 1974 exposé in *Consumer Reports*, "Is the Water Safe to Drink?",[1] concluded that industrial pollution in the Mississippi River had contaminated drinking water in New Orleans. This finding shocked the nation, which believed that public water supplies were safe ever since chlorination had eliminated the pathogens that had for made water consumption a risk for prior generations.[2] Congress responded by enacting the Safe Drinking Water Act (SDWA) of 1974, signed into law by President Ford just months after the explosive stories in *Consumer Reports* were published.[3]

SDWA basic requirements

The SDWA requires EPA to develop health-based standards for a list of potentially toxic contaminants found in water supplies, with 91 such chemicals now subject to regulation. The law covers six categories of contaminants: micro-organisms, inorganic chemicals (including lead), organic chemicals, radionuclides, disinfectants (notably chlorine, which has long been used to kill pathogens in water suppliers—with great success), and disinfection byproducts (a number of which arise from the chlorination process and have been identified as carcinogens).[4]

---

1 R.H. Harris and E.M. Brecher, *Is the Water Safe to Drink? Part I: The Problem*, 39 CONSUMER REP. 436 (1974); R.H. Harris and E.M. Brecher, *Is the Water Safe to Drink? Part II: How to Make it Safer*, 39 CONSUMER REP. 538 (1974); R.H. Harris and E.M. Brecher, *Is the Water Safe to Drink? Part III: What You Can Do*, 39 CONSUMER REP. 623 (1974).

2 DAVID SEDLAK, WATER 4.0: THE PAST, PRESENT, AND FUTURE OF THE WORLD'S MOST VITAL RESOURCE 91 (2014).

3 The 1974 Act built on Senate hearings on water quality in 1970 and a prior legislative initiative, the Pure Drinking Water Act of 1971, that had been blocked by President Nixon.

4 Safe Drinkng Water Act § 1412(b)(1), 42 U.S.C. § 300g-1(b)(1), https://www.law.cornell.edu/uscode/text/42/300g-1; National Primary Drinking Water Regulations: Maximum Contaminant

It also regulates underground injection wells for the disposal of toxic wastes.[5]

The law requires EPA to establish *National Primary Drinking Water Regulations* (NPDWRs)[6] based on *Maximum Contaminant Level Goals* (MCLGs), targets that would limit human exposure to these chemicals, with an adequate margin of safety,[7] if implemented. But the statute does not require EPA to implement these pure public health targets. Instead, it directs EPA to set *Maximum Contaminant Levels* (MCLs) that define the actual exposure levels permitted. The law provides that the MCLs are to be as close to the MCLGs as feasible after considering technology limits and costs.[8] But there is a final step in the process of setting drinking water rules: EPA must undertake a risk assessment of the MCLs and modify the legal standards to be promulgated based on a benefit-cost calculation. In requiring EPA to maximize "health risk reduction benefits at a cost that is justified by the benefits," the SDWA represents a quintessential *risk-balancing* law.[9]

The SDWA also requires information disclosure of both water quality in general and any violations of standards. Specifically, the law mandates that the 155 000 drinking water systems (both public and private) across America that provide water to 25 customers or more send out an annual *Consumer Confidence Report* to their water customers spelling out the source of the water being provided, the levels of contaminants that have been detected, and the system's record of compliance with SDWA standards.[10] But the tens of thousands of small water systems that often lack funding to do upgrades or even the capacity to stay

---

Levels and Maximum Residual Disinfectant Levels, 40 C.F.R. §§ 141.60-141.66 (2021), https://www.law.cornell.edu/cfr/text/40/part-141/subpart-G.

5 *Underground Injection Control (UIC)*, EPA, https://www.epa.gov/uic/underground-injection-control-regulations-and-safe-drinking-water-act-provisions.

6 SDWA § 1412(b)(1)(A), 42 U.S.C. § 300g-1(b)(1)(A), https://www.law.cornell.edu/uscode/text/42/300g-1.

7 SDWA § 1412(b)(4)(A), 42 U.S.C. § 300g-1(b)(4)(A), https://www.law.cornell.edu/uscode/text/42/300g-1.

8 SDWA § 1412(b)(4)(B), 42 U.S.C. § 300g-1(b)(4)(B), https://www.law.cornell.edu/uscode/text/42/300g-1.

9 SDWA § 1412(b)(6)(A), 42 U.S.C. § 300g-1(b)(6)(A), https://www.law.cornell.edu/uscode/text/42/300g-1.

10 *See Consumer Confidence Reports (CCR)*, EPA, https://ofmpub.epa.gov/apex/safewater/f?p=136:102; SDWA § 1414(c)(4), 42 U.S.C. § 300g-3(c)(4), https://www.law.cornell.edu/uscode/text/42/300g-3.

abreast of best practices in water testing and purification present an on-going risk to those who rely upon them.

Regulation of underground injection wells

The practice of pumping fluids into underground porous geological formations such as sandstone and limestone, which are referred to as *injection wells*, became popular in the 1930s. Today, injection wells are used for the disposal of waste and *brine*,[11] enhancement of oil production, mining, and, more recently, the storage of carbon dioxide. The SDWA also regulates pumping materials into the ground under EPA's *Underground Injection Control* (UIC) program.[12] EPA sets minimum requirements for injection practices in order prevent the contamination and "endangerment" of underground sources of drinking water.[13] EPA regulates injection wells under six classes[14] and has delegated *primacy* for all well classes to 33 states (and shares responsibility with seven) to implement UIC programs.

Although EPA does regulate *enhanced recovery wells*—when fluids are injected into oil-bearing geological formations to recover oil and natural gas—as Class II wells,[15] the Energy Policy Act of 2005 created a broad exemption for hydraulic fracturing from the UIC program such that EPA now does not regulate fracking, as is discussed below.[16]

Does fracking contaminate drinking water?

Extraction of *unconventional* oil and gas using a technique called hydraulic fracturing (or simply *fracking*) has created a contentious drinking water issue. To recover *shale gas* or *tight oil*, drillers fracture

---

11 Brine is a product of natural gas and oil production that often contains toxic metals and radioactive substances.

12 SDWA §§ 1423, 42 U.S.C. 300h; Underground Injection Control Program, 40 C.F.R § 144; *Protecting Underground Sources of Drinking Water from Underground Injection*, EPA, https://www.epa.gov/uic.

13 Underground sources of drink water is defined at 40 C.F.R § 144.3.

14 The six classes include industrial and municipal waste disposal wells, oil and gas related injection wells, solution mining wells, shallow hazardous and radioactive waste injection wells, wells that inject non-hazardous fluids into or above underground sources of drinking water, and geologic sequestration wells.

15 *Class II Oil and Gas Related Injection Wells*, EPA, https://www.epa.gov/uic/class-ii-oil-and-gas-related-injection-wells.

16 Energy Policy Act of 2005 § 322 (codified as amended at 42 U.S.C. § 300h(d)). The exemption does not include hydraulic fracturing when diesel fuel is used.

underground rock where the fossil fuels are trapped and inject a slurry of sand, chemicals, and water into the cracks, thereby releasing the gas or oil. This technique in combination with horizontal drilling has dramatically increased U.S. oil and gas production in recent years. Critics claim that fracking may contaminate nearby groundwater due to leaks of the fracking fluids or the natural gas (methane) itself.[17] As intuitively plausible as that may seem, the issue has been studied repeatedly, and very few examples of contamination of drinking water from fracking have been found and in most of those cases, the contamination resulted from well casings leaking rather than from the fracking process itself.[18] Skeptics suggest that the real goal of anti-fracking environmental advocates can be traced to their concerns about climate change and desire to substitute renewable energy sources for fossil fuels.

The national government does not regulate fracking except on federal land,[19] but states have stepped into the breach with fracking regulations of varying rigor.[20] For example, all oil and gas producing states require that brine, salty water than can be hazardous, be disposed of through injection into the originating or similar formation. Some states such as Pennsylvania also require double lining of well casings to minimize the risk of contaminating aquifers.

---

17 JAMES SALZMAN, DRINKING WATER: A HISTORY 120–25 (rev. ed., 2017) [hereinafter SALZMAN, DRINKING WATER], at 127–31; *see also Fracking: Regulatory Failures and Delays*, GREENPEACE, *https://www.greenpeace.org/usa/global-warming/issues/fracking/regulatory-failures-and-delays/; but see* Susan L. Brantley and Anna Meyendorff, *The Facts on Fracking*, N.Y. TIMES (Mar. 13, 2013), http://www.nytimes.com/2013/03/14/opinion/global/the-facts-on-fracking.html?pagewanted=all&_r=0 (suggesting environmental concerns about fracking are overblown).

18 A 2015 report by the Obama-era EPA concluded "there are above and below ground mechanisms by which hydraulic fracturing activities have the potential to impact drinking water resources. . . . We did not find evidence that these mechanisms have led to widespread, systemic impacts on drinking water resources in the United States." *Assessment of the Potential Impacts of Hydraulic Fracturing for Oil and Gas on Drinking Water Resources Executive Summary*, EPA (2015), http://www2.epa.gov/sites/production/files/2015-07/documents/hf_es_erd_jun2015.pdf; *see also* James Saiers, *Science as a Foundation for Policy*, in A BETTER PLANET: 40 BIG IDEAS FOR A. SUSTAINABLE FUTURE (Daniel C. Esty ed., 2019).

19 The federal government does prohibit the discharge of wastewater pollutants from unconventional oil and gas extraction facilities into surface waters and POTWs with some exceptions. *See Unconventional Oil and Gas Extraction Effluent Guidelines*, EPA, https://www.epa.gov/eg/unconventional-oil-and-gas-extraction-effluent-guidelines.

20 Barbara Warner and Jennifer Shapiro, *Fractured, Fragmented Federalism: A Study in Fracking Regulatory Policy*, 43 PUBLIUS 3:474-96 (2013) https://www.jstor.org/stable/42000297?seq=1.

Results and continuing challenges

Drinking water across the nation has improved as a result of the SDWA. Before the law was passed, 40 percent of U.S. drinking water systems could not meet minimum health standards; but, as of 2014, over 90 percent of U.S. citizens drink water that consistently meets all SDWA standards.[21]

But the law also has limits. First, the law only applies to public drinking water systems, not private wells—leaving the water supplies of more than 40 million Americans, as of 2015, beyond the reach of the SDWA.[22] Second, EPA has added no new contaminants to its list of regulated chemicals since 2000, despite substantial advances in both public health science and contaminant detection capacity.[23] This means that new exposure threats, such as endocrine disrupters—chemicals that may mimic hormones in the body[24]—and pharmaceuticals[25] are not subject to SDWA standards.[26] Third, compliance with the SDWA is often delegated to the states, which may not be very diligent in their oversight, particularly as the parties against which enforcement actions must be taken are often the local government entities that manage drinking water systems with little ability to pay fines or upgrade their treatment facilities, never mind the political blowback that might arise from an angry mayor.

---

21 Gina McCarthy, Administrator, EPA, Remarks Celebrating the 40th Anniversary of the Safe Drinking Water Act, As Prepared (Dec. 9, 2014), https://archive.epa.gov/epapages/newsroom_archive/speeches/21a0a07494e97f3985257da9006ad9d0.html.

22 *Contamination in U.S. Private Wells*, USGS, https://www.usgs.gov/special-topic/water-science-school/science/contamination-us-private-wells?qt-science_center_objects=0#qt-science_center_objects.

23 Charles Duhigg, *That Tap Water Is Legal but May Be Unhealthy*, N.Y. TIMES (Dec. 16, 2009), https://www.nytimes.com/2009/12/17/us/17water.html.

24 Sze Yee Wee and Ahmad Zaharin Aris, *Occurrence and Public-Perceived Risk of Endocrine Disrupting Compounds in Drinking Water*, 2 NPJ CLEAN WATER 1 (2019), https://doi.org/10.1038/s41545-018-0029-3.

25 Interestingly, EPA chose in 2018 to regulate pharmaceuticals entering water supplies after being flushed down the toilet under the Resource Conservation and Recovery Act (RCRA) not the SDWA. Rich Thompson, *Much ado about pharma residue: EPA rule aims to end waste flushing.* WASTEDIVE (Jan. 7, 2019), http://bit.ly/3pXK6WS.

26 SALZMAN, DRINKING WATER, *supra* note 17. But despite the statutory limitations, the Biden Administration has signaled its intention to address PFAS (per- and polyfluoroalkyl substances), a set of carcinogenic chemicals that have come under scrutiny in recent years, using existing SDWA authority. *The Biden Plan to Secure Environmental Justice and Equitable Economic Opportunity*, BIDEN HARRIS, https://joebiden.com/environmental-justice-plan/.

As a result, many Americans continue to be exposed to unsafe drinking water. Indeed, a 2009 *New York Times* investigation found that many drinking water systems across the country failed to meet SDWA standards at various times and that very few of these violations were punished.[27] Despite major revisions to the law in 1986 and 1996 and minor amendments in 2005, 2011 (known as the Lead in Drinking Water Act), and 2015, problems continue to seep through cracks in the statutory framework.[28]

Flint water crisis

The shortcomings of the SDWA came into sharp relief in 2015 when lead contamination in the drinking water of Flint, Michigan exposed residents, a majority of whom are persons of color, to lead levels in excess of legal standards. Flint, like many older cities with aging infrastructure, has lead water pipes that date back 100 years, and which had not been upgraded as the city fell into industrial decline and faced continuous budget crises over the past several decades. When the city's finances collapsed in 2011, the Governor put the city into *receivership* (equivalent to bankruptcy) and appointed an emergency manager to take over fiscal decisionmaking. As a money-saving opportunity, the new management team decided to stop the practice of buying water from the city of Detroit and instead to draw *free* drinking water from the nearby Flint River. But the river was laced with industrial chemicals that leached lead out of the old pipes—putting contaminated tap water into homes across Flint and creating a high-profile *environmental justice* crisis.

Those managing the water system also declined to purchase orthophosphate or other corrosion inhibitors that could have been used to treat the water supply and prevent lead from leaching into the water even as

27 SALZMAN, DRINKING WATER, supra note 17, at 125. Salzman notes that unlike the CWA, little enforcement of the SDWA has been done through citizen suits.

28 The 1986 Amendments sought to speed up EPA's regulation of contaminants, improve protection of ground water, and limit lead pipe installation in new water systems. The 1996 Amendments increased EPA's regulatory flexibility and increased funding to improve drinking water quality but implemented a risk-based approach to regulation. The remaining minor Amendments increased the stringency of the SDWA "lead free" definition and allowed EPA to address algal toxins in public drinking water. MARY TIEMANN, CONGRESSIONAL RESEARCH SERVICE, SAFE DRINKING WATER ACT (SDWA): A SUMMARY OF THE ACT AND ITS MAJOR REQUIREMENTS (2017), https://fas.org/sgp/crs/misc/RL31243.pdf.

it passed through old lead pipes. As a result, tens of thousands of Flint residents were exposed to high lead levels in their drinking water. Tests showed that thousands of children (who are particularly susceptible to the impacts of lead—a neurotoxin with well-established risks to brain development in the early years of childhood) ended up with excess lead levels in their blood.[29]

Despite the multiple layers of protection built into the SDWA, the safe drinking water governance structure failed. Local officials clearly made poor policy choices that could not be justified no matter how serious the financial straits the city faced.[30] Alerted to the problem by Flint residents and analyses from a Virginia Tech professor who was asked to help assess the health risk, state Department of Environmental Quality (DEQ) officials not only declined to intervene but also actively dismissed suggestions that Flint might have a water problem. It now appears they may also have faked water quality test results.[31]

A number of local and state officials, including former Michigan Governor Rick Snyder, have been indicted for their "alleged actions and inactions that created the historic injustice" that has now been become known as the Flint Water Crisis.[32] While steps have now been taken to ameliorate the problem in Flint, similar risks continue to exist in older industrial cities across the country where economic distress and limited tax bases make pipe replacement a budget challenge.[33] Lead and other toxic contaminates in water can be removed by activated charcoal water filters at the tap, but EPA lacks the authority to require them. As the Flint case makes clear, America's framework of environmental law still has gaps that can result in serious problems.

---

29 James Salzman, *Safe Drinking Water*, in Fifty Years at the US Environmental Protection Agency: Progress, Retrenchment, and Opportunities (A. James Barnes, John D. Graham, and David M. Konisky eds., 2021).

30 *Id.*

31 Elisha Anderson and John Wisely, *Records: Falsified report led to charges in Flint Water crisis*, Det. Free Press (Apr. 22, 2016, 11:21 PM), https://www.freep.com/story/news/local/michigan/flint-water-crisis/2016/04/22/warrant-request-charges-flint-water-crisis/83406590/.

32 Ken Haddad, *Flint water crisis investigation: Here's who was charged*, Click-On Det (Jan. 14, 2021, 5:31 PM), https://www.clickondetroit.com/news/michigan/2021/01/14/flint-water-crisis-investigation-heres-who-was-charged/.

33 *Millions of Americans still get their drinking water from lead pipes*, Economist (Dec. 3, 2020), https://www.economist.com/united-states/2020/12/03/millions-of-americans-still-get-their-drinking-water-from-lead-pipes.

PFAS: an emerging issue

One area on which the Trump and the Biden Administrations agreed was the need to expand regulation of per- and poly-fluoroalkyl substances (PFAS), although regulation was somewhat grudging under Trump and is likely to expand under Biden. PFAS are a large family of chemicals with over 4700 substances already identified and more being invented all the time.[34] They are formed when fluorine, a highly reactive gas, combines with a carbon backbone to form a chain.[35] Various species of PFAS have many useful functions and are currently used in hundreds of applications, including treating clothing, cookware, cosmetics, carpet treatments, firefighting foam, and even dental floss. They are sometimes called *forever chemicals* because they break down very slowly in nature and bioaccumulate in the body.[36] However, recent science has also discovered a number of adverse health effects from high doses of certain members of the PFAS family including increases in cholesterol and blood pressure, decreased birth weight, and increased risks of kidney or testicular cancer.[37]

The Trump Administration EPA developed a *PFAS Action Plan,*[38] but its primary regulatory action was to promulgate a *significant new use rule* (SNUR) under the Toxic Substances Control Act for two specific chemicals, perfluorooctanoic acid (PFOA) and perfluorooctanesulfonic acid (PFOS). The SNUR required notice and advance approval by EPA of new uses of these two specific chemicals in surface coatings.[39] The

---

34 *Perfluoroalkyl and Polyfluoroalkyl Substances (PFAS)*, NATIONAL INSTITUTE OF ENVIRONMENTAL HEALTH SCIENCES, https://www.niehs.nih.gov/health/topics/agents/pfc/index. cfm#:~:text=PFAS%20are%20used%20in%20hundreds,of%20this%20type%20of%20chemical.

35 *See generally What is PFAS—and Why Should You Care?*, ENVIRONMENTAL PROTECTION (June 15, 2017), https://eponline.com/articles/2017/06/15/what-is-pfas.aspx.

36 Annie Sneed, *Forever Chemicals Are Widespread in U.S. Drinking Water: Experts hope that with the incoming Biden administration, the federal government will finally regulate a class of chemicals known as PFASs*, SCIENTIFIC AMERICAN (Jan. 22, 2021), https://www.scientificamerican.com/article/forever-chemicals-are-widespread-in-u-s-drinking-water/.

37 For a good, accessible summary of what is and is not known about the potential adverse health effects of PFAS, see *Per- and Polyfluoroalkyl Substances (PFAS) and Your Health: What are the Health Effects of PFAS?*, AGENCY FOR TOXIC SUBSTANCES AND DISEASE REGISTRY, https://www. atsdr.cdc.gov/pfas/health-effects/index.html.

38 *EPA's PFAS Action Plan*, EPA, https://www.epa.gov/pfas/epas-pfas-action-plan.

39 *See* Chapter 8 for a general explanation of SNURs. For a summary of prior regulatory and voluntary actions on PFAS extending as far back as 2002, see *Risk Management for Per- and Polyfluoroalkyl Substances (PFAS) under TSCA*, EPA, https://www.epa.gov/assessing-and-managing-chemicals-under-tsca/risk-management-and-polyfluoroalkyl-substances-pfas.

Biden Administration EPA has indicated that it will propose drinking water standards for 26 chemicals in the PFAS family,[40] as drinking water contaminated with PFAS appears to be one of the primary exposure routes for humans. EPA has also reportedly sent a proposal for White House review to designate some members of the PFAS family as hazardous substances, which would facilitate clean-ups under CERCLA.[41] We can anticipate that regulation and litigation regarding various chemicals in the PFAS family will continue for many years.

Bottled water issues

Many people drink bottled water because they perceive it as heathier than tap water.[42] EPA does not regulate bottled water except to the extent the SDWA applies to the original water sources. Bottled water that is shipped across state lines is regulated by the Food and Drug Administration (FDA).[43] FDA has incorporated by reference EPA's safe drinking water standards and applies them to bottled water but it does little to inspect bottled water supplies.[44]

Drinking water safety in perspective

Americans drink safer water today than in years past due in part to the regulatory requirements of the SDWA. The outbreaks of waterborne disease that regularly plagued America in centuries past have largely been abated. But we cannot declare the law's promise of safe drinking water fulfilled as substantial risks remain.

---

40 EPA, Final Rule, Significant New Use Rule: Long-Chain Perfluoroalkyl Carboxylate and Perfluoroalkyl Sulfonate Chemical Substances (EPA-HQ-OPPT-2013-0225) (July 27, 2020), https://www.regulations.gov/document/EPA-HQ-OPPT-2013-0225-0232.

41 *See* Chapter 7.

42 Stephanie Strom, *Bottled Water Sales Rising as Soda Ebbs*, N.Y. TIMES (Oct. 25, 2013), https://www.nytimes.com/2013/10/26/business/bottled-water-sales-rising-as-soda-ebbs.html?smid=url-share.

43 Lauren M. Posnick and Henry Kim, *Bottled Water Regulation and the FDA*, FOOD SAFETY (Aug. 1, 2002), https://www.food-safety.com/articles/4373-bottled-water-regulation-and-the-fda.

44 CHARLES FISHMAN, THE BIG THIRST: THE SECRET LIFE AND TURBULENT FUTURE OF WATER 354 (2011).

Additional resources

Clark, Anna (2018). *The Poisoned City: Flint's Water and the American Urban Tragedy.* New York, NY: Metropolitan Books.

Fishman, Charles (2012). *The Big Thirst: The Secret Life and Turbulent Future of Water.* New York, NY: Free Press.

Pontius, Fredrick W. (2003). *Drinking Water Regulation and Health* (1st ed.). Hoboken, NJ: Wiley.

Salzman, James (2017). *Drinking Water: A History* (rev. ed.). New York, NY: Overlook Press.

Sedlack, David (2014). *Water 4.0: The Past, Present, and Future of the World's Most Vital Resource.* New Haven, CT: Yale University Press.

Tiemann, Mary (2017). Safe Drinking Water Act (SDWA): A Summary of the Act and Its Major Requirements. *Congressional Research Service.* https://fas.org/sgp/crs/misc/RL31243.pdf.

Weinmeyer, Richard et al. (2017). The Safe Drinking Water Act of 1974 and its Role in Providing Access to Safe Drinking Water in the United States. *AMA Journal of Ethics, 19*(10), 1018-1026. https://journalofethics.ama-assn.org/article/safe-drinking-water-act-1974-and-its-role-providing-access-safe-drinking-water-united-states/2017-10.

7   Hazardous waste: extreme measures in the wake of a crisis

Land is plentiful and therefore inexpensive in large sections of the United States. As a result, a common historic practice in the United States was to dispose of waste, including hazardous chemical liquids, by burying it in drums in *landfills*, which used to be called *dumps*. This practice resulted in a range of environmental problems that attracted attention from citizen activism movements in the mid-1970s, particularly as a result of *Love Canal*, a dump in upstate New York which leaked hazardous chemicals into nearby residences. Congress responded in 1980 with two of the more extreme U.S. environmental statutes: the Comprehensive Environmental Response Compensation and Liability Act (CERCLA), also known as the *Superfund* law for reasons we will explain later, which is designed to clean up historic sites on which hazardous substances have been disposed; and the Resource Conservation and Recovery Act (RCRA), which regulates the management and disposal of hazardous wastes, non-hazardous wastes, medical wastes, and underground storage tanks.

CERCLA: cleaning up historic hazardous waste sites

Many U.S. environmental laws have been passed in the wake of a crisis, but none more clearly than the CERCLA. In the mid-1970s, Love Canal became synonymous with inappropriate disposal of hazardous wastes in landfills and led to some of the strongest liability laws in U.S. history.[1] Hooker Chemical Company buried drums of hazardous chemicals in an abandoned canal, then deeded the property to the local community which built a school on the site. Eventually, the steel drums rusted and began leaking chemicals into nearby residential properties. Local activists, led by Lois Gibbs, skillfully used the media

---

1 The story of Love Canal is told in an article in the *EPA Journal*, which describes Love Canal as "one of the most appalling environmental tragedies in American history." *See* Eckardt C. Beck, *The Love Canal Tragedy*, EPA J. (Jan., 1979), https://archive.epa.gov/epa/aboutepa/love-canal-tragedy.html.

to publicize the incident, and Congress responded by passing CERCLA in 1980. Ms Gibbs went on to train environmental activists throughout the country. She exemplifies the critical role that citizen activists and media publicity have played in forcing the government to address environmental problems.[2]

CERCLA's goals

CERCLA has two different purposes. It aims to: (1) clean-up 47 000 abandoned hazardous waste sites throughout the United States; but also to (2) establish liability rules holding industries that generate hazardous waste responsible for the costs of cleaning-up disposal sites. CERCLA creates a process by which the federal government, states or private parties may clean-up sites at which hazardous substances have been deposited if they are leaking or threatening to release their contents, and establishes a liability scheme for four categories of *potentially responsible parties* (PRPs)—current owners of the waste site, former owners, transporters of the waste, and those who arranged for waste's disposal—all of whom can be asked to cover *response costs* at the site.[3] These are defined to include not only the costs of the clean-up but also damage to natural resources, costs of health assessments, and attorney's fees for government entities (but not for private parties). Despite its name, the Comprehensive Environmental Response, *Compensation* and Liability Act does not create a private cause of action for damages from exposure to hazardous substances; that is left to the states' common law of *toxic torts*.

CERCLA's liability structure

The CERCLA liability scheme for response costs is the most stringent known to U.S. environmental law. It holds parties *jointly and severally* liable *retroactively* for the costs of clean-up if they fall into four categories regardless of whether they were guilty of creating the problem:

---

2   *See generally* Lois Marie Gibbs, *Love Canal: The Start of a Movement*, BU.EDU, https://www.bu.edu/lovecanal/canal/; Kevin Konrad, *Lois Gibbs: Grassroots Organizer and Environmental Health Advocate*, 101 AM. J. PUB. HEALTH 1558 (2011), https://www.ncbi.nlm.nih.gov/pmc/articles/PMC3154230/.

    For how publicity changes political dynamics by focusing public attention on an issue, see E. Donald Elliott, Bruce A. Ackerman, and John C. Millian, *Toward a Theory of Statutory Evolution: The Federalization of Environmental Law*, 1 J.L. ECON. & ORG. 313 (1985), http://digitalcommons.law.yale.edu/fss_papers/147/.

3   CERCLA § 107(a)(4), 42 U.S.C. § 9607(a)(4), https://www.law.cornell.edu/uscode/text/42/9607.

(1)   the [current] owner and operator of a vessel or a facility,

(2)   any person who at the time of disposal of any hazardous substance owned or operated any facility at which such hazardous substances were disposed of,

(3)   any person who by contract, agreement, or otherwise arranged for disposal or treatment, or arranged with a transporter for transport for disposal or treatment, of hazardous substances owned or possessed by such person, by any other party or entity, at any facility or incineration vessel owned or operated by another party or entity and containing such hazardous substances, and

(4)   any person who accepts or accepted any hazardous substances for transport to disposal or treatment facilities, incineration vessels or sites selected by such person, from which there is a release, or a threatened release which causes the incurrence of response costs, of a hazardous substance, . . .[4]

The sweeping joint and several liability provisions mean that any one party (or small number of parties) can be held responsible for *all* the clean-up costs. With time having passed and many of companies that sent waste to a particular site having gone out of business or otherwise disappeared, it turned out in practice that companies with very modest responsibility for a site might be asked to pay tens of millions and sometimes hundreds of millions of dollars in clean-up costs. Moreover, liability under CERCLA is "subject *only* to the defenses"[5] that "the release or threat of release of a hazardous substance and the damages resulting therefrom were caused *solely*" by: an act of god, an act of war, or the actions of a third party with whom the liable party had no contractual relationship.[6] That the waste disposal was entirely legal at the time it was done is no defense.

This liability scheme has been criticized as *status liability,* the collection of a tax via litigation, or more colorfully, as "superdumb."[7] On the other hand, others have argued that by creating strong economic incentives holding generators of hazardous waste responsible for how toxic materials are handled from *cradle to grave,* Superfund got the attention

---

4   CERCLA § 107(a), 42 U.S.C. § 9607(a), https://www.law.cornell.edu/uscode/text/42/9607.

5   *Id.* (emphasis added).

6   CERCLA § 107(b), 42 U.S.C. § 9607(b). https://www.law.cornell.edu/uscode/text/42/9607.

7   Dashiell Shapiro, *Superdumb Discrimination in Superfund: CERCLA Section 107 Violates Equal Protection,* 1 U. CHI. LEGAL F. 331 (2002), http://chicagounbound.uchicago.edu/uclf/vol2002/iss1/13.

of industry, which changed its waste disposal practices, thereby preventing inappropriate disposal of hazardous waste in the future.[8]

What cannot be denied is that, in a pattern we have seen under other environmental statutes,[9] Congress did not fully appreciate the second-order incentive effects[10] set in motion by CERCLA. In particular, by making *current* owners of contaminated sites responsible for the costly clean-ups regardless of whether they had anything to do with putting the waste there in the first place, the liability framework created the *brownfields* problem, in which no one would redevelop contaminated properties for fear of Superfund liability. Instead, businesses would choose *greenfields* sites on the outskirts of cities, where there was much less risk of contaminated land or ground water. Carol Brower, EPA Administrator under President Clinton (and later White House environmental and energy *czar* under President Obama) made one of her signature issues at EPA solving the brownfields problem and encouraging redevelopment of old industrial sites. In another familiar pattern, EPA first addressed the problem ad hoc by regulatory interpretation, developing a practice of entering into *prospective purchaser agreements* in which EPA agreed not to sue a purchaser of contaminated property if the new owner took specified actions to minimize exposures and keep the problem from getting worse. Congress amended the statute in 2002 to codify this approach by creating a new defense for *bona fide prospective purchasers*.[11]

Superfund clean-ups

In addition to its liability provisions, Superfund is also a clean-up statute, which has spawned an industry of environmental consultants, lawyers, and mediators who allocate costs among the PRPs at

---

8 Adam Babich, *Understanding the New Era in Environmental Law*, 41 S.C. L. Rev 733 (1990), https://scholarcommons.sc.edu/sclr/vol41/iss4/4/.

9 *See* section of Chapter 3 discussing Prevention of Significant Deterioration (PSD) under the Clean Air Act.

10 *See generally* Henry Hazlitt, Economics in One Lesson (1946), https://fee.org/media/14946/economicsinonelesson.pdf (Condemning "the fallacy of overlooking secondary consequences . . . the whole of economics can be reduced to a single lesson, and that lesson can be reduced to a single sentence. *The art of economics consists in looking not merely at the immediate but at the longer effects of any act or policy; it consists in tracing the consequences of that policy not merely for one group but for all groups.*").

11 Small Business Liability Relief and Brownfields Revitalization Act, Pub. L. No. 107-118, 115 stat. 2356 (January 11, 2002), codified in part at 42 U.S.C. § 9601(40)(D), https://www.govinfo.gov/app/details/PLAW-107publ118.

Superfund sites. The process begins with EPA[12] ranking sites according to a *hazard ranking system,* which looks primarily at the potential for exposure and detrimental effects on human health. Roughly 150 of the highest ranked sites are included on a *National Priority List* (NPL). EPA then takes the lead in cleaning up these NPL sites, and they become eligible for clean-up financing out of the federal government's *Superfund trust fund,* which gives the statute its common name. The Superfund trust fund had spent over $32 billion funded by taxes toward cleaning up sites as of 2008, when it ran out of money because Congress repealed the tax on chemical feedstocks that supported it in 1995.[13] Site clean-ups at lower priority non-NPL sites are managed by the states or private parties.

The site clean-up process is governed by an extensive master rule, the National Contingency Plan (NCP),[14] some of which has been subsequently strengthened and codified by Congress in the 1986 Superfund Amendments and Reauthorization Act.[15] This is another familiar pattern in U.S. environmental law in which Congress legislates against the backdrop of agency interpretations. While the NCP is long and detailed, it leaves substantial discretion to balance seven factors in the agency's *record of decision* (ROD) selecting the remedy at a site.[16] Although timing is postponed until after the clean-up is completed, remedy selection is technically subject to judicial review. However, remedy selection is reviewed under a deferential standard for whether EPA's decision is *arbitrary and capricious* or supported

---

12 While this section describes the EPA clean-up process which applies to most sites, Superfund is in fact one of the few U.S. environmental statutes that explicitly grants authority to "the President," rather than the Administrator of EPA. The President has delegated his Superfund authority to the Department of Defense for military sites, and to EPA for most other sites. *See* Exec. Order No. 12,580, 3 C.F.R., 1987 Comp. (1987), as subsequently amended.

13 U.S. GOVERNMENT ACCOUNTABILITY OFFICE WASHINGTON, SUPERFUND: FUNDING AND REPORTED COSTS OF ENFORCEMENT AND ADMINISTRATION ACTIVITIES (July 18, 2008), https://www.gao.gov/products/GAO-08-841R.

14 National Oil and Hazardous Substances Pollution Contingency Plan, 40 C.F.R § 300, https://www.govinfo.gov/content/pkg/CFR-2015-title40-vol28/xml/CFR-2015-title40-vol28-part300.xml.

15 *The Superfund Amendments and Reauthorization Act (SARA),* EPA, https://www.epa.gov/superfund/superfund-amendments-and-reauthorization-act-sara.

16 *See* Lawrence E. Starfield, *The 1990 National Contingency Plan — More Detail and More Structure, But Still a Balancing Act,* 20 ENVTL. L. REP. 10222, https://elr.info/sites/default/files/articles/20.10222.htm.

by the administrative record on matters of *central relevance*[17] and the remedies selected by EPA are almost never overturned in practice.

Clean-ups are done in three phases. The first phase is a *removal action* to abate immediate risks to health such as by removing leaking drums, fencing off the site and providing an alternative water supply to replace contaminated drinking water. The next step is a *remedial investigation and feasibility study* (RIF) to design the remedy, followed by the *remedial action*, which is the permanent site clean-up, a process that typically takes years and costs millions of dollars.

If the PRPs do not agree to perform the remedy, EPA may hire contractors to do it, or EPA may issue a *unilateral administrative order* (UAO) directing one or more of the PRPs to clean up the site if it poses an *imminent and substantial endangerment*.[18] This standard as interpreted by EPA and upheld by the courts is not as demanding as it sounds. A mere *threat* or *risk of harm* is deemed sufficient even if it is not immediate and may not come about for many years.[19] Judicial review of a UAO is not permitted until after the clean-up is completed.[20] A party receiving such an order may, however, file a *substantial cause letter* outlining its reasons for refusing to comply,[21] but it does so at its peril; if it *wrongfully* refuses to do the clean-up *without substantial cause* it is subject to fines of $25 000 per day,[22] which, indexed for inflation, had risen to $58 328 per day as of 2020.[23] Faced with potentially huge fines, most PRPs decide to do the clean-up themselves under EPA supervision, in part because clean-ups typically cost only about half as much if managed by the PRPs rather than by EPA.

---

17 CERCLA § 113(j)(2), (4), 42 U.S.C. § 9613(j)(2), (4), https://www.law.cornell.edu/uscode/text/42/9613.

18 CERCLA § 106(a), 42 U.S.C. § 9606(a), https://www.law.cornell.edu/uscode/text/42/9606.

19 *See* Memorandum from Don R. Clay, Assistant Administrator Office of Solid Waste Emergency Response to Regional Administrators, Regions I-X, Guidance on CERCLA Section 106(a) Unilateral Administrative Orders for Remedial Designs and Remedial Actions (Mar. 7, 1990), https://www.epa.gov/sites/production/files/documents/cerc106-uao-rpt.pdf.

20 CERCLA § 113(h), 42 U.S.C. § 9613(h), https://www.law.cornell.edu/uscode/text/42/9613.

21 CERCLA § 106(b)(1), 42 U.S.C. § 9606(b)(1), https://www.law.cornell.edu/uscode/text/42/9606.

22 *Id.*

23 Memorandum from Kenneth Patterson, Director Regional to Regional Superfund Legal Branch Chiefs, Regions I-X, 2020 Revised Penalty Matrix for CERCLA § 106(b)(1) Civil Penalty Policy (Jan. 23, 2020). https://www.epa.gov/sites/production/files/2020-03/documents/106b-penalty-matrix-mem-2020.pdf.

To date, the lower courts have upheld the statutory scheme postponing judicial review until after the remedy is completed, but the Supreme Court has not addressed the issue. The Supreme Court, however, held in *Sackett v. EPA*[24] that a UAO under the CWA, prohibiting building in what EPA considered to be a wetland, was subject to immediate judicial review. Some court observers see this decision as a shot across EPA's bow warning that these provisions of Superfund coercing action with the threat of large penalties and postponing judicial review might be unconstitutional.[25] Although 77.5 percent of CERCLA remediation costs arise from waste disposed of prior to CERCLA's passage in 1980,[26] some going back a century or more ago, to date the courts have upheld the retroactive effect of the statute against constitutional challenges.[27]

Toxic waste site risk exposure

The primary potential pollution exposure route at a Superfund site is through drinking water from contaminated wells, but that risk is eliminated once an alternative source of drinking water is supplied to neighboring properties. Most of the risk reduction is accomplished at the removal stage, but the overwhelming majority of the cost is attributable to the exhaustive *permanent* clean-up efforts undertaken. As a result, Superfund has been the most controversial of U.S. environmental statutes because it produces relatively little benefit to health compared to air or water pollution statutes, but at a very high cost because relatively few people are exposed.[28]

When the Republicans retook Congress in 1994, they proposed legislative reforms to Superfund to make it more risk based.[29] The Clinton Administration staved off legislation by making a series of reforms administratively that greatly reduced the costs of Superfund clean-ups.

24 Sackett v. EPA, 566 U.S. 120 (2012), https://www.supremecourt.gov/opinions/11pdf/10-1062.pdf.

25 E. Donald Elliott, *EPA In The Trump Era: The Superfund Enforcement Initiative*, LAW360 (Feb. 21, 2018), http://digitalcommons.law.yale.edu/cgi/viewcontent.cgi?article=6118&context=fss_papers.

26 Dashiell Shapiro, *Superdumb Discrimination in Superfund: CERCLA Section 107 Violates Equal Protection*, 1 U. CHI. LEGAL F. 331, 332 (2002), http://chicagounbound.uchicago.edu/uclf/vol2002/iss1/13.

27 Gen. Elec. Co. v. Johnson, 362 F. Supp. 2d 327 (D.D.C. 2005), *aff'd*, Gen. Elec. Co. v. Jackson, 610 F.3d 110 (D.C. Cir. 2010), https://casetext.com/case/general-electric-company-v-johnson.

28 *See generally Unfinished Business: A Comparative Assessment of Environmental Problems Overview Report*, EPA, https://biotech.law.lsu.edu/blog/PB88127048.pdf.

29 *See* Reform of Superfund Act of 1995, H.R.2500, 104th Cong. (1995–1996), https://www.congress.gov/bill/104th-congress/house-bill/2500?s=1&r=1.

For example, rather than continuing to pump and treat groundwater for thirty years whether or not it was getting appreciably cleaner, which was formerly EPA's policy, today EPA only requires continuing to pump up and treat contaminated groundwater if there is a reasonable prospect of returning it to beneficial use. Otherwise, the rules simply require that the contaminated groundwater be contained in place.[30]

Historically, the discretion to select remedies was delegated from the EPA Administrator in Washington to the Regional Administrators, who are presidential appointees in EPA's eleven different geographic regions. However, Scott Pruitt, the EPA Administrator in the first years of the Trump Administration, took back personal authority over the selection of remedies at the fifty largest Superfund sites as part of his Superfund Enforcement Initiative.[31] This decision reflected his *back to basics* program to re-focus EPA on cleaning up air, water, and waste which he deemed to be its core mission as opposed to climate change.[32] His approach seems unlikely to continue as the Biden Administration has signaled that it has other priorities for the EPA.[33]

Liability refinement and reforms

Judicial interpretations have ameliorated some provisions of the Superfund liability system by interpreting them to be consistent with common law antecedents. For example, in Superfund's early years, most courts and commentators thought that joint and several liability was routine, which can result in a *deep pocket* that contributed only a small amount of waste to a site being held disproportionately liable for the total cost of clean-up.[34] In 2009, however, the Supreme Court

---

30 *How Superfund Addresses Groundwater Contamination*, EPA, https://www.epa.gov/superfund/how-superfund-addresses-groundwater-contamination.

31 *See* E. Donald Elliott, *EPA In The Trump Era: The Superfund Enforcement Initiative*, LAW360 (Feb. 21, 2018), http://digitalcommons.law.yale.edu/cgi/viewcontent.cgi?article=6118&context=fss_papers.

32 Alex Guillén, *The radical idea behind Trump's EPA rollbacks*, POLITICO (June 18, 2017, 7:13 AM), https://www.politico.com/story/2017/06/18/pruitts-predecessors-pan-epa-originalism-philosophy-239669.

33 *See e.g.*, *The Biden Plan for a Clean Energy Revolution and Environmental Justice*, BIDEN HARRIS, https://joebiden.com/climate-plan/; *See also* Sylvia Carignan, *Superfund Seen to Benefit From Biden's Climate, Justice Focus*, BLOOMBERG (Nov. 25, 2020, 6:00 AM), https://news.bloomberglaw.com/environment-and-energy/superfund-seen-to-benefit-from-bidens-climate-justice-focus.

34 Brennan F, Douglas, *Joint and Several Liability for Generators under Superfund: A Federal Formula for Cost Recovery*, 5 UCLA J. ENVTL. L. & POL'Y 101 (1986), https://escholarship.org/uc/item/5002x293.

applied traditional common law principles to make it easier to apportion liability fairly among responsible parties.[35] In theory, this could result in larger *orphan shares*—shares of clean-up costs for which no solvent PRP is currently responsible due to companies going out of business. These shares were formerly paid by the other jointly and severally liable parties but now arguably must be made up by EPA out of the Superfund trust fund. In practice, however, EPA usually racks up substantial oversight costs, which it can then waive as its contribution toward the orphan share.[36]

In the 1990 amendments, Congress made clear that a PRP who pays to clean-up a site under a judicial or administrative order may bring a *contribution action* under CERCLA section 113(f) against other PRPs for their equitable shares.[37] *Voluntary* clean-ups cannot form the basis for contribution suits under that section, but under some circumstances, PRPs that do a clean-up without a judicial or administrative order may be able to sue other PRPs under CERCLA section 107 provided that the clean-up was "consistent with the national contingency plan."[38]

RCRA: preventing future Superfund sites

The Resource Conservation and Recovery Act (RCRA), which provides a statutory framework for appropriate waste handling, creates a legal approach dominated by definitions. It applies to *solid wastes*, which

---

35 Burlington Northern & S. F. R. Co. v. United States, 556 U.S. 599 (2009), https://supreme.justia.com/cases/federal/us/556/599/.

36 *Guidance: Orphan Share Compensation Through the Compromise of Future Oversight Costs (Model Language)*, EPA, https://www.epa.gov/enforcement/guidance-orphan-share-compensation-through-compromise-future-oversight-costs-model.

37 CERCLA § 113(f), 42 U.S.C. § 9613(f), https://www.law.cornell.edu/uscode/text/42/9613. In apportioning liability among PRPs, courts often rely on six "Gore factors," which were proposed by then-Representative Al Gore in an unsuccessful attempt to amend CERCLA in 1980, as well as other equitable factors. *See generally* Justin R. Pidot and Dale Ratliff, *Common Law of CERCLA Claims*, 70 STAN. L. REV. 191 (2018), https://review.law.stanford.edu/wp-content/uploads/sites/3/2018/01/70-Stan.-L.-Rev.-191.pdf.

38 *Compare* Cooper Indus., Inc. v. Aviall Servs., Inc., 543 U.S. 157, 158 (2004), https://supreme.justia.com/cases/federal/us/543/157/ *with* United States v. Atl. Research Corp., 551 U.S. 128, 131–32 (2007), https://supreme.justia.com/cases/federal/us/551/128/. These complexities are explored in detail in Jeffrey M. Gaba, *The Private Causes of Action under CERCLA: Navigating the Intersection of Sections 107(a) and 113(f)*, 5 MICH. J. ENVTL & ADMIN. L. 117 (2015), https://repository.law.umich.edu/cgi/viewcontent.cgi?article=1045&context=mjeal.

as a general matter are materials that have been *discarded*.[39] However, with logic that only a lawyer could love, solid wastes may include gases and liquids! Solid wastes, which include ordinary municipal trash, are lightly regulated under Subtitle D of RCRA. However, a subset of solid wastes, called *hazardous wastes*, are regulated in excruciating detail under Subtitle C. In recent years, EPA has developed an intermediate level of regulation for *universal wastes*, substances such as batteries, pesticides, mercury-containing equipment, and lamps that require proper management, but not the high degree of regulation for Subtitle C hazardous wastes.[40]

A solid waste becomes a hazardous waste, and thus subject to stringent regulation under Subtitle C, in two ways:

(1) if it is *listed* specifically by EPA, usually because it is the residue from a specified production process (for example, "Spent Catalysts From Dual-Purpose Petroleum Hydroprocessing Reactors") of which there are currently 724 such listings;[41] or

(2) if it is classified as a *characteristic* hazardous waste because it exhibits one of four properties that might make it hazardous (corrosivity, ignitability, reactivity, and toxicity).[42]

EPA supposedly chose these four properties "because for each characteristic, succinct, low-cost analytical tests can be used to determine whether or not the waste exhibits a given characteristic."[43] For example, a solid waste is considered *ignitable*, and therefore regulated as a *hazardous waste*, if it is a "liquid[] with flash points below 60°C, non-liquids that cause fire through specific conditions, ignitable compressed gases and oxidizers."[44] A material is still regulated as a hazardous waste if it is mixed or derived from a hazardous waste, a rule that

---

39 American Mining Congress v. EPA, 824 F.2d 1177 (D.C. Cir. 1987), https://law.justia.com/cases/federal/appellate-courts/F2/824/1177/121718/.

40 *Universal Waste*, EPA, https://www.epa.gov/hw/universal-waste.

41 For listed wastes, see Identification and listing of hazardous waste, 40 C.F.R § 261, https://www.law.cornell.edu/cfr/text/40/part-261.

42 *Id.*

43 *RCRA 101 Part 3: Listed and Characteristic Wastes*, NEW PIG, https://www.newpig.com/rcra-101-part-3-listed-and-characteristic-wastes/c/8017?show=All.

44 *Defining Hazardous Waste: Listed, Characteristic and Mixed Radiological Wastes*, EPA, https://www.epa.gov/hw/defining-hazardous-waste-listed-characteristic-and-mixed-radiological-wastes.

is justified as necessary to prevent generators of waste from diluting or mixing them with other substances to escape regulation.[45]

There are a number of exemptions and exclusions to these rules, with some materials that would otherwise qualify exempted from being considered solid wastes[46] and others still being considered solid wastes but excluded from regulation as hazardous wastes. Perhaps the most important in the latter category of exclusions is the exemption of *household hazardous wastes* from the regulations that would apply if the same material were being handled by industry,[47] but there are also several other important exclusions as listed in Table 7.1 below.

The process of deciding whether a material is a hazardous waste regulated by Subtitle C is summarized in Figure 7.1.

The generator of a waste has the legal obligation to determine whether it is a solid or hazardous waste.[48] Ignorance of the law or that a material is regulated is no excuse, even in a criminal case. This system has been criticized as unduly complex. And other critics note that the environment does not care whether the material released into it is a *waste* as opposed to some other type of material.

Regulation of hazardous wastes comes in two types: for *generators* of waste, and for *treatment storage and disposal facilities* (TSDFs). The regulatory provisions for both are very detailed and prescriptive and are summarized in an excellent article by EPA attorney Randolph Hill with a revealing title: An Overview of RCRA: The "Mind-Numbing" Provisions of the Most Complicated Environmental Statute.[49]

---

45 Jeffrey M. Gaba, *The Mixture and Derived-From Rules Under RCRA: Once a Hazardous Waste Always a Hazardous Waste?*, 21 ENVTL. L. REP., 10033 (1991), https://elr.info/news-analy sis/21/10033/mixture-and-derived-rules-under-rcra-once-hazardous-waste-always-hazardous-waste.

46 *Criteria for the Definition of Solid Waste and Solid and Hazardous Waste Exclusions*, EPA, https:// www.epa.gov/hw/criteria-definition-solid-waste-and-solid-and-hazardous-waste-exclusions; *see also* 40 C.F.R § 261.4(a), https://www.law.cornell.edu/cfr/text/40/part-261.

47 40 C.F.R § 261.4(b)(1), https://www.law.cornell.edu/cfr/text/40/part-261.

48 Hazardous waste determination and recordkeeping, 40 C.F.R § 262.11, https://www.law.cornell. edu/cfr/text/40/262.11.

49 Randolph L. Hill, *An Overview of RCRA: The "Mind-Numbing" Provisions of the Most Complicated Environmental Statute*, 21 ENVTL. L. REP. 10254 (1991), https://elr.info/sites/default/files/arti cles/21.10254.htm.

Table 7.1   Solid wastes which are not hazardous wastes

CFR Citation for the Exclusion	Category of Solid Waste
§ 261.4(b)(1)	Household Hazardous Waste
§ 261.4(b)(2)	Agricultural Waste
§ 261.4(b)(3)	Mining Overburden
§ 261.4(b)(4)	Fossil Fuel Combustion Waste (Bevill)
§ 261.4(b)(5)	Oil, Gas, and Geothermal Wastes (Bentsen Amendment)
§ 261.4(b)(6)	Trivalent Chromium Wastes
§ 261.4(b)(7)	Mining and Mineral Processing Wastes (Bevill)
§ 261.4(b)(8)	Cement Kiln Dust (Bevill)
§ 261.4(b)(9)	Arsenical-Treated Wood
§ 261.4(b)(10)	Petroleum Contaminated Media & Debris from Underground Storage Tanks
§ 261.4(b)(11)	Injected Groundwater
§ 261.4(b)(12)	Spent Chlorofluorocarbon Refrigerants
§ 261.4(b)(13)	Used Oil Filters
§ 261.4(b)(14)	Used Oil Distillation Bottoms
§ 261.4(b)(15)	Landfill Leachate or Gas Condensate Derived from Certain Listed Wastes

Source: *Criteria for the Definition of Solid Waste and Solid and Hazardous Waste Exclusions,* EPA, https://www.epa.gov/hw/criteria-definition-solid-waste-and-solid-and-hazardous-waste-exclusions.

Most RCRA regulation is delegated to states that submit their proposed programs to EPA for approval. If accepted, the delegated state or territory is granted authority to enforce RCRA within its borders. Currently, fifty states and territories have such authority, but some are approved to administer some but not all RCRA provisions.[50] As is typical of many U.S. environmental statutes, states may regulate more, but not less, strictly than the federal requirements.

The basic requirement applicable to all waste generators is to create a *manifest* that identifies the nature of the material and the entity which generated it. The manifest is supposed to accompany the waste when

---

50   *State Authorization under the Resource Conservation and Recovery Act (RCRA),* EPA, https://www.epa.gov/rcra/state-authorization-under-resource-conservation-and-recovery-act-rcra.

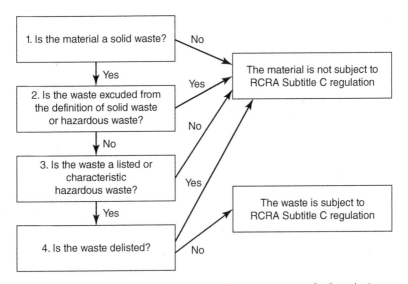

Source: *Learn the Basics of Hazardous Waste*, EPA, https://www.epa.gov/hw/learn-basics-hazardous-waste#hwid.

Figure 7.1   Hazardous waste identification process

it is sent to a TSDF for disposal. The purpose is to make it easier to identify responsible parties if a problem should later occur. Regulation of generators is very detailed and prescriptive and varies depending upon the volume of hazardous waste being created, and how long it is accumulated on site, as shown in Table 7.2.

TSDFs are also regulated in detail[51] and are usually only permitted to receive and dispose of or treat certain specified types of waste. EPA has promulgated regulations defining permissible disposal methods for particular wastes, which are called *best demonstrated available technologies* (BDATs). Most liquids may no longer be disposed of in landfills.[52] As a general matter, a characteristic waste may be *decharacterized* by treatment so that it no longer exhibits a hazardous waste characteristic. For example, an acid may be neutralized so that it is

51 *See* 40 C.F.R. §§ 264-266, summarized at *Hazardous Waste Management Facilities and Units*, EPA, https://www.epa.gov/hwpermitting/hazardous-waste-management-facilities-and-units.

52 Land Disposal Restrictions, 40 C.F.R. § 268, https://www.law.cornell.edu/cfr/text/40/part-268.

Table 7.2   Regulatory requirements for generators

Requirement	Very Small Quantity Generators	Small Quantity Generators	Large Quantity Generators
Quality Limits	*40 CFR § 260.10*	*40 CFR § 260.10*	*40 CFR § 260.10*
The amount of hazardous waste generated per month determines *how a generator is categorized* and what regulations must be complied with.	≤ 100 kg/month, and ≤ 1 kg/month of acute hazardous waste, and ≤ 100 kg/month of acute spill or soil residue	> 100 and < 1,000 kg/month	≥ 1,000 kg/month, or > 1 kg/month of acute hazardous waste, or > 100 kg/month of acute spill residue or soil
EPA ID Number		*40 CFR § 262.18*	*40 CFR § 262.18*
Acquire a unique EPA identification number that identifies generators by site.	Not Required	Required	Required

Source: *Hazardous Waste Generator Regulatory Summary*, EPA, https://www.epa.gov/hwgenerators/hazardous-waste-generator-regulatory-summary.[53]

no longer caustic. However, these decharacterized wastes may still contain *underlying hazardous constituents* (UHCs), that also must be treated.[54]

An interesting and potentially controversial feature of RCRA is that, historically, *corrective action* to clean up environmental contamination at RCRA-regulated generators and TSDFs was deferred until the facility closed. However, in recent years EPA has been moving to create priority lists for RCRA corrective action while facilities continue to operate.[55]

---

53   EPA's Hazardous Waste Generator Regulatory Summary summarizes the detailed provisions applicable to generators prescribed in 40 C.F.R. § 262.

54   *Treatment Standards for Hazardous Wastes Subject to Land Disposal Restrictions*, EPA, https://www.epa.gov/hw/treatment-standards-hazardous-wastes-subject-land-disposal-restrictions.

55   *Learn about Corrective Action*, EPA, https://www.epa.gov/hw/learn-about-corrective-action.

International regulation of transboundary shipment of hazardous waste: the Basel Convention and OECD

Transboundary shipments of hazardous waste are governed by the 1989 Basel Convention, which was signed by President George H.W. Bush and ratified by the U.S. Senate, but has not been implemented by legislation. Therefore, the United States is considered a *non-party* to the convention.[56] Originally designed to ensure *informed consent* by countries receiving hazardous waste from other countries, the Convention and its 120 pages of annexes have gradually morphed into an international regulatory regime.[57] Some provisions only allow signatories to accept waste from other signatories, which does not at present include the United States. However, the Organization for Economic Cooperation and Development (OECD), of which the United States is a member, has its own system regulating transboundary shipments among OECD countries.[58]

Additional resources

Garrett, Theodore L. (ed.) (2014). *The RCRA Practice Manual* (3d ed.). Chicago, Illinois: ABA Publishing.

Gray, Peter L. (ed.) (2016). The Superfund Manual: *A Practitioner's Guide to CERCLA Litigation*. Chicago, Illinois: ABA Publishing.

McMichael, Susan M. (2011). *RCRA Permitting Deskbook*. Washington, D.C.: Environmental Law Institute.

Rumsey, Allison and Daneker, Michael (2014). *Superfund Deskbook* (2d ed.). Washington, D.C.: Environmental Law Institute.

---

56 *Basel Convention on Hazardous Wastes*, U.S. DEPT. OF STATE, https://2001-2009.state.gov/g/oes/env/c18124.htm.

57 For a brief summary of the main provisions, see *Basel Convention*, WIKIPEDIA, https://en.wikipedia.org/wiki/Basel_Convention. For an official, but less useful, "overview" by the Convention Secretariat, see *Overview*, BASEL CONVENTION, http://www.basel.int/TheConvention/Overview/tabid/1271/Default.aspx. The full text of the *Basel Convention on the Control of Transboundary Movements of Hazardous Wastes and Their Disposal* is available at http://archive.basel.int/text/documents.html.

58 *The OECD Control System for waste recovery*, OECD, http://www.oecd.org/env/waste/theoecdcontrolsystemforwasterecovery.htm. *See also Frequent Questions on International Agreements on Transboundary Shipments of Waste*, EPA, https://www.epa.gov/hwgenerators/frequent-questions-international-agreements-transboundary-shipments-waste.

8 Regulation of chemicals: from toxic substance control to chemical safety

National environmental law in the United States has attempted to protect people from harmful exposures to chemicals for over a century. Initially, federal law only addressed chemicals with special purposes, such as drugs and pesticides.[1] The first general national regulation of potentially toxic substances dates back nearly fifty years to the enactment of the Toxic Substances Control Act in 1976 (TSCA).[2]

Many experts view the 1976 version of TSCA as the *least* successful of all U.S. environmental statutes. It proved to have a number of flaws including the assumption built into the original legislation that substances that occur in nature are safer because our bodies have learned to adapt to them while the newer generation of synthetic chemicals are more likely to be toxic.[3] As plausible as this sounds, toxicologists who study the harmful properties of substances have known for a long time that almost every substance can be harmful under the wrong exposure conditions—or as they sometimes put it, "the phrase 'toxic chemical' is redundant."[4] Nonetheless, as originally drafted in 1976, TSCA focused

---

1 The federal Pure Food and Drugs Act, the predecessor of today's Food Drug and Cosmetic Act, dates back to 1906. *See* U.S. Food and Drug Administration, *80 Years of the Federal Food, Drug, and Cosmetic Act* (last updated July 11, 2018), https://www.fda.gov/about-fda/virtual-exhibits-fda-history/80-years-federal-food-drug-and-cosmetic-act. The Insecticide Act, the predecessor of today's regulation of pesticides under the Federal Insecticide, Fungicide, and Rodenticide Act (FIFRA), dates back to 1910. 36 Stat. 331; 61 Stat. 163.

2 Toxic Substances Control Act of 1976, 15 U.S.C. §§ 2601–2629.

3 This is sometimes called the *familiarity principle*. It was a theme in a best-selling book, RACHEL CARSON, SILENT SPRING (1962), which opposed the widespread misuse of synthetic pesticides such as DDT. Many credit that book with inspiring the modern environmental movement. *See* Eliza Griswold, *How 'Silent Spring' Ignited the Environmental Movement*, N.Y. TIMES MAG. (Sept. 21, 2012), https://www.nytimes.com/2012/09/23/magazine/how-silent-spring-ignited-the-environmental-movement.html.

4 For a good summary of the factors that influence toxicity, see *Tox Tutor*, U.S. National Library of Medicine, https://toxtutor.nlm.nih.gov/03-002.html (noting that "[v]irtually all chemicals can be acute toxicants if sufficiently large doses are administered.").

on regulating *new* chemicals that were not already in general use,[5] and its provisions for regulating existing chemicals were cumbersome and proved ineffective in the few instances that EPA tried to use them. Much of the problem was attributable to the fact that 1976 TSCA put the *burden of proof* on the government to prove that an *existing chemical*, one that was already in use, was hazardous.[6]

Congress amended TSCA in 2016 with the Frank R. Lautenberg Chemical Safety for the 21st Century Act[7] in an attempt to improve regulation of existing chemicals. It remains to be seen how effective these changes will be, but the initial signs are encouraging. The title of the amendments captures a fundamental change in how policymakers think about protecting the public from *control of toxic chemicals* to ensuring *chemical safety*. It is also notable that the 2016 TSCA amendments, which stand out as the most significant change to any U.S. environmental statute in the past several decades, were adopted by broad bipartisan majorities with support from both environmental groups and the chemical industry, despite deep political polarization on many other issues.[8]

New chemical regulation under TSCA

The 1976 TSCA adopted a *licensing* approach to chemical regulation. The 1976 statute was modeled on the framework of older statutes such as the 1938 Food, Drug, and Cosmetics Act (FDCA) and the 1947 Federal Insecticide, Fungicide, and Rodenticide Act (FIFRA). In short,

---

5 Leonardo Trasande, *Updating the Toxic Substances Control Act to Protect Human Health*, 315 JAMA 1565 (2016). As noted previously regarding *grandfathering* of existing plants under the CAA, it is often easier politically to regulate pollution sources that do not already exist because they are less powerful politically. *See* discussion on Fixing Unintended Consequences Part II – Non-Attainment in Chapter 3).

6 *See* Sarah A. Vogel and Jody A. Roberts, *Why the Toxic Substances Control Act Needs an Overhaul, and How to Strengthen Oversight of Chemicals in the Interim*, 30 HEALTH AFFS. 898 (2011); Richard A. Denison, *Ten Essential Elements in TSCA Reform*, 39 ENV'T L. REP. 10020 (2009) (criticizing § 6 of 1976 TSCA the burden of proof imposed on the government under the 1976 statute to show that a chemical poses an *unreasonable risk* before it may regulate).

7 Frank R. Lautenberg Chemical Safety for the 21st Century Act, Pub. L. No. 114–18, 130 Stat. 448 *et seq.* (June 22, 2016).

8 *See* E. Donald Elliott, *Politics Failed, Not Ideas*, 28 ENV'T FORUM 42 (Sept./Oct. 2011) (criticizing environmentalists for an almost exclusive focus on the divisive issue of climate change and suggesting it would be possible to make progress on a bipartisan basis on other issues such as TSCA reform, which happened five years later).

an entity seeking to distribute a *new chemical*, one not already in use in commerce, was required to seek prior approval from the government to do so.

The first step in the process was to compile an *inventory*[9] of the *chemical substances*[10] that were already in commerce. As of 2021, 86 229 chemicals are listed in the inventory of which 40 655 are actively distributed in commerce. Of this total, approximately 1600 are classified as *hazardous* and roughly 20 percent, or about 8300, are confidential in the sense that the formula will not be disclosed to the public.[11]

Under the 1976 TSCA, chemicals on the inventory were presumed to be safe, although EPA had some limited authority to regulate them if it could convince a court that they presented an *unreasonable risk*.[12] EPA was also given authority to regulate *significant new uses* of existing chemicals but there too the burden of proof was on the agency to show that the significant new use rule (SNUR) was necessary to prevent an "unreasonable risk of injury to health or the environment."[13]

For new chemicals not listed in the inventory, an entity was required to submit a *premanufacture notification* (PMN) to EPA for permission to distribute the substance in commerce in the United States.[14] Unlike the REACH program in the European Union, 1976 TSCA did not require PMNs to be accompanied by any prescribed testing results. However, the applicant was required to supply, along with the PMN, any existing data they possessed regarding effects of the chemical on human

---

9 TSCA § 8(a), 15 U.S.C. § 2607; EPA, TSCA Chemical Substance Inventory, https://www.epa.gov/tsca-inventory.

10 The term "chemical substance" is defined as "a particular molecular identity" but excludes mixtures, pesticides, tobacco, nuclear material and foods, drugs and cosmetics. TSCA § 2, 15 U.S.C. § 2602(2). Some but not all of those substances are regulated under other statutes.

11 *Chemical Safety and Pollution Prevention, EPA Releases First Major Update to Chemicals List in 40 Years*, EPA, (Feb. 19, 2019), https://www.epa.gov/newsreleases/epa-releases-first-major-update-chemicals-list-40-years.

12 TSCA § 6, 15 U.S.C. § 2606.

13 TSCA § 6, 15 U.S.C, § 2605; Section 5(f) Actions: Protection Against Unreasonable Risk, EPA, https://www.epa.gov/reviewing-new-chemicals-under-toxic-substances-control-act-tsca/actions-under-tsca-section-5#5(f). The 2016 amendments specify that these unreasonable risk determinations must now be made "without consideration of cost or other non-risk factors, including . . . unreasonable risk[s] to a potentially exposed subpopulation." *Id.*

14 TSCA § 5, 15 U.S.C. § 2605.

health or the environment.[15] As a result, 67 percent of applications for approval of new chemicals included no test data and 85 percent included no health data, according to a 2003 study.[16] After a PMN filing, EPA had 90 days (which could be extended once for another 90 days) to decide whether the chemical presents an unreasonable risk to human health or the environment. If the Agency failed to act, the chemical would be approved automatically.

Despite these limitations, the new-chemicals program under 1976 TSCA worked reasonably well even prior to the 2016 amendments. As of 2003, while about 90 percent of applications to distribute new chemicals in commerce were approved, 4 percent of PMNs were withdrawn and 5 percent resulted in regulatory restrictions.[17] In the absence of test data submitted by manufacturers, EPA developed a computer modeling system to predict the possible toxic properties of chemicals using *qualitative structure activity relationships* (QSARs),[18] which EPA insists is as good as or better than animal testing.[19] If EPA's computer models suggest that a new chemical may be hazardous because its molecular structure is similar to other chemicals that have proven hazardous in the past, EPA will either use its authority under Section 4 of TSCA to require additional testing[20] or negotiate regulatory restrictions in a consent decree as conditions for regulatory approval.[21]

As a result, very few chemicals are in wide distribution in the United States but not in Europe, despite claims that the European system for regulating chemicals is more *precautionary*.[22] But note that what may be keeping dangerous chemicals off the U.S. market is the vigorous

---

15 40 C.F.R. § 720.50. *See generally* Reviewing New Chemicals under the Toxic Substances Control Act (TSCA), EPA, https://www.epa.gov/reviewing-new-chemicals-under-toxic-substances-control-act-tsca.

16 Battelle, *Overview: Office of Pollution Prevention And Toxics Programs*, EPA, (Dec. 24, 2003), http://chemicalspolicy.org/downloads/TSCA10112-24-03.pdf.

17 *Id.*

18 Toxicity Estimation Software Tool (TEST), EPA, https://www.epa.gov/chemical-research/toxicity-estimation-software-tool-test.

19 U.S. Gen. Accountability Office, GAO-05-458, *Chemical Regulation: Options Exist to Improve EPA's Ability to Assess Health Risks and Manage Its Chemical Review Program* (2005).

20 TSCA § 4, 15 U.S.C. § 2605 and implementing regulations at 40 C.F.R. §§ 790–799.

21 Ortwin Renn and E. Donald Elliott, *Precautionary Regulation of Chemicals in the US and EU*, in THE REALITY OF PRECAUTION: COMPARING RISK REGULATION IN THE UNITED STATES AND EUROPE 223–56 (Jonathan B. Wiener, Michael D. Rogers, James K. Hammitt and Peter H. Sand eds., 2011).

22 *Id.*

system of common law tort liability for injuries due to chemical exposures rather than preventive regulation under TSCA.[23] This framework is typical of the U.S. approach to regulation: multiple, redundant systems of national and state regulation overlaid with common law tort liability.

The 2016 amendments changed the process for reviewing new chemicals by making it easier for EPA to require testing if it had reasonable doubts about the safety of a new chemical proposed to be distributed in commerce.[24] TSCA as amended in 2016 now requires that EPA make an affirmative finding that a chemical proposed to be distributed or imported is safe under the conditions of intended use (including foreseeable misuse).[25] But because EPA's decision to require more testing and keep a chemical off the market or limit its use can be challenged in court, as a practical matter even the 2016 version of TSCA still puts a burden of proof—albeit a lesser one—on the government to show a reasonable basis for its conclusion that a chemical may be hazardous and to require additional testing or impose other restrictions.

Existing chemical regulation under TSCA

The law that eventually became TSCA was drafted by the Council on Environmental Quality in the early 1970s, at the same time as the bills that became the Clean Air and Clean Water Acts. Due to opposition from the chemical industry, a Congressional committee held up the bill to create a national system of chemical regulation until an incident focused public attention on chemical hazards. A small pesticide manufacturer released a pesticide called Kepone into the James River in Virginia, where it injured numerous people—including causing uncontrollable nervous shakes—and led to fishing bans that lasted for 45 years.[26] Although, as a pesticide, Kepone would have been exempt

---

23 *Id.*

24 *See An Abbreviated Guide to the Frank R. Lautenberg Chemical Safety for the 21st Century Act*, SAFER CHEMICALS, HEALTHIER FAMILIES, https://saferchemicals.org/public-policy/an-abbreviated-guide.

25 Highlights of Key Provisions in the Frank R. Lautenberg Chemical Safety for the 21st Centure Act, EPA, https://www.epa.gov/assessing-and-managing-chemicals-under-tsca/highlights-key-provisions-frank-r-lautenberg-chemical#changes.

26 Tamara Dietrich, *VIMS: Kepone Could Soon be History in the James River*, DAILY PRESS (July 8, 2017, 8:35 PM), https://www.dailypress.com/news/dp-nws-kepone-update-vims-20170624-story.html.

from regulation under TSCA, the attendant publicity focused public attention squarely on the risks of chemicals and changed the political dynamic such that it was no longer possible to block federal regulation of chemicals. This high-profile environmental disaster played a role in the push for Congressional action on toxic substances similar to that of the Cuyahoga River fire, which helped to spur enactment of the 1972 Clean Water Act.[27]

As a result, the chemical industry changed its strategy from preventing federal legislation to supporting amendments that required EPA to conduct so-called *hybrid rulemaking*, which include oral hearings with cross-examination, as opposed to the *paper hearing* that is the usual approach for notice and comment rulemaking under the Administrative Procedure Act,[28] and to select the *least burdensome alternative* before regulating an existing chemical. These provisions made it difficult for EPA to use its TSCA authority to regulate existing chemicals as opposed to regulating them under other statutes with less burdensome administrative provisions.

This challenging legal framework had a profound effect. In fact, EPA regulated almost no existing chemicals under TSCA until 1989, when the Agency attempted to use TSCA on a precautionary basis to ban five uses of asbestos. EPA took this action because asbestos had proven deadly in uses such as insulation where it could be inhaled and had resulted in tens of thousands of deaths and lawsuits.[29] EPA's regulatory action was set aside by the Fifth Circuit Court of Appeals in the (in)famous *Corrosion Proof Fittings* case on the grounds that EPA had failed to show that its ban was the least burdensome approach possible.[30] Though EPA sought to appeal the Fifth Circuit's ruling to the Supreme Court, the Department of Justice turned down the request because there was no conflict among the circuit courts of appeal on the issue, which is the main ground for review by the Supreme Court. The *Corrosion Proof Fittings* decision convinced EPA that it would be very difficult to use its authority under the 1976 version of TSCA to regulate existing chemicals. Instead, EPA negotiated a voluntary agreement to gradually phase out many, but not all, uses of asbestos by industry and

27 *See* Chapter 5.
28 *See* Administrative Procedure Act, 5 U.S.C. § 553.
29 54 Fed. Reg. 29,460 (1989) (TSCA § 6 rule banning five uses of asbestos).
30 Corrosion Proof Fittings v. EPA, 947 F.2d 1201 (5th Cir. 1991).

turned to using its authority under other statutes to regulate existing uses of chemicals.

The widespread perception that EPA regulation of existing chemicals was ineffective encouraged states to promulgate their own regulations of chemicals, which confronted the chemical industry with the prospect of a hodgepodge of differing state regulations.[31] In addition, public perception that citizens could not rely on EPA regulation to protect them led to a proliferation of sites on the internet warning the public about the dangers of various chemicals.[32] The rise of these private *alarm systems* confronted the chemical industry with a situation not unlike the one that the automobile industry faced in 1965. At that time, the automobile industry switched from opposing to supporting federal regulation on the condition that federal law would pre-empt a rising tide of state regulation.[33] As a result, unlike in the 1970s, when the chemical industry opposed federal regulation, the American Chemistry Council—the chemical industry's main trade association—supported the 2016 TSCA reforms, noting "[m]ore effective federal oversight of chemicals will give Americans greater confidence that chemicals in commerce are being used safely and reduce the number of inconsistent state-based chemical initiatives that impede interstate commerce and send mixed messages to consumers."[34] Likewise, the environmental community played an active role in the TSCA reform process. Indeed, Richard Denison of the Environmental Defense Fund, who took the lead for environmentalists, wrote and helped to negotiate many of the key provisions of the 2016 amendments.[35]

Perhaps the most controversial issue in the 2016 TSCA reform was whether to pre-empt state authority to regulate chemicals such as

---

31 For a discussion of the most prominent of these state laws regulating chemicals, California's Proposition 65, see Chapter 14. As we discuss there, unlike 1976 TSCA, Proposition 65 created incentives for the distributors of chemicals whose safety had been questioned to prove that they were safe. *See generally* David Roe, *Barking Up the Right Tree: Recent Progress in Focusing the Toxics Issue*, 13 COLUM. J. ENV'T L. 275 (1988).

32 *See, e.g.*, RACHEL'S NETWORK, https://rachelsnetwork.org/?s=chemicals; ENVIRONMENTAL WORKING GROUP, https://www.ewg.org/key-issues/toxics.

33 See E. Donald Elliott, Bruce A. Ackerman and John C. Millian, *Toward a Theory of Statutory Evolution: The Federalization of Environmental Law*, 1 J.L. ECON & ORG. 313 (1985).

34 *Toxic Substances Control Act (TSCA)*, AMERICAN CHEMISTRY COUNCIL, https://www.ameri canchemistry.com/TSCA.

35 Richard Denison, EDF, https://www.edf.org/people/richard-denison (noting that "Richard played a central role in pressing for reform of the Toxic Substances Control Act and represented EDF in its advocacy work to secure passage in 2016 of the Lautenberg Act that overhauled TSCA").

California's Proposition 65. The final bill enacted an elaborate compromise by providing that pre-existing state regulation of chemicals could continue in force, but new state regulation would be pre-empted if EPA has either examined a chemical and decided it is safe or has regulated the chemical.[36] However, if EPA has done neither, states may continue to enact new regulations or act pursuant to a law already in effect in 2003. (That date was picked to leave California's Proposition 65, which is discussed in Chapter 14, unaffected.) In addition, states may also request waivers and continue to enforce laws that are identical to federal requirements.[37]

Other key changes the 2016 Lautenberg Act enacted include:[38]

- A risk-based system for prioritizing reviews of existing chemicals;
- Deadlines for EPA to begin 20 high-priority chemical risk evaluations;
- New standards for determining *unreasonable risk* that excludes consideration of costs or non-risk factors and requires consideration of risks to susceptible and highly exposed populations—but allowing EPA to consider costs and the availability of alternatives when determining appropriate action to address risks;
- A provision that overrules the *Corrosion Proof Fittings* case by repealing requirement that regulation must be *least burdensome* alternative;
- A mechanism by which manufacturers may request that EPA evaluate the safety of specific chemicals, but must pay for the associated costs if they were not already on EPA's priority list;
- Requirements for obtaining treatment of chemicals as *confidential business information* that is protected against public disclosure; and
- Authorization for EPA to collect up to $25 million annually in user fees.

---

36 TSCA § 18, 15 U.S.C. § 2617; Highlights of Key Provisions in the Frank R. Lautenberg Chemical Safety for the 21st Century Act, EPA, https://www.epa.gov/assessing-and-managing-chemicals-under-tsca/highlights-key-provisions-frank-r-lautenberg-chemical#changes.

37 *Id.*

38 Highlights of Key Provisions in the Frank R. Lautenberg Chemical Safety for the 21st Century Act, EPA, https://www.epa.gov/assessing-and-managing-chemicals-under-tsca/highlights-key-provisions-frank-r-lautenberg-chemical#changes; *see also An Abbreviated Guide to the Frank R. Lautenberg Chemical Safety for the 21st Century Act*, SAFER CHEMICALS, HEALTHIER FAMILIES, https://saferchemicals.org/public-policy/an-abbreviated-guide/.

It is too early to say for sure how effective these amendments will be. EPA is only now completing its first few risk evaluations of existing chemicals under the new structure. Initial signs, however, suggest the 2016 reforms may address many of the TSCA's past shortcomings effectively.

The road not taken: REACH and harmonization

While the 2016 reforms to TSCA aimed at improving implementation, particularly with regard to existing chemicals, TSCA's basic structure based on risk assessment and regulating risks from chemicals deemed by government to be unreasonable was left unchanged. Meanwhile, between 1976 and 2016, the European Union developed a different, *precautionary principle*[39]-based approach entitled Registration, Evaluation, Authorization, and Restriction of Chemicals (REACH). REACH places the burden on manufacturers to conduct testing to show that chemicals are safe and to develop less harmful substitutes for hazardous chemicals they obtain authorization to continue to use.[40] Some had hoped the United States would mirror REACH by adopting some of these principles,[41] but that was not the approach enacted in the 2016 TSCA reforms.

For many years, proponents of international trade have advocated for harmonization of regulatory approaches for chemicals, particularly between major trading partners such as the United States and the European Union.[42] The science of human exposure and epidemiological effects doesn't vary across nations, so there are economies of scale in assessing the science once, rather than separately by every country. Moreover, inconsistent regulatory standards of chemicals among trade partners can constitute non-tariff barriers to international trade and

---

39 *See* Jonathan B. Wiener et al., The Reality of Precaution: Comparing Risk Regulation in the United States and Europe (2011).

40 *See generally* European Commission, REACH in Brief (2007), https://ec.europa.eu/environment/chemicals/reach/pdf/publications/2007_02_reach_in_brief.pdf.

41 Adam D.K. Abelkop, Ágnes Botos, Lois R. Wise & John D. Graham, *Regulating Industrial Chemicals: Lessons For U.S. Lawmakers from the European Union's REACH Program*, 42 Env't L. Rep. 1042 (2012).

42 Daniel C. Esty, *Regulatory Competition in Focus*, 3 J. Int'l. Econ. L. 215 (2000). Other authorities are collected in Congressional Research Service, Transatlantic Regulatory Cooperation: Background and Analysis (2008), https://www.everycrsreport.com/files/20081022_RL34717_3bb20bbcf90f2c12fbd2b7742aa5032cd224d928.pdf.

increase costs to consumers. On the other hand, others have argued that "regulatory competition" among different jurisdictions can be a good thing.[43]

In his 2013 State of the Union address, then-President Barack Obama proposed a free trade agreement between the United States and the European Union. Negotiations for a proposed Transatlantic Trade and Investment Partnership (TTIP) began almost immediately. Both the United States and the European Union identified the chemical industry as a particularly promising sector for coordination, and some scholars and think tanks thought TTIP held promise to bring about greater regulatory cooperation and harmonization in regulating chemicals.[44] However, the in-coming Trump Administration cancelled the TTIP negotiations in 2016 to focus on re-negotiating the North American Free Trade Agreement (NAFTA) with Canada and Mexico. TTIP negotiations resumed in 2018, but the European Union called them off in 2019, stating that the TTIP negotiations were "obsolete and no longer relevant."[45] Meanwhile, EPA and the European Chemicals Agency (ECHA) continue to share information and coordinate at the staff level.

A number of other countries, including China, South Korea, Russia, Thailand, Cambodia, and Turkey all regulate chemicals with national systems loosely modeled on the European Union's REACH program. Other countries such as Brazil are also considering developing their own national systems. As a practical matter, recommendations from international organizations such as the Organization for Economic Cooperation and Development (OECD)[46] and the International Programme on Chemical Safety (IPCS) of the World Health Organization (WHO)[47] are influential, albeit not binding, on national

43 Roberta Romano, *Is Regulatory Competition a Problem or Irrelevant for Corporate Governance?*, 21 Oxford Rev. Econ. Pol'y 212 (2005).

44 E. Donald Elliott and Jacques Pelkmans, *Greater TTIP Ambition in Chemicals: Why and How*, in Rule-Makers or Rule-Takers? Exploring the Transatlantic Trade and Investment Partnership (Daniel S. Hamilton and Jacques Pelkmans eds., 2015).

45 European Commission, The Transatlantic Trade and Investment Partnership (TTIP), https://ec.europa.eu/trade/policy/in-focus/ttip/.

46 *Chemical Safety*, OECD, https://www.oecd.org/gov/regulatory-policy/chemicalsafety.htm#:~:te xt=OECD%20governments%20have%20significant%20and,environmental%20risks%20posed%20 by%20chemicals.&text=This%20is%20done%20by%20testing,results%2C%20and%20taking%20 appropriate%20action.

47 *Chemical Safety*, WTO, https://www.who.int/health-topics/chemical-safety#tab=tab_1.

regulatory programs. But the vision of reformers for a single regulatory system for chemicals worldwide is still just that—a vision.

Additional resources

Applegate, John S. (2008). Synthesizing TSCA and REACH: Practical Principles for Chemical Regulation Reform, *Ecology Reform*, 35, 721–768. https://www.repository.law.indiana.edu/cgi/viewcontent.cgi?article=1441&context=facpub.

Hathaway, Carolyne R., Hatcher, Julia A., and Rawson, William K. (2012). *TSCA Deskbook* (2d ed.), Washington; Environmental Law Institute.

Lerner, Steve and Brown, Phil (2010). *Sacrifice Zones: The Front Lines of Toxic Chemical Exposure in the United States.* MIT Press.

Markell, David (2010). New Directions of Environmental Law: An Overview of TSCA, its History and Key Underlying Assumptions, and its Place in Environmental Regulation, *Washington University Journal of Law and Policy*, 32, 333–375. https://openscholarship.wustl.edu/cgi/viewcontent.cgi?article=1084&context=law_journal_law_policy.

Safer Chemicals, Healthy Families. *An Abbreviated Guide to the Frank R. Lautenberg Chemical Safety for the 21st Century Act.* https://saferchemicals.org/public-policy/an-abbreviated-guide/.

9 FIFRA: from misbranding to reasonable certainty of no harm

The predecessors of today's *Federal Insecticide, Fungicide, and Rodenticide Act* (FIFRA)[1] date back to 1910, when then-President William Howard Taft signed into law the Federal Insecticide Act.[2] The primary purpose of the 1910 law was to protect farmers against false claims about misbranded pesticides that were ineffective against the pests they claimed to kill, not to protect the environment. Major amendments in 1947, 1972, and 1996 refocused the statute.[3] The 1972 amendments are particularly important for our purposes as they transferred responsibility for regulating pesticides from the Department of Agriculture to the (then) recently created EPA and expanded the grounds for regulation to include protecting public health and the environment.

From 1972 until 1996, FIFRA—like the original 1976 TSCA, discussed in Chapter 8—was a classic example of a statute that balanced risks and benefits and only regulated *unreasonable risks*. Thus, when the authors served at EPA in the late 1980s and early 1990s, EPA would sometimes register a pesticide even though the scientific evidence suggested that some people could get cancer from exposure to the pesticide residues on food. The theory under the balancing framework of FIFRA at that time was that the benefits to agriculture and lower prices for food to consumers outweighed the costs in terms of public health.[4]

---

1 Federal Insecticide, Fungicide, and Rodenticide Act §§ 1–35, 7 U.S.C. §§ 136 *et seq*, https://www. law.cornell.edu/uscode/text/7/chapter-6/subchapter-II.

2 Federal Insecticide Act of 1910, Pub.L.61-152, 36 Stat. 331 (1910), https://govtrackus.s3.amazonaws. com/legislink/pdf/stat/36/STATUTE-36-Pg331.pdf.

3 'For a good account of the history, see LYNN L. BERGESON, FIFRA: FEDERAL INSECTICIDE, FUNGICIDE, AND RODENTICIDE ACT (2020).

4 *See generally* Pesticide Safety Education Program, *Risk/Benefit Balancing Under FIFRA*, CORNELL UNIVERSITY COOPERATIVE EXTENSION, http://psep.cce.cornell.edu/issues/risk-benefit-fifra.aspx.

This approach was changed—much to the better, in our opinion—by the 1996 Food Quality Protection Act (FQPA),[5] which put the burden of proof on the company seeking approval of an agricultural pesticide to show that the residues left on food would result in "reasonable certainty . . . [of] no harm" from the proper use of the pesticide in accordance with its instructions. This requirement, however, only applies to pesticide residues on food crops and not to other uses of pesticides such as by homeowners.

In assessing "reasonable certainty . . . [of] no harm," FQPA specifically requires consideration of the effects on particularly sensitive populations such as infants and the elderly.[6] This attention to possible effects on particularly sensitive populations was attributable to a famous 1993 report by the National Academy of Sciences, *Pesticides in the Diets of Infants & Children*.[7] The FQPA mandated an extra tenfold *safety factor* (sometimes also called an *uncertainty factor*[8]) must be used, absent empirical data proving that the material was safe for sensitive populations. The present authors endorse the aspects of the 1996 amendments that brought greater focus on differential impacts on sensitive subpopulations, which is an important environmental justice issue.[9]

---

5 Food Quality Protection Act of 1996, Pub.L.104-170, 110 Stat. 1489, https://www.govinfo.gov/content/pkg/PLAW-104publ170/pdf/PLAW-104publ170.pdf. For a good summary of the multiple mid-course corrections mandated by the FQPA, see *Accomplishments under the Food Quality Protection Act (FQPA)*, EPA (Aug. 3, 2006), https://archive.epa.gov/pesticides/regulating/laws/fqpa/web/html/fqpa_accomplishments.html.

6 FQPA § 408(b)(2)(A)(ii), 21 U.S.C. § 346a(b)(2)(A)(ii), https://www.law.cornell.edu/uscode/text/21/346a:

> As used in this section, the term 'safe', with respect to a tolerance for a pesticide chemical residue, means that the Administrator has determined that there is a reasonable certainty that no harm will result from aggregate exposure to the pesticide chemical residue, including all anticipated dietary exposures and all other exposures for which there is reliable information.

7 National Research Council, *Pesticides in the Diets of Infants and Children*, THE NATIONAL ACADEMIES OF SCIENCES, ENGINEERING, MEDICINE (1993), https://doi.org/10.17226/2126.

8 For an explanation of uncertainty factors and how they work, see *Uncertainty Factor*, GREENFACTS, http://bit.ly/3r25mMs.

9 Critics argue FQPA still fails to address a number of other issues of environmental justice adequately including farmworker exposure, residential fumigant exposure in low-income areas, and cumulative pesticide exposure patterns that may affect some ethnic groups differentially. *See, e.g.,* Valerie Watnick, *Risk Assessment: Obfuscation of Policy Decisions in Pesticide Regulation and the EPA's Dismantling of the Food Quality Protection Act's Safeguards for Children*, 31 ARIZ. ST. L.J. 1345 (1999); *see generally* JOHN WARGO, OUR CHILDREN'S TOXIC LEGACY: HOW SCIENCE AND LAW FAIL TO PROTECT US FROM PESTICIDES (1997).

In addition, we have suggested elsewhere that the evolution of FIFRA toward a goal of reasonable certainty of no harm on food crops— instead of balancing harms to some people against benefits to others— should be adopted as a fundamental equity principle and guide the future of environmental law more generally.[10] However, at the end of this chapter, we suggest that it is time for Congress to mandate a thorough review by outside experts of how well the many reforms put in place in response to the FQPA, as well as recent improvements in the science of assessing chemical safety, are working, and how they might be improved.

Pesticidal claims trigger FIFRA regulation

Unlike other statutes, such as TSCA, that regulate particular chemical identities, FIFRA regulates *pesticidal claims*, which is perhaps a vestige of its genesis in the 1910 Insecticide Act against misbranding and false claims. FIFRA defines a *pesticide* in relevant part as "any substance or mixture of substances intended for preventing, destroying, repelling, or mitigating any pest."[11] EPA interprets these terms broadly, so for example, a plant that has been genetically engineered to release a substance that repels or kills pests, which is referred to as a *plant incorporated protectant*, is regulated by EPA as a pesticide.[12] Similarly, a cleaning product can become a *pesticide* and require EPA registration if the company distributing it makes claims, either on the product itself or in its advertising, that the product cleans away dust mite allergens[13] on the theory that such claims amount to "mitigating [a] pest." Microbes and germs are also considered *pests*, so a substantial part of EPA's regulation of pesticides concerns the use of *anti-microbials* (disinfectants) on hard surfaces,[14] as well as the chemical pesticides used in agriculture.

10 Daniel C. Esty and E. Donald Elliott, *The End Environmental Externalities Manifesto: A Rights-Based Foundation for Environmental Law*, NYU ENVTL. L.J. (forthcoming 2021), https://ssrn.com/abstract=3762022.

11 FIFRA § 2(u), 7 U.S.C. § 136(u), https://www.law.cornell.edu/uscode/text/7/136.

12 *Introduction to Biotechnology Regulation for Pesticides*, EPA, https://www.epa.gov/regulation-biotechnology-under-tsca-and-fifra/introduction-biotechnology-regulation-pesticides. Genetically engineering plants to be resistant to particular pests may reduce the need to use broad spectrum chemical pesticides that may be hazardous to a variety of other organisms as well as the pests that are being targeted.

13 *Determining If a Cleaning Product Is a Pesticide Under FIFRA*, EPA, https://www.epa.gov/pesticide-registration/determining-if-cleaning-product-pesticide-under-fifra.

14 *Antimicrobial Pesticide Registration*, EPA, https://www.epa.gov/pesticides/antimicrobial-pesticides.

But note that if a product claims to prevent or cure disease by kill-ing germs, it can become a *drug* or *medical device* regulated by the Food and Drug Administration (FDA) rather than EPA—or more likely, require registration with both EPA and FDA for different uses.[15] These jurisdictional distinctions are complex and can become a trap for the unwary. For example, FDA approval of an active ingredient in hand sanitizers will not protect a company against a penalty for sell-ing an unregistered pesticide if the product is promoted to kill germs on restaurant tabletops rather than on hands, even though the claim is entirely truthful. Similarly, a collar for dogs or cats that claims to repel fleas must be registered as a pesticide with EPA,[16] and even a bug zapper that uses electricity to kill mosquitos is regulated, albeit less stringently, as a *pesticidal device*.[17]

On the other hand, EPA's regulations implementing FIFRA have long provided that if an article is treated with a properly registered pesticide solely to protect the article itself, then the article does not have to be registered separately as a pesticide. This *treated article exception*[18] has resulted in lots of litigation, as EPA frequently takes the position that the articles treated with anti-microbial pesticides are making "implied or explicit public health claims against human pathogens" and thus are outside the scope of the exception.[19] For example, EPA will not allow

---

15   *See generally What's the difference between products that disinfect, sanitize, and clean surfaces?*, EPA, https://www.epa.gov/coronavirus/whats-difference-between-products-disinfect-sanitize-an d-clean-surfaces ("At EPA, products used to kill viruses and bacteria on surfaces are registered as antimicrobial pesticides. Sanitizers and disinfectants are two types of antimicrobial pesticides. The Food and Drug Administration (FDA) regulates hand sanitizers, antiseptic washes, and anti-bacterial soaps for use on people.").

16   *See Companies Agree to Stop Selling Pet Collars Containing Pesticide to Protect Children*, EPA, https://www.epa.gov/safepestcontrol/companies-agree-to-stop-selling-pet-collars-containing-pesticide-protect-children#2.

17   *Examples of Regulated Pesticide Devices*, EPA, https://www.epa.gov/safepestcontrol/pesticide-devices-guide-consumers#6. Mercifully, EPA has decided that "any device that depends more upon the performance of the user than the performance of the device itself to be effective (such as a fly swatter) is not regulated. Also, traps for vertebrate animals are not regulated." *The Differences between Pesticide Devices and Pesticide Products and How They Are Regulated*, EPA, https://www.epa.gov/safepestcontrol/pesticide-devices-guide-consumers#1.

18   40 C.F.R 152.25(a) (2020), https://www.law.cornell.edu/cfr/text/40/152.25 ("Treated articles or substances. An article or substance treated with, or containing, a pesticide to protect the article or substance itself (for example, paint treated with a pesticide to protect the paint coating, or wood products treated to protect the wood against insect or fungus infestation), if the pesticide is registered for such use.").

19   *See Pesticide Registration (PR) Notice 2000 – 1*, EPA (Mar. 6, 2000), https://www.epa.gov/sites/production/files/2014-04/documents/pr2000-1.pdf.

a plastic cutting board treated with an anti-microbial pesticide to state or imply that it will reduce the potential for bacteria to grow on the cutting board and thereby reduce the risk of disease. Even if that claim is true scientifically, EPA insists that the product must "carry an appropriately qualifying statement, such as: This product does not protect users or others against food-borne bacteria."[20] EPA wants the article to go through the registration process as a pesticide so that the agency can verify the claims to kill bacteria and prevent the spread of disease. In other words, in the world of pesticides, it is not enough that claims made *are* true; EPA must have verified them as true and approved them as part of the label.

How EPA regulates pesticides

To obtain regulatory approval for a product as an EPA-approved pesticide, a company must first obtain registration as an *establishment* that produces pesticides, and each pesticide must be labeled with the number of the establishment that made it.[21] The applicant must also submit a draft label, which includes claims, cautions, and instructions for use. EPA maintains an elaborate 282-page pesticide registration *label review manual*[22] which summarizes what must, may, and may not be included on a pesticide label. For example, the front panel must contain the following:

1. Whether use is restricted to trained applicators only. 40 C.F.R 156.10(j)(2). (If only specially trained applicators may apply the pesticide, it is called a "restricted use pesticide.")
2. Product name, brand or trademark. 40 C.F.R 156.10(b)(1).
3. Name and percentage by weight of each active ingredient and the total percentage by weight of all other/inert ingredients. 40 C.F.R 156.10(g)(2).

---

20 *Consumer Products Treated with Pesticides*, EPA, https://www.epa.gov/safepestcontrol/con sumer-products-treated-pesticides; *see also* In re Microban Prods. Co., 9 E.A.D. 674 (EAB 2001), https://yosemite.epa.gov/OA/EAB_WEB_Docket.nsf/Case~Name/B6DE118815 1CFC0B8525706 9005F7CF4/$File/microban.pdf.

21 FIFRA § 7, 7 U.S.C. § 136e, https://www.govinfo.gov/content/pkg/USCODE-2011-title7/html/ USCODE-2011-title7-chap6-subchapII-sec136e.htm; *Pesticide Establishment Registration and Reporting*, EPA, https://www.epa.gov/compliance/pesticide-establishment-registration-and-reporting.

22 *Pesticide Registration Label Review Manual*, EPA, https://www.epa.gov/pesticide-registration/ label-review-manual.

4. Statement "Keep Out of Reach of Children," unless waiver by EPA. 40 C.F.R 156.66.
5. A *signal word* ("poison," "danger" "warning" or "caution") for the highest/most toxic acute toxicity category to which a pesticide product is assigned. 40 C.F.R 156.64.
6. First aid instructions. 40 C.F.R 156.68.
7. Net contents/net weight. According to EPA: "There is no required location for this statement, but the preferred location is at the bottom of the front panel below the company name and address."[23]

The label is the centerpiece of how EPA regulates pesticides. In fact, getting a pesticide approved is frequently called *getting a label*. As a general matter, the only claims that are legally permitted for a pesticide, even an approved pesticide, are those on the label. Even truthful claims are not allowed unless they were approved in advance by EPA.[24]

In addition to the draft label, an applicant for approval of a new pesticide must submit studies and/or references to the published scientific literature to support a finding by EPA that use of the pesticide in accordance with its instruction for proper use will not "generally cause unreasonable adverse effects on the environment."[25] These data requirements include:

- Product Chemistry
- Product Performance
- Data from Studies that Determine Hazard to Humans and Domestic Animals

---

23 EPA, PESTICIDE REGISTRATION LABEL REVIEW MANUAL, CHAPTER 3: GENERAL LABELING REQUIREMENTS (March 2018), https://www.epa.gov/sites/production/files/2018-04/documents/chap-03-mar-2018_1.pdf.
24 For a good summary of the requirements that must be met to distribute a pesticide in the United States, see *The Federal Insecticide, Fungicide, and Rodenticide Act: Frequently Asked Questions*, BERGESON AND CAMPBELL PC, https://www.lawbc.com/knowledge-resources/faq-fifra/.
25 FIFRA § 3, 7 U.S.C. § 136a(a), https://www.law.cornell.edu/uscode/text/7/136a; *Summary of the Federal Insecticide, Fungicide, and Rodenticide Act*, EPA, https://www.epa.gov/laws-regulations/summary-federal-insecticide-fungicide-and-rodenticide-act ("Before EPA may register a pesticide under FIFRA, the applicant must show, among other things, that using the pesticide according to specifications 'will not generally cause unreasonable adverse effects on the environment.'").

- Data from Studies that Determine Hazard to Nontarget Organisms
- Post-Application Exposure Studies
- Applicator/User Exposure Studies
- Pesticide Spray Drift Evaluation
- Environmental Fate
- Residue Chemistry.[26]

EPA may waive certain data requirements as unnecessary or deem them satisfied by *reading across*—which means projecting the results from data on similar substances.[27] In addition, EPA may, and often does, grant *conditional registrations* whereby a company is allowed to begin selling a pesticide, subject to conducting further studies to fill any remaining data gaps. As of 2020, the list of conditional registrations granted by EPA ran to over seventy-eight pages of fine print.[28] But proceeding to market under a conditional registration has become increasingly controversial and subject to court challenges.[29]

Finally, after the period of exclusive use (generally ten years) granted to the first registrant of a pesticide, EPA allows other applicants with similar products to rely on the data developed by the original producer in support their later applications. But note that, as a result of a 1984 Supreme Court case which held that requiring one company to allow others to piggyback on its data without just compensation constitutes an unconstitutional *taking*,[30] the law now provides an arbitration procedure for determining fair compensation to the original registrant that developed the data.[31]

---

26 *Data Requirements for Pesticide Registration*, EPA, https://www.epa.gov/pesticide-registration/data-requirements-pesticide-registration.

27 *Grouping of Chemicals: Chemical Categories and Read-Across*, OECD, https://www.oecd.org/env/ehs/risk-assessment/groupingofchemicalschemicalcategoriesandread-across.htm.

28 *Status of Conditional Registrations under FIFRA sec.3(c)(7)(C) from 2000 through 2020*, EPA, (August 2020), https://www.epa.gov/sites/production/files/2020-08/documents/conditional-reg-updates_8-4-2020.pdf.

29 *See* Keith A. Matthew, *Ninth Circuit Invalidates Nanosilver Conditional Pesticide Registration*, WILEY (June 2017), https://www.wiley.law/newsletter-June_2017_PSSR-Ninth_Circuit_Invalidates_Nanosilver_Conditional_Pesticide_Registration.

30 Ruckelshaus v. Monsanto Co., 467 U.S. 986 (1984), https://supreme.justia.com/cases/federal/us/467/986/.

31 FIFRA §3 (c)(1)(F)(iii), 7 U.S.C § 136a(c)(1)(F)(iii), https://www.law.cornell.edu/uscode/text/7/136a.

Evaluating FIFRA

Critics argue that slow regulatory procedures and gaps have plagued FIFRA, leaving the public unnecessarily at risk from chemical exposure.[32] The 1989 Alar apple scandal is symbolic of these problems. In that notorious case, EPA announced a special review of Alar, a chemical (daminozide) used to extend the shelf life of apples, but ten years passed, and EPA had not succeeded in getting the product registration cancelled. Finally, in 1989, under media and public pressure, the producer, Uniroyal Chemical Co., voluntarily withdrew Alar from the market in the face of public outrage over a study released by the Natural Resources Defense Council (with the actress Meryl Streep serving as the spokesperson for the group) that suggested one in 4200 children would get cancer as a result of their exposure to daminozide on apples.[33] While later analyses indicated that the NRDC study overstated the cancer risk to children by at least a thousand times,[34] the episode damaged both EPA's reputation and Alar's marketability—and a year's worth of Washington state apples sprayed with the pesticide went unsold.[35]

We note that the FQPA went some distance toward addressing this problem. Food-use pesticides now must be registered under FIFRA—and also have appropriate tolerances under the Federal Food, Drug, and Cosmetic Act (FFDCA).[36] EPA is also supposed to review all registrations every fifteen years so that pesticides presenting a dietary exposure are regularly re-assessed based on current science. But note that this enhanced regulatory review does not apply to other pesticides,

---

32 Jennifer Sass and Mae Wu, NRDC, Superficial Safeguards: Most Pesticides Are Approved by Flawed EPA Process (March 2013), https://www.nrdc.org/sites/default/files/flawed-epa-approval-process-IB.pdf.

33 See, e.g., Timur Kuran and Cass R. Sunstein, Availability Cascades and Risk Regulation, 51 Stan. L. Rev. 683 (1999), https://papers.ssrn.com/sol3/papers.cfm?abstract_id=138144.

34 Id.

35 David Shaw, Alar Panic Shows Power of Media to Trigger Fear: 60 Minutes' broadcast created scare at time when the industry was already moving away from use of the chemical, L.A. Times (Sept. 12, 1994, 12:00 AM), https://www.latimes.com/archives/la-xpm-1994-09-12-mn-37733-story.html; see also Adam M. Finkel, Alar: the aftermath, 255 Science 664 (Feb. 7, 1992), https://science.sciencemag.org/content/255/5045/664; Edward Groth, Alar in Apples letter, 244 Science 755 (May 19, 1989), https://science.sciencemag.org/content/244/4906/755.1; An Unhappy Anniversary: The Alar 'Scare' Ten Years Later, American Council on Science and Health (Feb. 1, 1999), https://www.acsh.org/news/1999/02/01/an-unhappy-anniversary-the-alar-scare-ten-years-later; but see Charles Fulwood, The campaign to sugar-coat Alar, Tampa Bay Times (Oct. 4, 2005), https://www.tampabay.com/archive/1995/11/26/the-campaign-to-sugar-coat-alar/.

36 Federal Food, Drug, and Cosmetic Act, 21 U.S.C. § 301, https://www.law.cornell.edu/uscode/text/21/chapter-9.

such as household insecticides, where the traditional FIFRA *unreasonableness* standard continues to apply.

EPA furthermore faces on-going criticism for failing to move quickly to *cancel* the registration of products where new science suggests that the prior tolerance may not be appropriate. For example, recent studies have concluded that certain pesticides (called neonicotinoids) are killing bees and other pollinators.[37] But EPA has declined to ban these products.[38] In EPA's defense, it must overcome significant legal hurdles to make the case for removing a product from the marketplace in the face of competing scientific studies and commercial interests willing to fight to protect the status quo. For non-food-use pesticides, the statutory requirement to balance risks and benefits remains an obstacle.

As a result of FIFRA's burden of proof, inescapable scientific uncertainty, and the *unreasonableness* hurdle that EPA must overcome in many circumstances, Agency officials often negotiate *voluntary cancellation* of pesticides where they suspect a product of causing risks to health, rather than go through the arduous process of formal cancellation or suspension.[39] While not always truly voluntary,[40] this alternative often works to the registrant's benefit because EPA typically allows the sale of existing pesticide stocks if the Agency "determines that such sale or use is not inconsistent with the purposes of (FIFRA) and will not have unreasonable adverse effects on the environment,"[41] plus the registrant avoids the adverse publicity that accompanies a mandatory cancellation for safety reasons.

Regulatory skeptics similarly decry the slow pace of the *data call-ins* and *special reviews* launched when EPA questions the safety of

---

37 Nadejda Tsvetkov et al., *Chronic exposure to neonicotinoids reduces honeybee health near corn crops*, 356 SCIENCE 1395 (2017), https://science.sciencemag.org/content/356/6345/1395. For what EPA is doing to address this issue, see *Protecting Bees and Other Pollinators from Pesticides*, EPA, https://www.epa.gov/pollinator-protection.

38 Britt E. Erickson, *Neonicotinoid pesticides can stay in the US market, EPA says*, CHEMICAL & ENGINEERING NEWS (Feb. 3, 2020) https://cen.acs.org/environment/pesticides/Neonicotinoid-pesticides-stay-US-market/98/web/2020/02.

39 *Voluntary Cancellation of a Pesticide Product or Use*, EPA, http://bit.ly/3kyujwQ.

40 For example, EPA may issue a *data call in* requiring registrants of already approved pesticides to supply information confirming their safety. Rather than comply, registrants often choose to cancel that pesticide. See *Voluntary Cancellation of a Pesticide Product or Use*, EPA, http://bit.ly/3kyujwQ.

41 Existing Stocks of Pesticide Products; Statement of Policy, 56 Fed. Reg. 29362, 29363 (June 26, 1991), https://www.epa.gov/sites/production/files/2015-04/documents/56-fr-29362.pdf.

a particular pesticide. FIFRA's legal framework provides pesticide makers with an extensive adjudicatory process that can lead to years of delay before a product gets taken off the market, unless EPA declares it to be an *imminent hazard* and pursues *suspension* of its registration.[42] Even then, the producer can demand hearings and invoke judicial review and other procedural safeguards that may result in months or even years of delay.[43] EPA can short circuit this process only by demonstrating the existence of an *emergency*, which, if proven, enables the Agency to go forward with *immediate suspension* of the product,[44] or by negotiating a voluntary cancellation as discussed above.

Reformers have long argued that EPA should use a *cumulative risk* model that goes beyond the pesticide-by-pesticide and crop-by-crop regulatory approach.[45] Since 2002, however, EPA has conducted some cumulative analyses of pesticides having the same or similar *modes of action*.[46] In view of these and other reforms introduced in response to FQPA, as well as dramatic gains in recent years in understanding how chemicals produce toxicity in the body[47] and increased capacity to detect and model low levels of exposure to chemical residues from pesticides in food, we believe it is time to review FIFRA—25 years since its last major overhaul in 1996. Congress should ask the National Academy of Sciences or another body of outside experts to assess how well FIFRA is working and make recommendations for its improvement—perhaps including application of the more stringent

---

42 FIFRA § 6(b)(2), 7 U.S.C. § 136d(b)(2), https://www.law.cornell.edu/uscode/text/7/136d.

43 Chlorpyrifos provides a case in point. NRDC filed a citizen petition in 2007 asking EPA to revoke the registration of this product, which has been in use since the 1960s, on the basis that there was no safe tolerance. A 2015 EPA risk assessment confirmed this conclusion, but Chlorpyrifos continues to be registered for use on food crops (although it has been withdrawn from the market in other applications). Litigation over Chlorpyrifos continues with a case still pending in the 9th Circuit as of March 2021. https://www.epa.gov/pesticides/epa-takes-next-step-review-process-insecticide-chlorpyrifos-making-draft-risk-assessments.

44 FIFRA § 6(c)(3), 7 U.S.C. § 136d(c)(3), https://www.law.cornell.edu/uscode/text/7/136d.

45 Sanne H. Knudsen, *Regulating Cumulative Risk*, 101 Minn. L. Rev. 2213 (2017), https://papers.ssrn.com/sol3/papers.cfm?abstract_id=2856011.

46 *Guidance on Cumulative Risk Assessment of Pesticide Chemicals that have a Common Mechanism of Toxicity*, EPA, https://www.epa.gov/pesticide-science-and-assessing-pesticide-risks/guidance-cumulative-risk-assessment-pesticide; *see also* EPA Office of Pesticide Programs, Pesticide Cumulative Risk Assessment Framework Final (Apr. 12, 2016), https://www.regulations.gov/document/EPA-HQ-OPP-2015-0422-0019.

47 *See, e.g.,* National Research Council, Toxicity Testing In The Twenty-First Century: A Vision And A Strategy (2007), https://www.nap.edu/catalog/11970/toxicity-testing-in-the-21st-century-a-vision-and-a.

FQPA safety standards and burden shifting to all pesticides, not simply those used on food crops.[48]

Additional resources

Environmental Law Institute (2001). *Pesticide Regulation Deskbook* (1st ed.). Washington, D.C.: Environmental Law Institute.

Fisher, Linda J. et al. (1994). Practitioner's Guide to the Federal Insecticide, Fungicide, and Rodenticide Act: Part II. *Environmental Law Reporter, 24*(9), 10507. https://elr.info/news-analysis/24/10507/practitioners-guide-federal-insecticide-fungicide-and-rodenticide-act-part-ii.

Hornstein, Donald T. (1993). Lessons from Federal Pesticide Regulation on the Paradigms and Politics of Environmental Law Reform. *Yale Journal on Regulation, 10*(2), 369–446. https://digitalcommons.law.yale.edu/cgi/viewcontent.cgi?article=1264&context=yjreg.

Knudsen, Sanne H. (2017). Regulating Cumulative Risk. *Minnesota Law Review, 101*(6), 2312–2396. https://scholarship.law.umn.edu/mlr/177/.

Racke, Kenneth D. et al. (eds.) (2012). *Pesticide Regulation and the Endangered Species Act.* Oxford University Press.

Sass, Jennifer and Wu, Mae (2013). *Superficial Safeguards: Most Pesticides Are Approved by Flawed EPA Process* (Issue Brief No. 13-01-B). NRDC. https://www.nrdc.org/sites/default/files/flawed-epa-approval-process-IB.pdf.

---

48 For an argument that consensus recommendations by experts are a promising way around the political "logjam" in Congress, see E. Donald Elliott, *Portage Strategies for Adapting Environmental Law and Policy During a Logjam Era,* 17 NYU ENVTL. L.J. 24 (2008), http://digitalcommons.law.yale.edu/fss_papers/2221/.

10 Occupational Safety and Health Act: making environments safe on the job

The average American spends about 87 percent of his or her time indoors,[1] but ironically, most U.S. environmental laws focus on the outdoor environment. One exception, however, is the *Occupational Safety and Health Act* (OSH Act),[2] which was enacted in 1970, at about the same time as the Clean Air Act and the National Environmental Policy Act. Its purpose is "to assure so far as possible every working man and woman in the Nation safe and healthful working conditions."[3] *The Occupational Safety and Health Administration* (OSHA), which is part of the Department of Labor, implements the OSH Act, rather than EPA. While many courses in U.S. environmental law ignore OSHA, we believe that a brief summary offers a useful comparison to the EPA-administered statutes and that the indoor environment in which we spend most of our time is also a proper subject of environmental law.

OSHA exercises regulatory authority over environmental exposures in the workplace for any employer engaged in a business that may affect commerce[4] and also prescribes rules designed to prevent work-place injuries such as falls or traumatic amputations. OSHA regulates through a combination of inspections, recordkeeping and injury report-ing requirements, and specific regulatory rules (called occupational safety and health standards) that generally apply to specific industries

---

1 Neil E. Klepeis et. al., *The National Human Activity Pattern Survey (NHAPS): a resource for assess-ing exposure to environmental pollutants*, 11 J. EXPOSURE SCI. & ENVTL. EPIDEMIOLOGY 231 (2001), https://escholarship.org/uc/item/1zg3q68x.
2 Occupational Safety and Health Act, 29 U.S.C. §§ 651–678, https://www.law.cornell.edu/uscode/text/29/chapter-15.
3 OSH Act, 29 U.S.C. § 651(b), https://www.law.cornell.edu/uscode/text/29/651.
4 OSH Act, 29 U.S.C. § 652(5), https://www.law.cornell.edu/uscode/text/29/652. Some OSHA rules exempt employers with fewer than ten employees from certain requirements, such as maintaining an injury log, but it is a myth that the OSH Act only applies to employers with a certain number of employees. Eric J. Conn and Amanda R. Strainis-Walker, *The So-Called "Rule of 10": A Myth about OSHA's Lack of Jurisdiction Over Small Employers*, EPSTEIN, BECKER & GREEN, P.C., (Jan. 9, 2012), https://www.workforcebulletin.com/2012/01/09/the-so-called-rule-of-10-a-myth-of-oshas-lack-of-jurisdiction-over-small-employers/.

or industrial processes. In regulating exposures to toxic substances in the workplace, OSHA promulgates substance-specific *permissible exposure limits* (PELs), which typically set a maximum concentration exposure limit over an eight-hour work day.[5] While engineering controls are the preferred means of limiting workplace exposure to toxic substances, *personal protective equipment* (PPE) such as safety glasses, face masks, or respirators may be required, or permitted, for work in areas that would otherwise exceed the PEL.[6]

In addition to requiring compliance with these specific requirements, the OSH Act also contains a *General Duty Clause* requiring every employer must "furnish to each of his employees employment and a place of employment which are free from recognized hazards that are causing or are likely to cause death or serious physical harm to his employees."[7] In other words, even where no specific standard applies, OSHA inspectors may issue citations for unsafe conditions as violations of the *General Duty Clause*. These citations are, however, more difficult to enforce than specific requirements.[8]

Like many other environmental laws, the OSH Act is enforced through *cooperative federalism*.[9] OSHA has approved twenty-two

---

5 OSH Act, 29 U.S.C. § 655(b)(5), https://www.law.cornell.edu/uscode/text/29/655 (authorizing promulgation of PELs by OSHA). Original OSHA PEL standards are published in the Z-tables of 29 C.F.R. § 1910.1000. Recognizing these standards were published shortly after the OSH Act in 1970, OSHA has published annotated Z-tables listing Recommended Exposure Limits (RELs) for the benefit of employers available at https://www.osha.gov/annotated-pels.

6 *See generally Personal Protective Equipment*, OSHA, https://www.osha.gov/personal-protective-equipment.

7 OSH Act, 29 U.S.C. § 654(a)(1), https://www.law.cornell.edu/uscode/text/29/654.

8 Alan Ferguson, *OSHA's General Duty Clause*, HEALTH & SAFETY MAG. (Dec. 20, 2019), https://www.safetyandhealthmagazine.com/articles/19258-oshas-general-duty-clause; *see also* E. Donald Elliott, *U.S. Environmental Law in Global Perspective: Five Do's and Five Don'ts from Our Experience*, 2010 NAT'L TAIWAN UNIV. L. REV. 144, 147–49 (2010), https://digitalcommons.law.yale.edu/fss_papers/2717/ (arguing that one of the best features of U.S. environmental law is its practice of translating general goals into facility-specific permit conditions that are easier to enforce).

9 *See, e.g.*, Clean Air Act, 42 U.S.C. § 7401, https://www.law.cornell.edu/uscode/text/42/7401 (emphasizing "air pollution control at its source is the primary responsibility of States and local governments," but that federal leadership "is essential for the development of cooperative Federal, State, regional, and local programs to prevent and control air pollution"); Clean Water Act, 33 U.S.C. §§ 1251(a)-(b), https://www.law.cornell.edu/uscode/text/33/1251 (establishing the "objective of [the CWA] to restore and maintain the chemical, physical, and biological integrity of the Nation's waters" but also "[i]t is the policy of Congress to recognize, preserve, and protect the primary responsibilities and rights of States to prevent, reduce, and eliminate pollution, to plan the

state-operated workplace safety and health programs (called *State Plans*), which the states implement under OSHA monitoring, rather than narrowly applying federal OSHA standards. To be approved, the State Plan must be at least as effective as federal OSHA in protecting workers and in preventing work-related injuries, illnesses, and deaths.[10]

Unlike EPA, where scientific assessments are generally subject to political oversight and control,[11] the OSH Act set up an independent science agency, the National Institute of Occupational Safety and Health (NIOSH), which is now part of the Center for Disease Control and Prevention (CDC), to make non-binding, scientific findings and recommendations to OSHA.[12]

An important 1980 Supreme Court precedent interpreted the OSH Act as only authorizing regulation of "significant" workplace hazards and not requiring employers to make workplaces as safe as technologically feasible.[13] The decision suggested, though it did not require, that quantitative risk assessment using benefit-cost analysis might be one way to determine whether a risk was significant under the court's new standard. Subsequently, OSHA has generally used quantitative risk assessment and benefit-cost analysis in setting standards.[14] This trend has carried over to other instances of environmental standard-setting under a series of executive orders requiring review of proposed major rules by the White House Office of Information and Regulatory Affairs (OIRA).[15]

---

development and use . . . of land and water resources, and to consult with the Administrator in the exercise of his authority under this chapter").

10 OSH Act, 29 U.S.C. § 667, https://www.law.cornell.edu/uscode/text/29/667; *State Plans*, OSHA, https://www.osha.gov/stateplans.

11 *See generally* E. Donald Elliott, *Strengthening Science's Voice at EPA*, 66 L. & CONTEMP. PROBS. 45 (2003), https://scholarship.law.duke.edu/lcp/vol66/iss4/3/.

12 OSH Act, 29 U.S.C. § 671(c)(1), https://www.law.cornell.edu/uscode/text/29/671.

13 Indus. Union Dept., AFL-CIO v. Am. Petrol. Inst., 448 U.S. 607 (1980), https://supreme.justia.com/cases/federal/us/448/607/ (remanding the OSHA benzene standard for failure to find a "significant" risk to health).

14 John F. Martonik et al., *The History of OSHA's Asbestos Rulemakings and Some Distinctive Approaches that They Introduced for Regulating Occupational Exposure to Toxic Substances*, 62 AM. INDUST. HYGIENE ASSN. J. 208, 213 (2001), https://pubmed.ncbi.nlm.nih.gov/11331993/ ("quantitative assessment of risk was a result of the . . . 1980 benzene decision requiring OSHA to perform such an analysis when appropriate data are available").

15 Exec. Order No. 12,291, 3 C.F.R. § 127 (1982) (reprinted in 5 U.S.C. § 601 app. at 431–34 (1982)), https://www.archives.gov/federal-register/codification/executive-order/12291.html. *See also* Exec. Order No. 12,866, 3 C.F.R. § 638 (1994) (reprinted as amended in 5 U.S.C. § 601 app. at 86–91 (2006 & Supp. V 2011)), https://www.archives.gov/files/federal-register/executive-orders/pdf/12866.pdf.

Overall, the U.S. system for regulating workplace environments is typically less stringent than the system for regulating exposures to the general population. Risk levels deemed tolerable for workers who consent to such exposures to hazardous substances in the workplace are roughly ten times higher than for involuntary exposures to the general public. However, unlike the general population, workers are entitled to no-fault compensation under state workers' compensation systems for illness or injuries that can be traced to workplace hazards.[16] Workers are also entitled to accurate information about the extent of risks to which they are exposed.[17] Elsewhere the present authors have argued that members of the general population who are exposed to pollution should also be entitled to these two features of the workplace system: compensation for the risks that remain after the application of feasible pollution control technology and accurate information about the extent of such risks.[18]

Additional resources

Currie, David P. (1976). OSHA. *American Bar Foundation Research Journal*, *1*(4), 1107–1160.

U.S. Dept. of Labor, Occupational Safety and Health Administration, All About OSHA (OSHA 3302-01R 2020), https://www.osha.gov/Publications/all_about_OSHA.pdf.

U.S. Dept. of Labor, Employment Law Guide Safety and Health Standards: Occupational Safety and Health, https://webapps.dol.gov/elaws/elg/osha.htm.

---

16 *See* Arthur Larson, *Nature and Origins of Workmen's Compensation*, 37 CORNELL L. REV. 206 (1952), https://scholarship.law.cornell.edu/clr/vol37/iss2/2/; *see also, e.g.* N.Y. Workers' Comp. Law § 10 (McKinney 2020).

17 *See* OSHA Hazard Communication Rule, 29 C.F.R. § 1910.1200, https://www.osha.gov/laws-regs/regulations/standardnumber/1910/1910.1200.

18 E. Donald Elliott and Daniel C. Esty, *The End Environmental Externalities Manifesto: A Rights-Based Foundation for the Next Fifty Years of Environmental Law*, NYU ENVTL. L. J. (forthcoming, 2021), https://papers.ssrn.com/sol3/papers.cfm?abstract_id=3762022.

11 OPA90: why economic incentives only work sometimes

"Only a crisis—actual or perceived—produces real change. When that crisis occurs, the actions that are taken depend on the ideas that are lying around," writes Milton Friedman, a Nobel Prize-winning economist.[1] The crisis that led to passage of *the Oil Pollution Act of 1990* (OPA90) occurred on March 24, 1989, when an oil tanker, the *Exxon Valdez*, ran aground near Price William Island in Alaska. Eleven million gallons of black, viscous crude oil spilled into a narrow channel and washed ashore, doing enormous damage to wildlife and a sensitive Arctic ecosystem.[2] The *Exxon Valdez* oil spill was the largest in U.S. history at the time and Congress responded with OPA90.

In the case of OPA90, the ideas that were "lying around" were borrowed from the environmental laws of the 1970s and 1980s but also augmented by the growing intellectual influence of the *law and economics* movement. Pioneered by academics such as Guido Calabresi,[3] later dean of the Yale Law School and a judge on the Second Circuit Court of Appeals, and Richard Posner[4] of the University of Chicago Law School, later a judge on the Seventh Circuit Court of Appeals, the first generation of law and economics presumed that the actors the law desires to regulate are, at least in the aggregate, continuously calculating risks and benefits and responding rationally to the *incentives*

---

1 Milton Friedman, Capitalism and Freedom xiv (1962).

2 *The Exxon Valdez Oil Spill: A Report to the President (Executive Summary)*, EPA, https://archive. epa.gov/epa/aboutepa/exxon-valdez-oil-spill-report-president-executive-summary.html.

3 Guido Calabresi, The Costs of Accidents: A Legal and Economic Analysis (1970); Guido Calabresi and A. Douglas Melamed, *Property Rules, Liability Rules and Inalienability: One View of the Cathedral*, 85 Harv. L. Rev. 1089 (1972), https://digitalcommons.law.yale.edu/ cgi/viewcontent.cgi?article=3043&context=fss_papers. Both Elliott and Esty were students of Calabresi's at Yale Law School and acknowledge his influence on their work.

4 Richard Posner, Economic Analysis of Law (1st ed. 1973).

created by the system of legal rules.[5] For example, in one article,[6] Calabresi claims that all legal systems either are, or are in the process of *becoming*, optimally economically efficient in the sense that no further moves are available to improve the welfare of some without harming others. Economists call a situation in which no changes are possible that will benefit some without harming others a *Pareto optimal* state, after the Italian economist Vilfredo Pareto.[7]

Regulating by creating economic incentives to spur the behavior desired has proven to be a powerful tool in U.S. environmental law for addressing problems as diverse as improving the management of hazardous waste,[8] reducing the toxic chemicals in consumer products,[9] and reallocating pollution allotments more efficiently than government can do itself through a market-based trading system.[10] However, understanding why regulating via economic incentives sometimes succeeds and sometimes fails to achieve its desired goals is key not only for understanding why oil spills continue to occur but also for designing the next generation of environmental regulations more generally.

Main provisions of OPA90

Preventing oil spills

OPA90 did not attempt to use economic incentives alone to reduce the damage to the environment from oil spills. Rather, like most other U.S. environmental laws, the nation's approach to oil spill regulation relies on multiple techniques (a strategy sometimes called *redundancy*

---

5 For an excellent summary of the law and economics movement including its reliance on the rational actor model, see Lewis Kornhauser, *The Economic Analysis of Law*, STANFORD ENCYCLOPEDIA OF PHILOSOPHY (Edward N. Zalta ed., Fall 2017), https://plato.stanford.edu/archives/fall2017/entries/legal-econanalysis.

6 Guido Calabresi, *The Pointlessness of Pareto: Carrying Coase Further*, 100 YALE L.J. 1211 (1991), https://digitalcommons.law.yale.edu/fss_papers/2014/.

7 Vilfredo Pareto, LIBRARY OF ECONOMICS AND LIBERTY, https://www.econlib.org/library/Enc/bios/Pareto.html. Interestingly, Pareto himself came to believe late in life that people do not actually always act rationally. *Id.*

8 *See* Chapter 14; Adam Babich, *Understanding the New Era in Environmental Law*, 41 S.C.L. REV. 733, 749–62 (1990), https://scholarcommons.sc.edu/cgi/viewcontent.cgi?article=2947&context=sclr (arguing that the expanded liability provisions of Superfund create incentives for companies to reduce their releases of hazardous substances to the environment).

9 *See* Chapter 14 discussing California's Proposition 65.

10 *See* Chapter 3 regarding the 1990 Acid Rain Trading system.

or *hybrid* regulation[11]). The first line of defense by U.S. environmental law against oil spills is to ban oil drilling in particularly sensitive ecological areas where a spill could be particularly damaging, such as in the Arctic National Wildlife Refuge (ANWR)[12] or the continental shelf off the east and west coasts. The second line of defense is traditional command-and-control regulation under detailed rules governing the drilling process issued by a federal government regulatory agency.[13] This form of regulation is particularly pervasive for offshore oil exploration in that an off-shore driller must file a detailed drilling plan with federal regulators for their approval and subsequently obtain written approval for even seemingly minor changes.

In addition to these traditional techniques, OPA90 added a third line of defense by amending Section 311 of the Clean Water Act to add massive civil and criminal penalties for unpermitted releases of oil into waters of the United States.[14] Previously, the penalty for violations of the CWA was only $25 000 per day for each day that the violation continued. Thus, only a trivial penalty might result from an oil spill that lasts just a few days. OPA90, however, added an alternative penalty of $1000 for every barrel of oil spilled and $3000 per barrel in cases of gross negligence or violation of regulations, amounts that are indexed

---

11 The characteristic tendency of U.S. legal culture to attack a problem with multiple approaches was identified by a sage nineteenth century political scientist who wrote: "The English constitution, in a word, is framed on the principle of choosing a single sovereign authority, and making it good; the American, upon the principle of having many sovereign authorities, and hoping that their multitude will atone for their inferiority." WALTER BAGEHOT, THE ENGLISH CONSTITUTION AND OTHER POLITICAL ESSAYS 296 (rev. ed. 1901), https://www.goodreads.com/author/quotes/182994.Walter_Bagehot.

12 For a summary of the controversy that has raged since 1977 over whether to allow drilling in ANWR, see Elizabeth Shogren, All Things Considered, *For 30 Years, a Political Battle Over Oil and ANWR*, NATIONAL PUBLIC RADIO (Nov. 10, 2005, 12:00 AM), https://www.npr.org/templates/story/story.php?storyId=5007819.

13 At the time of the 2010 *Deepwater Horizon* spill, the regulatory agency responsible for regulating offshore drilling was the Minerals Management Service (MMS). In response to that spill, it was renamed the Bureau of Ocean Energy Management, Regulation and Enforcement (BOEMRE). *The Reorganization of the Former MMS*, BOEM, https://www.boem.gov/about-boem/reorganization/reorganization-former-mms. Reorganizing existing agencies and changing their names is one way that governments sometimes attempt to appear to address problems without making substantial changes.

14 For a more detailed description of the provisions of OPA90, see *Oil Pollution Act Overview*, EPA, https://archive.epa.gov/emergencies/content/lawsregs/web/html/opaover.html; E. Donald Elliott and Mary Beth Houlihan, *A Primer on the Law of Oil Spills*, ALI-ABA ADVANCED ENVTL. L. CONF. (2011); Brian P. Flanagan, *Recovering Damages for Oil Spills*, BOHONNON (May, 2011), https://www.bohonnon.com/firm-news-and-articles/recovering-damages-for-oil-spills.

to increase with inflation.[15] Generally OPA90 limited legal liability to the cost of clean-up plus $75 million in the case of an off-shore facility and $350 million for an onshore facility.[16] These limits are only rarely exceeded.[17] Moreover, the liability limits do not apply in the event of gross negligence or willful misconduct, violation of federal safety, construction, or operating regulations, or failure to report an incident.[18] For major oil spills, there is almost always gross negligence or a violation of regulations involved, and thus the civil penalties under OPA90 can add up to *billions* of dollars.[19] Under OPA90, the total cost to BP and the other companies involved of the 2010 *Deepwater Horizon* spill totaled over $65 billion.[20]

A true success story

By many measures, OPA90 has been "a true success story" as the number of oil spills has "precipitously dropped . . . from over 600 in 1990 to less than 100 in 2012."[21] The public concern and adverse publicity following the *Exxon Valdez* and *Deepwater Horizon* spills as well as the increased legal liability under OPA90 spurred the oil industry to form a consortium to take collective action to respond more effectively to future spills.[22] This is an example of a strategy called *resilience*, which means trying to reduce the harm when accidents do occur, as well as

---

15 *Water*, U.S. DEPARTMENT OF JUSTICE, https://www.justice.gov/enrd/water ("With inflation adjustments, the current amounts [as of 2020] are $32,500 per day, or $1,100 per barrel or unit; $4,300 per barrel in the event of gross negligence or willfulness.").

16 OPA90 § 1004, 33 U.S.C. § 2704, https://www.law.cornell.edu/uscode/text/33/2704.

17 U.S. COAST GUARD, OIL POLLUTION ACT LIABILITY LIMITS IN 2019: REPORT TO CONGRESS (Feb. 25, 2020), https://www.uscg.mil/Portals/0/NPFC/docs/PDFs/Reports/2020-02-25-Oil-Pollution-Act-Liability-Limits-in-2019.pdf?ver=2020-02-25-133009-910.

18 OPA90 § 1004(c)(1), 33 U.S.C. §§ 2704(c)(1)-(2), https://www.law.cornell.edu/uscode/text/33/2704.

19 For example, as a result of the 2010 *Deepwater Horizon* spill, BP paid a civil penalty of $5.5 billion, plus other costs for a total settlement with the national and state governments of $20 billion. *Proposed Consent Decrees: Deepwater Horizon*, U.S. DEPARTMENT. OF JUSTICE, https://www.justice.gov/enrd/deepwater-horizon#:~:text=Under%20the%20Consent%20Decree%20BP,of%20accrued%20interest)%20for%20adaptive.

20 Ron Bousso, *BP Deepwater Horizon costs balloon to $65 billion*, REUTERS (Jan. 16, 2018 2:20 AM), https://www.reuters.com/article/us-bp-deepwaterhorizon/bp-deepwater-horizon-costs-balloon-to-65-billion-idUSKBN1F50NL.

21 Paul Hankins, *A closer look at OPA 90's success*, MARINE LOG 36 (March 2014), http://www.americansalvage.org/marine-log/ML-Mar2014.pdf.

22 Henry Berry, *How Did the Oil Industry Change Post Deepwater Horizon*, ENVTL. PROT. (Nov. 9, 2020), https://eponline.com/articles/2020/11/09/how-did-the-oil-industry-change-post-deepwater-horizon.aspx#.

trying to prevent them.[23] Today oil spills are typically much less damaging to the environment than in the past. This result can be attributed to two additional underappreciated developments: a requirement in OPA90 for facilities to develop response plans (an idea borrowed from the 1986 Emergency Planning and Community Right to Know Act (EPCRA))[24] and the development of chemical dispersants and other technologies for preventing oil from coming ashore and harming sensitive coastal areas.[25] In addition, the oil industry trade association, the American Petroleum Institute (API), develops and maintains a system of 700 *industry consensus standards*, which amounts to a non-binding private regulatory system of best practices.[26]

Despite putting in place enormous economic incentives to take precautions to prevent oil spills, OPA90 failed to prevent the massive 2010 *Deepwater Horizon* oil spill, which was about 20 times larger than the 1989 *Exxon Valdez* spill.[27] Before we turn to diagnosing why this huge oil spill occurred despite ample economic incentives to prevent it, we describe a second issue on which the economic incentive approach of OPA90 also worked.

Incentives to compensate victims

OPA90 aimed not only to prevent oil spills like the 1989 Alaska oil spill but also to compensate victims promptly and fairly for any future spills that do occur. Almost twenty years after the *Exxon Valdez* spill, litigation by victims was still pending,[28] which brings to mind the adage

---

23 AARON WILDAVSKY, SEARCHING FOR SAFETY (1988) (arguing for great reliance on resilience as opposed to anticipation and prevention in environmental law and policy).

24 Emergency Planning and Community Right to Know Act, 42 U.S.C. § 11003, https://www.law.cornell.edu/uscode/text/42/11003.

25 *Oil Spill Prevention + Response: Dispersants*, API. https://www.oilspillprevention.org/oil-spill-cleanup/oil-spill-cleanup-toolkit/dispersants.

26 *Standards*, AMERICAN PETROLEUM INSTITUTE, https://www.api.org/products-and-services/standards/. For a thoughtful exploration of the interplay between mandatory government regulation and API's voluntary standards, see Russell W. Mills and Christopher J. Koliba, *The challenge of accountability in complex regulatory networks: The case of the Deepwater Horizon oil spill*, 9 REG. & GOVERNANCE 77 (2015), https://onlinelibrary.wiley.com/doi/abs/10.1111/rego.12062.

27 For a summary of the *Deepwater Horizon* spill and its aftermath, see *Deepwater Horizon Oil Spill*, BRITANNICA, https://www.britannica.com/event/Deepwater-Horizon-oil-spill; *see also Deepwater Horizon Oil Spill*, WIKIPEDIA, https://en.wikipedia.org/wiki/Deepwater_Horizon_oil_spill.

28 *See* Exxon Shipping Co. v. Baker, 554 U.S. 471 (2008), https://supreme.justia.com/cases/federal/us/554/471/ (reducing $5 billion award of punitive damages to $1 billion).

justice delayed is justice denied. In addition, a 1927 Supreme Court case restricted the rights of plaintiffs who did not sustain physical injuries to their persons or property to recover for purely economic losses under traditional maritime law.[29]

The drafters of OPA90 were determined to get more compensation to victims promptly. The heart of OPA90 is the concept of a "responsible party,"[30] which was modeled loosely on the concept of *potentially responsible parties* under Superfund.[31] Both statutes create *status liability* for the owner or operator of the facility in the first instance,[32] but allow the responsible party to seek contribution or indemnification from others whose actions may have contributed to causing spill.[33] The idea was to eliminate the finger-pointing[34] among the companies about which of them caused the spill in order to get compensation to the victims quickly. OPA90 provides that the responsible party is liable for *removal costs*—to abate and clean-up the spill[35]—and six categories of economic damages,[36] including natural resource damages (another concept borrowed from Superfund). Following the pattern of many previous U.S. environmental laws, the federal OPA90 rights and

---

29 Robbins Dry Dock & Repair Co. v. Flint, 275 U.S. 303 (1927), https://supreme.justia.com/cases/federal/us/275/303/ (no recovery for purely economic losses unless the plaintiff sustained physical damage to property in which she had a proprietary interest).

30 OPA90 § 1001(32), 33 U.S.C. § 2701(32), https://www.law.cornell.edu/uscode/text/33/2701.

31 CERCLA, 42 U.S.C. § 9601, https://www.law.cornell.edu/uscode/text/42/9601. *See* Chapter 7.

32 JOEL MOSKOWITZ, ENVIRONMENTAL LIABILITY AND REAL PROPERTY TRANSACTIONS 49 (2d ed. 1995) ("[T]his liability [under Superfund] is more appropriately called 'absolute' or 'status' liability as it dispenses with the prerequisite of causation, as well as fault.").

33 Thus, the term "responsible party" is potentially misleading; a better term would be the *initially* responsible party. A design flaw in OPA90 (for which Elliott takes some responsibility as he was involved in the drafting for EPA) is that the statute allows the parties to rearrange the incentives for safety through private contracts.

34 John Broder and Helene Cooper, *Obama Vows End to 'Cozy' Oversight of Oil Industry,* N.Y. TIMES (May 14, 2010), https://www.nytimes.com/2010/05/15/us/politics/15obama.html ("President Obama on Friday angrily assailed the finger-pointing among the three companies involved in the oil spill in the Gulf of Mexico as a 'ridiculous spectacle.'").

35 Clean Water Act §§ 311(a)(25), (b)(10), 33 U.S.C. §§ 1321(a)(25), (b)(10), https://www.law.cornell.edu/uscode/text/33/1321.

36 OPA90 § 1002, 33 U.S.C. §§ 2702(b)(2)(A)-(F), https://www.law.cornell.edu/uscode/text/33/2702. The categories are (1) damages for natural resources, (2) damages or economic losses resulting from destruction of real or personal property, (3) loss of subsistence use of natural resources, (4) loss of taxes, royalties or fees by a state, a political subdivision or the national government, (5) loss of profits or earning capacity, and (6) additional costs of public services.

liabilities are in addition to and do not preempt existing liability under state and maritime law.[37]

OPA90 also created an economic incentive for a responsible party to compensate victims promptly. When assessing civil penalties for a spill, the judge has discretion to take into account the extent to which responsible parties have been forthcoming in abating the spill and compensating victims.[38] This has prompted many companies, including BP, to set up alternative dispute resolution (ADR) systems run by a mediator to compensate victims more promptly, rather than litigating cases in court.[39]

Why economic incentives don't always work

The question remains: why was OPA90 effective in reducing the number and severity of oil spills and in getting compensation paid to victims more promptly but not in preventing a massive incident such as the *Deepwater Horizon* spill? This is not the place to rehearse in detail the many factors that contributed to the *Deepwater Horizon* spill, but suffice it to say that the drilling of that particular well in water 10 000 feet deep involved complex technology and a number of mistakes combined to produce the spill. Later studies revealed that BP and its contractors omitted many cost-effective precautions that might have prevented the disaster.[40] These include, for example, a relatively inexpensive cement log bore test that would have detected that the cement lining of the well had not set and hardened properly which allowed explosive methane gas to leak into the well and rise to the surface where it caught fire.

Why didn't the company take economically efficient precautions to prevent an avoidable spill as predicted by the law and economics models? It wasn't for lack of proper incentives, both economic and

---

37 OPA90 § 1018, 33 U.S.C. §§ 2718(a), (c), https://www.law.cornell.edu/uscode/text/33/2718.

38 CWA§ 311(b)(8), 33 U.S.C. § 1321(b)(8), https://www.law.cornell.edu/uscode/text/33/1321.

39 For a critical review of the administration of BP's $20 billion victim compensation fund for the *Deepwater Horizon* spill, see David F. Partlett and Russell L. Weaver, *BP Oil Spill: Compensation, Agency Costs, and Restitution*, 68 WASH. & LEE L. REV. 1341 (2011), https://scholarlycommons. law.wlu.edu/wlulr/vol68/iss3/19/.

40 NATIONAL ACADEMY OF SCIENCES, MACONDO WELL DEEPWATER HORIZON BLOWOUT: LESSONS FOR IMPROVING OFFSHORE DRILLING SAFETY 3–9 (2012), http://www.nap.edu/down load.php?record_id=13273.

otherwise. As noted earlier, the spill cost BP and its partners a total of over $65 billion.[41] Perhaps more dramatically, a number of the people who made the mistaken decisions ended up in the water, 50 miles from shore surrounded by burning oil. The drilling company and the well owner did not take economically efficient precautions due to a lack of sufficient human *foresight* to predict accurately the consequences of taking a series of actions each with a low level of risk in itself, but which in combination have the potential to create huge damages.[42] Human beings struggle to predict risks that result from a complex combination of factors. Because of this and numerous other cognitive failures, decisionmakers do not always behave as predicted by the rational actor model of human nature that underlies traditional law and economics.[43]

There is no doubt that in the absence of proper incentives to internalize costs, regulated parties may be tempted to invest insufficiently in preventing harm to the environment. However, the converse is not necessarily true: proper incentives do not automatically guarantee that regulated entities will take all the actions necessary to prevent harm to others and the environment even when it would be economically efficient for them to do so. Rather, they are more likely to respond rationally to incentives in simple situations in which they can take discrete actions to reduce their liability—such as by cooperating in abating a spill and paying victims promptly—than in more complex situations that are more difficult for human beings to analyze accurately.[44]

The frailties of human judgment have led some to argue that technologies such as nuclear power or off-shore drilling in deep water are

41 *See supra* note 19; *see also* David M. Uhlmann, *BP paid a steep price for the Gulf oil spill but for the US a decade later, it's business as usual*, THE CONVERSATION (Apr. 23, 2020), https://theconversation.com/bp-paid-a-steep-price-for-the-gulf-oil-spill-but-for-the-us-a-decade-later-its-business-as-usual-136905.

42 *See, e.g.,* E. Donald Elliott, *The Tragi-Comedy of the Commons: Evolutionary Biology, Economics and Environmental Law*, 20 VA. ENVTL. L. J. 17 (2001), https://digitalcommons.law.yale.edu/cgi/viewcontent.cgi?article=3186&context=fss_papers (explaining environmental problems as caused not only by the absence of proper incentives such as the tragedy of the commons, but also as a failure of humans and their institutions to foresee the consequences of their actions).

43 RICHARD H. THALER AND CASS R. SUNSTEIN, NUDGE: IMPROVING DECISIONS ABOUT HEALTH, WEALTH, AND HAPPINESS (2008) (arguing humans are not "econs" who continuously estimate costs and benefits accurately as assumed by classic law and economics models); Christine Jolls, Cass R. Sunstein, and Richard H. Thaler, *A Behavioral Approach to Law and Economics*, 50 STAN. L. REV. 1471 (1998), https://papers.ssrn.com/sol3/papers.cfm?abstract_id=2292029.

44 E. Donald Elliott, *Re-Inventing Defenses/Enforcing Standards: The Next Stage of the Tort Revolution?*, 23 RUTGERS L. REV. 1069 (1991) (The Pfizer Distinguished Lecture in Tort Law).

just too complex for fallible human beings to manage safely.[45] Perhaps automated systems and artificial intelligence will eventually correct for the errors of human judgment.[46] On the other hand, others argue for a new style of regulation in which regulators try to build intelligent decisions into the regulations rather than leaving them to fallible human beings on the scene who are subject to a variety of pressures and cognitive failures. For example, in perhaps the most thoughtful of the *after action* reports on the *Deepwater Horizon* spill, a Committee of the National Academy of Sciences proposed to make the inexpensive cement log bore test that would have prevented the *Deepwater Horizon* spill mandatory rather than leaving that decision to the fallible discretion of those drilling the well.[47]

Perhaps the lesson from the *Deepwater Horizon* oil spill is that proper economic incentives are a necessary, but not always a sufficient, condition to prevent avoidable harm to the environment.

Additional resources

Boebert, Earl and Blosson, James M. (2016). *Deepwater Horizon: A Systems Analysis of the Macondo Disaster.* Cambridge, Massachusetts: Harvard University Press.

Elliott, E. Donald and Houlihan, Mary Beth (2011). *A Primer on the Law of Oil Spills.* ALI-ABA Advanced Environmental Law Conference, Washington, D.C., United States, http://ssrn.com/abstract=2007604.

Randle, Russell V. (2012). *Oil Pollution Deskbook* (2nd. ed.). Washington, DC: Environmental Law Institute, https://www.eli.org/eli-press-books/oil-pollution-deskbook-second-edition.

Safina, Carl (2011). *A Sea in Flames: The Deepwater Horizon Oil Blowout.* New York: Crown Publishers.

---

45 PETER LEHNER WITH BOB DEANS, IN DEEP WATER: THE ANATOMY OF A DISASTER, THE FATE OF THE GULF, AND ENDING OUR OIL ADDICTION (2010); CHARLES PERROW, NORMAL ACCIDENTS: LIVING WITH HIGH RISK TECHNOLOGIES (rev. ed., Princeton 1999).

46 Cary Coglianese, *A Framework for Governmental Use of Machine Learning,* ADMINISTRATIVE CONFERENCE OF THE U.S. (Dec. 7, 2020), https://www.acus.gov/report/framework-governmental-use-machine-learning-final-report.

47 NATIONAL ACADEMY OF SCIENCES, MACONDO WELL DEEPWATER HORIZON BLOWOUT: LESSONS FOR IMPROVING OFFSHORE DRILLING SAFETY 111–27 (2012), http://www.nap.edu/download.php?record_id=13273.

12 From protecting endangered species to promoting biodiversity and healthy ecosystems

As we get older and our death looms, we take comfort in the thought that our progeny and proteges will carry on after we are gone. Perhaps as a result, human beings are haunted by images of the hapless dodo bird,[1] the last passenger pigeon, or other species that have been killed off by humans. Extinction is forever—or at least so it seemed until recently.[2] Reacting to our collective abhorrence at the prospect of being responsible for the extinction of other species, Congress adopted the 1973 Endangered Species Act (ESA)[3] with the aim of protecting species from becoming extinct as a result of the effects of humans on nature. Upon signing the ESA into law, President Richard Nixon declared: "Nothing is more priceless and more worthy of preservation than the rich array of animal life with which our country has been blessed."[4]

More recent ecological research suggests, however, that the number of surviving species is not necessarily a good measure of *biodiversity* or ecosystem health.[5] As a result, the policy goals in this area of U.S. environmental law have gradually morphed from merely preserving species from extinction per se to the broader goals of preserving critical habitats and promoting healthy ecosystems in support of

---

1 The dodo bird became extinct in the seventeenth century and has become a modern symbol of the impact of human progress and development on species diversity. ENCYCLOPEDIA BRITANNICA, Dodo: extinct bird, https://www.britannica.com/animal/dodo-extinct-bird.

2 Recently, scientists have been experimenting with using cloning to recreate extinct species. *See* David Shultz, *Should we Bring Extinct Species back from the Dead?*, SCIENCE (Sep. 26, 2016), https://www.sciencemag.org/news/2016/09/should-we-bring-extinct-species-back-dead.

3 Endangered Species Act, 16 U.S.C. § 1531 *et seq.*, https://www.law.cornell.edu/uscode/text/16/chapter-35.

4 *40 Years Ago – RN Signs the Endangered Species Act*, RICHARD NIXON FOUNDATION (Dec. 28, 2013), https://www.nixonfoundation.org/2013/12/40-years-ago-rn-signs-endangered-species-act/.

5 *See* ENCYCLOPEDIA BRITANNICA, Species Richness, https://www.britannica.com/science/species-richness.

biodiversity—which refers to the scope and variety as well as genetic make-up of plants, animals, and even micro-organisms across the planet.[6]

Scientists tell us that while some species do become extinct from natural causes, the rate of extinction due to human alterations of the environment is 100 to 1000 times greater.[7] In addition, some people believe that our moral responsibilities are different if a species becomes extinct due to the activities of human beings, because we are aware of the consequences of our actions, and thus have a duty to manage our effects on other species in ways that arguably other creatures do not.[8] At the same time, many people are uncomfortable with "playing God" by deciding which species will survive and which will not. This uneasy tension is reflected in the informal term the *God Squad*, that refers to a special Cabinet-level committee set up in a 1979 amendment to ESA following the Supreme Court's (in)famous *TVA v. Hill* decision,[9] which halted construction of the Tellico dam to protect a small fish, the snail darter.[10] Made up of the heads of a number of environment-related federal government departments and agencies, the so-called God Squad is empowered to grant exceptions from the ESA and thus to determine which species survive and which will be allowed to go extinct,[11] but it has rarely been called upon to exercise this awesome power.[12]

---

6 *See* Thomas E. Lovejoy, *A Habitable Earth: Protecting Biodiversity Through Natural Systems*, in A BETTER PLANET: 40 BIG IDEAS FOR A Sustainable FUTURE 1 (Daniel C. Esty ed., 2019); *see generally* E.O. Wilson, BIODIVERSITY (1988).

7 William K. Stevens, *How Many Species Are Being Lost? Scientists Try New Yardstick*, N.Y. TIMES (July 25, 1995), https://www.nytimes.com/1995/07/25/science/how-many-species-are-being-lost-scientists-try-new-yardstick.html.

8 *See generally* E. Donald Elliott, *The Tragi-Comedy of the Commons: Evolutionary Biology, Economics and Environmental Law*, 20 VA. ENVTL. L. J. 17, 29 (2001), https://www.jstor.org/stable/24787274 ("Some even argue that because humans are the only species capable of consciously managing the environment on a worldwide scale, we have a moral responsibility to do so for the benefit of other species as well as ourselves.") (citing ROBERT ORNSTEIN AND PAUL EHRLICH, NEW WORLD NEW MIND: MOVING TOWARD CONSCIOUS EVOLUTION (1989)).

9 TVA v. Hill, 437 U.S. 153 (1978), https://supreme.justia.com/cases/federal/us/437/153/.

10 Ironically, it turned out that the snail darter was not endangered at all; we were just looking for them in the wrong place. Cass Peterson, *Darter Is Doing Swimmingly, Quits Endangered Species List*, WASHINGTON POST (Aug. 17, 1983), https://www.washingtonpost.com/archive/politics/1983/08/17/darter-is-doing-swimmingly-quits-endangered-species-list/fb84de8a-f351-4d4c-bb7d-687278a5321c/.

11 *See* Benjamin Rubin, *Calling on the "God Squad"*, NOSSMAN LLP (Apr. 23, 2014), http://bit.ly/2NNfYAw.

12 EARTHJUSTICE, CITIZENS' GUIDE TO THE ENDANGERED SPECIES ACT 39 (2017) [hereinafter, "Earthjustice, Citizens Guide"], https://earthjustice.org/sites/default/files/library/reports/Citi

Although enacted by a near-unanimous Congress in 1973, the ESA has become a flashpoint in environmental policy in recent decades. Pitched battles have broken out between environmentalists on the one hand and loggers (and other commercial interests) on the other about whether and how to balance a commitment to species protection (and now biodiversity, as a broader goal), against the economic burdens and restrictions on private property rights that such policies can impose.

How the ESA protects species

Distinguishing one species from another on a scientific basis is not always easy,[13] but the definition of a species in common parlance is a group of animals or plants that are capable of interbreeding with one another.[14] However, the ESA goes even farther and defines a *species* to include subspecies that are capable of interbreeding[15] but excludes insects regarded as pests from protection.[16] For example, some grizzly bears may be threatened with extinction, even though other brown bears with which they could interbreed are not.

The first step toward protecting a species or subspecies under the ESA is for the U.S. Fish and Wildlife Service (FWS), acting on a delegation from the Secretary of the Interior (or in a limited number of cases, the Secretary of Commerce[17]), to designate it as either an *endangered species* or a *threatened species.* An *endangered species* is defined as one "which is in danger of extinction throughout all or a significant portion

---

zens_Guide_ESA.pdf. The "God squad" was asked to exempt the snail darter from the ESA, but declined to do so. Congress then amended the statute to exempt the Tellico Dam from its reach. *Id.*

13 *Species Definition*, SCITABLE, https://www.nature.com/scitable/definition/species-312/.

14 *Species*, OXFORD ENGLISH DICTIONARY, https://www.lexico.com/en/definition/species.

15 ESA § 3(16), 16 U.S.C. § 1532(16) ("The term 'species' includes any subspecies of fish or wildlife or plants, and any distinct population segment of any species of vertebrate fish or wildlife which interbreeds when mature."), https://www.law.cornell.edu/uscode/text/16/1532.

16 ESA § 3(6), 16 U.S.C. § 1532(6) (excluding from the definition of an "endangered species" to be protected "a species of the Class *Insecta* determined by the Secretary [of Agriculture] to constitute a pest whose protection under the provisions of this chapter would present an overwhelming and overriding risk to man"), https://www.law.cornell.edu/uscode/text/16/1532.

17 The ESA is administered by the Fish and Wildlife Service in the Department of Interior for terrestrial and freshwater species and by the National Oceanographic and Atmospheric Administration in the Department of Commerce for marine species, including species that spend part of their lives in freshwater (e.g., anadromous fish).

of its range" other than certain insects that are "determined . . . to constitute a pest whose protection . . . would present an overwhelming and overriding risk to man."[18] On the other hand, a *threatened species* is defined as one "which is likely to become an endangered species within the foreseeable future throughout all or a significant portion of its range."[19] These designations are made through notice-and-comment rulemaking, often in response to citizens' petitions, and are subject to judicial review, but the consequences are different, as is explained below.

In addition, for some but not all listed species, the Secretary may also designate *critical habitat,* which are those places that are deemed *essential* to preserve in order for the species to survive.[20] Section 4(b) regarding designation of critical habitat is the only part of the ESA that expressly permits consideration of economic impacts.[21] Designation of critical habitat balances the economic impact or impact on national security against the benefits to the species from survival.[22] This balancing approach has been criticized because it seeks to compare economic impacts, usually expressed in dollars, with a more qualitative assessment of the benefits of habitat preservation, the importance of which typically depends on expert opinion.

Both those who want to see more robust protection of biodiversity and those who believe that implementation of the ESA has led to government overreach agree that more refined methods to assess the benefits from the preservation of species are needed. Today, many of those benefits are anecdotal. For example, medical researchers derived Taxol, a drug used to treat several types of cancer from

---

18 ESA § 3(6), 16 U.S.C. § 1532(6), https://www.law.cornell.edu/uscode/text/16/1532#6.
19 ESA § 3(20), 16 U.S.C. § 1532(20), https://www.law.cornell.edu/uscode/text/16/1532#20.
20 ESA § 3(5), 16 U.S.C. § 1532(5)(i), https://www.law.cornell.edu/uscode/text/16/1532#5:

    the specific areas within the geographical area occupied by the species, at the time it is listed . . . on which are found those physical or biological features (I) essential to the conservation of the species and (II) which may require special management considerations or protection; and (ii) specific areas outside the geographical area occupied by the species at the time it is listed . . . upon a determination by the Secretary that such areas are essential for the conservation of the species.

21 ESA § 4(b), 16 U.S.C. § 1533(b)(2) ("The Secretary shall designate critical habitat, . . . after taking into consideration the economic impact, the impact on national security, and any other relevant impact, of specifying any particular area as critical habitat.").
22 Critical habitat designations have been made for just over half of the 1655 species administered by FWS.

the bark of the Pacific Yew tree.[23] But what value should we place on future cancer cures or other societal advances that remain to be discovered in the as-of-yet-unexplored reaches of our planet's biological diversity?

Finally, the statute requires the government to develop and implement *recovery plans*, which are plans designed to bring listed species back to a self-sustaining state, for both threatened and endangered species, unless the government finds that for some reason a recovery plan would not promote the conservation of the species.[24] Funding for recovery plans has typically focused on *charismatic megafauna*, like gray wolves and panthers, with which people can easily identify, but many listed species are plants and invertebrates that would otherwise receive no protection, and their survival can in turn help to keep ecosystems healthy.[25]

Enforcement mechanisms

The ESA contains two primary mechanisms that give effect to the statute's goal of protecting endangered or threatened species. Section 7 requires consultation by federal agencies with the FWS or the National Marine Fisheries Service (NMFS) when their actions might affect a listed species. Section 9 prohibits anyone, including private parties, from *taking* an endangered species. In some cases, this protection extends to threatened species, as explained in more detail below.

Section 7 consultations

Under Section 7:

> [e]ach Federal agency shall, in consultation with and with the assistance of the Secretary, insure that any action authorized, funded, or carried out by such agency . . . is not likely to jeopardize the continued existence of any endangered species or threatened species or result in the destruction

---

23 *Success Story: Taxol*, NATIONAL CANCER INSTITUTE, https://dtp.cancer.gov/timeline/flash/suc cess_stories/S2_Taxol.htm#:~:text=Taxol%C2%AE%20(NSC%20125973),as%20well%20as%20 Kaposi's%20sarcoma.

24 ESA § 4(f), 16 U.S.C. § 1533(f), https://www.law.cornell.edu/uscode/text/16/1533.

25 *Endangered Species*, U.S. FISH AND WILDLIFE SERVICE, https://www.fws.gov/endangered/spe cies/us-species.html.

or adverse modification of [critical] habitat of such species ... unless such agency has been granted an exemption by the God Squad.[26]

This *no jeopardy* requirement has proven to be a surprisingly effective mechanism for forcing government agencies to take the potential effect of their actions on threatened or endangered species and critical habitats into account. The Act's simple language has been taken as a command to all federal agencies with significant consequences for how decisions get made. For example, EPA evaluates pesticide impacts on endangered species using its ecological risk assessments. But note that EPA did not regularly consult with the FWS or NMFS until 2004. In recent years, however, pesticide consultations spurred all the agencies involved to engage with the National Academy of Sciences to develop more effective impact analyses.[27]

Section 9 *take* prohibition

ESA Section 9 prohibits any *take* of an endangered species by anyone, including private parties on their own land. The statute defines this term broadly to cover all actions that "harass, harm, pursue, hunt, shoot, wound, kill, trap, capture, or collect" such species.[28] Unlike the Section 7 consultation requirement described above, which applies to both endangered and threatened species, Section 9 applies automatically only to endangered species,[29] but the statute provides FWS and NMFS discretion to extend the prohibitions to threatened species as well, by using *section 4(d) rules*.[30] Stiff

---

26 ESA § 7 (a)(2), 16 U.S.C. § 1536(a)(2), https://www.law.cornell.edu/uscode/text/16/1536.

27 Wash. Toxics Coal. v. EPA, 413 F.3d 1024 (9th Cir. 2005), https://casetext.com/case/wash-toxics-coal-v-environ-protect-agen required consultation between the EPA and the FWS, National Oceanographic, and Atmospheric Administration on 54 pesticides and started the process of instituting consultation into the pesticide regulation process. The National Academy of Sciences report changed the analysis process for these consultations. *See Implementing NAS Report Recommendations on Risk Assessment Methodology for Endangered and Threatened Species*, EPA, https://www.epa.gov/endangered-species/implementing-nas-report-recommendations-risk-assessment-methodology-endangered.

28 ESA § 3(19), 16 U.S.C. § 1532(19), https://www.law.cornell.edu/uscode/text/16/1532.

29 ESA § 4(b), 16 U.S.C. § 1538(b), https://www.law.cornell.edu/uscode/text/16/1538.

30 ESA § 4(d), 16 U.S.C. § 1538(d), https://www.law.cornell.edu/uscode/text/16/1538:

   Whenever any species is listed as a threatened species pursuant to subsection (c) of this section, the Secretary shall issue such regulations as he deems necessary and advisable to provide for the conservation of such species. The Secretary may by regulation prohibit with respect to any threatened species any act prohibited under section 9(a)(1), in the case of fish or wildlife.

criminal as well as civil penalties, including possible imprisonment, back up the take prohibition.[31]

Building on the broad statutory definition, the Interior Department and the courts have interpreted the prohibition on any take of an endangered species very broadly. In a famous Supreme Court case, *Babbitt, Secretary of the Interior v. Sweet Home Chapter of Communities for a Great Oregon*,[32] the Court upheld by a six-to-three vote an Interior Department interpretation of the word "harm" in the definition of a "take" to including logging on a company's own land if it entails "significant habitat modification or degradation where it actually kills or injures wildlife."[33] This broad interpretation has had a significant impact on private landowners and consequently has been highly controversial. Some view it as commandeering private property for species protection purposes without compensation to the affected property holders.

There is, however, one important escape hatch: a 1982 amendment to the ESA allows the Secretary to issue *incidental take* permits "if such taking is incidental to, and not the purpose of, the carrying out of an otherwise lawful activity."[34] However, an application for an

---

However, under a 1975 rule, the FWS reversed the presumption and stated that all threatened species are covered by the "take" prohibition unless the Service specifically exempts them. Proposal to Reclassify the American Alligator and Other Amendments, 40 Fed. Reg. 44,425 (Sept. 26, 1975), https://ecos.fws.gov/docs/federal_register/fr72.pdf. This rule was criticized as creating disincentives for private parties to protect threatened species because recovery from endangered to threatened status would not result in fewer restrictions. *See* Robert Gordon, *Take It Back: Extending the Endangered Species Act's "Take" Prohibition to All Threatened Animals Is Bad for Conservation*, HERITAGE FOUND. (Dec. 7, 2017), https://www.heritage.org/government-regulation/report/take-it-back-extending-the-endangered-species-acts-take-prohibition. However, FWS also developed species-specific 4(b) rules, reducing some of the protections for many threatened species. Some have argued that species-specific rules better promote species conservation than providing the same protections to both threatened and endangered species because species-specific rules provide necessary protection while also not restricting activities that do not impact the species. In 2019, the Trump Administration revised the 1975 rule to provide newly designated threatened species with protection only if FWS develops a species-specific 4(b) rule. Regulations for Prohibitions to Threatened Wildlife and Plants, 84 Fed. Reg. 44,753 (Aug. 27, 2019) (to be codified at 50 C.F.R. pt. 17), https://www.federalregister.gov/documents/2019/08/27/2019-17519/endangered-and-threatened-wildlife-and-plants-regulations-for-prohibitions-to-threatened-wildlife. Thus, today, threatened species are provided protection against "takes" by the FWS only on a case-by-case basis, but the fate of this policy under the Biden Administration remains uncertain.

31 ESA § 11, 16 U.S.C. § 1540, https://www.law.cornell.edu/uscode/text/16/1540.

32 Babbitt v. Sweet Home Chapter of Cmtys. For a Great Or., 515 U.S. 687 (1995), https://supreme.justia.com/cases/federal/us/515/687/.

33 *Id.* at 708 (quoting 50 C.F.R § 17.3).

34 ESA § 10(a)(1)(B), 16 U.S.C. § 1539(a)(i)(B), https://www.law.cornell.edu/uscode/text/16/1539.

incidental take permit must include a *habitat conservation plan* that shows how the applicant proposes to minimize the adverse effect on the endangered or threatened species.[35]

ESA controversies

Given the reach of the ESA and the fact that economic activities on private lands can be—and have been—prohibited when endangered species are threatened by the destruction of their habitat, it should perhaps come as no surprise that the law came under fire. The most notable of these controversies arose from efforts to protect the Northern Spotted Owl, which was listed as *threatened* in 1990, triggering the prospect that critical habitat might be designated covering vast swaths of timberlands in the Pacific Northwest. The threat to logging interests and lumber jobs led to significant pushback on those advocating protection for the Spotted Owl and the old-growth forests the birds occupied. The political debate that ensued over a decade led to heated debates in Congress, calls for the God Squad to be convened to override the Owl protection efforts, protests by both loggers and environmentalists (and sometimes heated confrontations across these battlelines), and demands for the ESA to be rewritten or even repealed.[36]

In the latest twist in the on-going debate over how to balance species protection and competing economic goals, the Trump Administration introduced in 2019 sweeping changes to the ESA regulations that it described as "modernizing the implementation of the ESA in order to improve collaboration, efficiency, and effectiveness."[37] Both environmental advocates and ecosystem scientists pushed back on the new regulations which they decried as weakening the ESA[38] and curtailing

---

35 ESA § 10(a)(2), 16 U.S.C. § 1539(2), https://www.law.cornell.edu/uscode/text/16/1539. For more specifics about habitat conservation plans, see *Endangered Species Habitat Conservation Plan Handbook*, FWS, https://www.fws.gov/endangered/what-we-do/hcp_handbook-chapters.html.

36 *See Spotted Owl Timeline*, FOREST HISTORY SOCIETY, https://foresthistory.org/research-explore/us-forest-service-history/policy-and-law/wildlife-management/spotted-owl-timeline/.

37 *ESA Implementation: Regulation Revisions*, U.S. FISH AND WILDLIFE SERVICE, https://www.fws.gov/endangered/improving_ESA/regulation-revisions.html [https://web.archive.org/web/2021011 6195600/https://www.fws.gov/endangered/improving_ESA/regulation-revisions.html].

38 Jonathan Lambert, *Trump Administration Weakens Endangered Species Act*, NATURE, (Aug. 12, 2019), https://www.nature.com/articles/d41586-019-02439-1; *Trump Administration Releases Regulations Endangering Imperiled Wildlife*, DEFENDERS OF WILDLIFE (Aug. 12, 2019), https://defenders.org/newsroom/trump-administration-releases-regulations-endangering-imperiled-wildlife.

the government's ability to protect species and their critical habitats.[39] During the first year of the Biden Administration, the U.S. Fish and Wildlife Service and the National Marine Fisheries Service "announced a plan to improve and strengthen implementation of the Endangered Species Act" by repealing the Trump Administration's 2019 and 2020 regulations.[40]

Evaluating the ESA

Despite the controversies, by many measures the ESA has been a great success. According to one of its prominent supporters, the environmental group Earthjustice, "[t]he protection afforded by the ESA currently extends to over 1,250 species, and most of them have completely recovered, partly recovered, had their habitat protected, or had their populations stabilized or increased as a result."[41] In addition, "[a]ccording to the FWS, as of April 2003, 541 [Habitat Conservation Plans] had been approved, covering approximately 38 million acres and involving more than 525 endangered or threatened species."[42]

Another environmental NGO, the Center for Biological Diversity, argues that the ESA has been a "wild success" and observes:

> The Endangered Species Act is the strongest law for protecting biodiversity passed by any nation. . . . Currently the Act protects more than 1,600 plant and animal species in the United States and its territories, many of which are successfully recovering. Over the past four-plus decades, the Endangered Species Act has repeatedly demonstrated that—when used to the full extent of the law—it works. The Act has been more than 99 percent successful at preventing extinction. Were it not for the Act, scientists have estimated, at least 227 species would have likely gone extinct since the law's passage in 1973.[43]

39 Ya-Wei Li, et al. *Species Protection will take more than Rule Reversal*, 370 SCIENCE 665 (6 November 2020). https://science.sciencemag.org/content/370/6517/665.abstract.

40 *ESA Implementation: Regulation Revisions*, U.S. FISH AND WILDLIFE SERVICE, https://www.fws.gov/endangered/improving_ESA/regulation-revisions.html.

41 Earthjustice, Citizens Guide at 5.

42 Earthjustice, Citizens Guide at 35.

43 *The Endangered Species Act: A Wild Success*, CENTER FOR BIOLOGICAL DIVERSITY, https://www.biologicaldiversity.org/campaigns/esa_wild_success/.

On the other hand, critics argue that most of the attention under the ESA has focused on protecting *charismatic megafauna* that appeal to humans, whereas it might have been better to focus on maintaining healthy ecosystems that support biodiversity rather than centering policy efforts on preserving individual species.[44] For example, the International Union for Conservation of Nature (IUCN) recognizes the need for ecosystem protection in addition to threatened and endangered species protection.[45] Ecology teaches the two cannot really be separated, because the more diverse habitats that are available, the more species that can be supported.[46]

Biodiversity as a critical policy focus

Scientists have recently identified threats to biodiversity as one of the critical *planetary boundaries* at risk of being transgressed by human impacts with potentially profound consequences for life on Earth as the "safe operating space for humanity" gets overstepped.[47] In parallel, frustration has mounted with the narrow focus of the ESA and the lack of policy tools to promote biodiversity more broadly. In response to growing documentation of the loss of biodiversity,[48] environmental groups and their science partners have pushed the issue up the policy agenda. Some of the biodiversity activists launched the *Half-Earth Project*, which aims to set aside half of the land and oceans as protected areas that would provide sufficient habitat to avoid further biodiversity loss.[49]

---

44 *See generally* Edward O. Wilson, *The Biological Diversity Crisis: Despite unprecedented extinction rates, the extent of biological diversity remains unmeasured*, 35 BIOSCIENCE 700 (1985), https://liberiafti.files.wordpress.com/2013/08/wilson_biological-diversity-crisis.pdf; *see also* Damian Carrington, *What is Biodiversity and why does it Matter to us?*, THE GUARDIAN (Mar. 12, 2018), https://www.theguardian.com/news/2018/mar/12/what-is-biodiversity-and-why-does-it-matter-to-us.

45 *IUCN Red List for Ecosystems*, INTERNATIONAL UNION FOR CONSERVATION OF NATURE, https://www.iucn.org/sites/dev/files/content/documents/rle_2pager_nov18_final.pdf.

46 *See* Marc W. Cadotte, Kelly Carscadden, and Nicholas Mirotchnick, *Beyond Species: Functional Diversity and the Maintenance of Processes and Services*, 48 J. ECOLOGY 1079 (2011), https://besjournals.onlinelibrary.wiley.com/doi/full/10.1111/j.1365-2664.2011.02048.x.

47 Johan Rockstrom et al., *A Safe Operating Space for Humanity*, SCIENCE (23 Sept. 2009); *see generally* JOHAN ROCKSTROM AND MATTIAS KLUM, BIG WORLD, SMALL PLANET: ABUNDANCE WITHIN PLANETARY BOUNDARIES (2015).

48 ELIZABETH KOLBERT, THE SIXTH EXTINCTION: AN UNNATURAL HISTORY (2014); *see also* IUCN, WILDLIFE IN A CHANGING WORLD: AN ANALYSIS OF THE 2008 IUCN RED LIST OF THREATENED SPECIES (Jean-Christophe Vie, et al., eds. 2009).

49 EDWARD O. WILSON, HALF-EARTH: OUR PLANET'S FIGHT FOR LIFE (2016).

Private initiatives to preserve species

Recognizing the limits of the ESA, private parties have launched a number of efforts to promote species recovery. The Sage Grouse Initiative,[50] for example, provides an innovative approach to protecting a species at risk of becoming threatened but not yet listed under the ESA. Specifically, it provides that farmers and ranchers who voluntarily maintain grouse conservation strategies for thirty years will be considered by the FWS to comply with any future ESA requirements if the sage grouse is eventually listed. Over eight million acres of grouse habitat in public and private lands have been protected under this public-private cooperative agreement.

Recent ESA policy changes

The Trump Administration revised several aspects of endangered species regulations and weakened some of the law's protections.[51] In particular, the Trump regulations redefined *critical habitat* to require "resources to support at least one life process" already be present in the habitat rather than considering a species' entire historical range. The new rules also limited the circumstances in which threatened species would be provided the same protections against *takes* as endangered species. In addition, the criteria for designating recovery were loosened such that species are considered *recovered* without achieving all the indicators of healthy populations. Many, if not all, of these changes are likely to be revisited by the Biden Administration, with the U.S. Fish and Wildlife Service and the National Marine Fisheries Service proposing in 2021 a rollback of these regulations.[52] As with other policy areas where the Trump Administration has been seen as rolling back environmental protection, the role of states has come

---

50 *Tracking Success 2016 Report*, THE SAGE GROUSE INITIATIVE, https://www.sagegrouseinitiative. com/report/; *see also BLM Drops Sage-Grouse Habitat from Oil & Gas Auction*, INSIDE ENERGY & ENVIRONMENT (Nov. 8, 2018), https://www.insideenergyandenvironment.com/2018/11/blm-drops-sage-grouse-habitat-from-oil-gas-auction/.

51 Katie Bleau, *Biodiversity on the Brink: The Consequences of a Weakened Endangered Species Act*, YALE ENV'T REV. (Jan. 28, 2020), https://environment-review.yale.edu/biodiversity-brink-consequences-weakened-endangered-species-act.

52 *ESA Implementation: Regulation Revisions*, *supra* note 40.

into sharper focus as many have substantial state law protections for endangered species and wildlife more broadly.[53]

International efforts to protect species and promote biodiversity

Concerns about species loss and diminished biodiversity stretch across national boundaries—both because some species move across borders and because the loss of a species anywhere is a loss to humankind. As discussed below, the Convention on International Trade in Endangered Species of Wild Fauna and Flora (CITES) provides an international analogue to the domestic ESA, with 183 signatory countries now working together to protect endangered and threatened species. And global efforts to promote biodiversity led to the creation in 1992 of a Convention on Biological Diversity (CBD).

CITES Convention

Negotiated in the wake of the first *Earth Summit* in Stockholm in 1972, CITES regulates trade in endangered or threatened species as identified in an annex to the agreement that builds on the IUCN's *Red List*, which inventories the conservation status of species across the globe. As a party to CITES, the United States prevents import, export, or re-export of any ESA-listed species.[54] Similarly, the Migratory Bird Treaty Act protects the take (killing, capturing, trading, selling, transporting) of migratory birds without prior authorization from the FWS.[55] The Act applies to both intentional and non-intentional take.

Convention on Biological Diversity

After years of rising concern in the scientific world, the environmental community, and some policy circles that the species focus of CITES did not fully address the need to protect biodiversity, in 1988 the UN Environment Programme[56] launched a working group to address the

---

53 Eric Biber, *A Survey of State Wildlife and Endangered Species Protections*, IDAHO L. REV (2020). https://lawcat.berkeley.edu/record/1181395.

54 ESA § 11, 16 U.S.C. § 1540, https://www.law.cornell.edu/uscode/text/16/1540.

55 Migratory Bird Treaty Act, 16 U.S.C. § 703, https://www.law.cornell.edu/uscode/text/16/703.

56 For more on the history and role of UNEP, see MARIA IVANOVA, THE UNTOLD STORY OF THE WORLD'S LEADING ENVIRONMENTAL INSTITUTION: UNEP AT FIFTY (2021).

problem. This process led to international negotiations that produced the Convention on Biological Diversity (CBD), which was introduced at the 1992 Earth Summit in Rio de Janeiro. Now with 196 members and a secretariat based in Montreal, the CBD builds on the idea that biodiversity is a "common concern of humankind" and important to conserve across the world. Implementation of the agreement centers on National Biodiversity Strategies and Action Plans that each member nation is asked to develop, as well as national reports on their biodiversity efforts that countries periodically submit. The United States has signed but not ratified the CBD, so its provisions are not binding in the United States.[57] U.S. ratification of the CBD became a victim of the partisan break over the environment that emerged in 1992 and the suggestion that the intellectual property provision of the proposed Convention might obstruct biotechnology progress. Specifically, opponents of the agreement declared that the CBD would "coerce the transfer of technology by the United States and other developed countries to the developing countries."[58] This dispute illustrates once again the continuing controversy over how to balance commercial development and the protection of nature.

Additional resources

Earthjustice (2017). *A Citizens' Guide to the Endangered Species Act*. https://earthjustice.
org/sites/default/files/library/reports/Citizens_Guide_ESA.pdf.
Kolbert, Elizabeth (2014). *The Sixth Extinction: An Unnatural History*. New York, N.Y.:
Henry Holt and Company.
Lovejoy, Thomas and Lee, Hannah (2019). *Biodiversity and Climate Change:
Transforming the Biosphere*. New Haven, C.T.: Yale University Press.
Rockström, Johan and Klum, Mattias (2015). *Big World, Small Planet: Abundance within
Planetary Boundaries*. New Haven, C.T.: Yale University Press.
U.S. Fish and Wildlife (1998). *Endangered Species Consultation Handbook*. https://www.
fws.gov/endangered/esa-library/pdf/esa_section7_handbook.pdf.
Goble, Dale et al. (eds.) (2017). *Wildlife Law: Cases and Materials*. (3rd ed.). Foundation
Press.

---

57 For an excellent account of the history of the CBD and the reasons that the United States remains
the only notable country in the world not to ratify it, see *Robert F. Blomquist, Ratification Resisted:
Understanding America's Response to the Convention on Biological Diversity, 1989–2002*, 32
GOLDEN GATE U. L. REV. 493 (2002), http://digitalcommons.law.ggu.edu/ggulrev/vol32/iss4/5.
58 138 Cong. Rec. S 8375 (daily ed. June 17, 1992) (statement of Sen. Nickles), https://www.govinfo.
gov/app/details/GPO-CRECB-1992-pt25/GPO-CRECB-1992-pt25-1/context.

13 National parks and wilderness preservation: "America's best idea"[1]

Setting aside lands as a natural area for the enjoyment of the public and the benefit of future generations is an idea that originated in America and has now been emulated around the world.[2] Perhaps there is nothing more emblematic of the environmental movement than wilderness preservation. In the latter half of the nineteenth century, expeditions returning from the West captured the public's imagination with photographs and accounts of an ecosystem largely unaffected by humans that was vastly different from the Eastern United States.[3] Prominent naturalists and conservatists[4] wrote of the spiritual renewal afforded by nature and argued for preserving some of it before it was destroyed. By 1872, when Congress established our first national park, Yellowstone, as a "public park or pleasuring ground for the benefit and enjoyment of the people," the western frontier was already vanishing as population increased and moved west.[5] Congress provided that the timber, mineral deposits, and natural wonders within the park were to be preserved, but also mandated the construction of roads, bridal paths, and accommodations for visitors. From the first to the most recent park, an uneasy tension exists between preservation and promotion of other uses.

By 1916, Congress had established thirty-five national parks and monuments.[6] The creation of the National Park Service (NPS) replaced

---

1 Ken Burns and Dayton Duncan, THE NATIONAL PARKS: AMERICA'S BEST IDEA (PBS 2009).

2 For a brief history, see *Origin of the National Park Idea*, NPS, https://www.nps.gov/articles/npshistory-origins.htm.

3 This rich history is documented in Steven Ives (Director) & Ken Burns (Executive Producer), THE WEST: A PBS MINISERIES (PBS 1996).

4 Henry David Thoreau, who advocated nature preserves in *The Maine Woods* and John Muir, who eloquently described the spiritual experience of nature in his many books and articles, are two of the early influential writers.

5 Yellowstone National Park Protection Act, 16 U.S.C. § 21, https://www.law.cornell.edu/uscode/text/16/21.

6 The difference between national parks and national monuments turns on the reason for which the federal government sets the land aside. "National parks are protected due to their scenic,

the patchwork management of these lands by the War Department, Interior Department and Forest Service with more uniform management. The parks are to "conserve the scenery, natural and historic objects, and wild life in the System units and to provide for the enjoyment of the . . . [same] in such manner . . . as will leave them unimpaired for the enjoyment of future generations."[7] The dual nature of parks as places of solitary contemplation of nature as well as tourist destinations creates tension and sometimes active conflict between these competing uses. Setting aside land as a *park* requires a compromise between allowing people to use and enjoy the land and providing solitude and untouched *wilderness*.[8] The notion that the parks should be used to meet nature on its own terms and allow a visitor to become a better person influences the types of amenities and public access provided in some parks.[9] Managing these federal lands therefore requires a delicate balance between preservation and recreation.

Establishing a new national park may require compromise between the Park Service and the surrounding community, resulting in allowing some uses to facilitate park formation. National parks may permit hunting and fishing on park lands. Mining claims and oil and gas rights that predate the formation of a park remain valid, as do grazing rights predating the park.[10]

Private *inholdings*, lands under private ownership within the boundaries of a national park, are common and can be quite extensive in Western states and Alaska. The Park Service's longstanding policy has

---

inspirational, education, and recreational value. National monuments have objects of historical, cultural, and/or scientific interest, so their content is quite varied." Ashley M. Biggers, *The Difference Between National Parks and Monuments*, OUTSIDE (Mar. 13, 2019), https://www.outsideonline.com/1785161/whats-difference-between-national-parks-and-national-monuments#:~:text=The%20primary%20difference%20lies%20in,their%20content%20is%20quite%20varied.

7 National Park Service Organic Act, 54 U.S.C.§ 100101(a), https://www.law.cornell.edu/uscode/text/54/100101.

8 In his iconic book, *Walden; or, Life in the Woods*, Thoreau celebrates not just the value of wilderness, but also of *wildness*, declaring: "In Wildness is the preservation of the world." HENRY DAVID THOREAU, WALDEN; OR, LIFE IN THE WOODS (1995).

9 For an excellent presentation of preservationist view of park management, even at the expense of limiting visitors and the range of their experiences, see JOHN SAX, MOUNTAINS WITHOUT HANDRAILS (1980), https://www.nps.gov/parkhistory/online_books/sax/.

10 Pub.L 113-287 and 43 C.F.R. § 3811.2-2 (preserving existing mining claims in the National Parks); 36 C.F.R. § 9, Subpart B (regulating oil and gas extraction in the National Parks); 16 U.S.C. § 3 (preserving existing grazing rights).

been that the Park Service may regulate activities on such inholdings. However, the question of whether and to what the extent the federal government can regulate private property in the national parks has not yet been definitively resolved by the Supreme Court. Exceptions to the Park Service policy have arisen on a case-by-case basis. Congress may limit the Park Service's regulatory power by setting up alternative systems.[11] Hunting may not be banned on private lands within a park even when it is prohibited on park land.[12]

The degree to which the Park Service permits commercial operations and recreational facilities is a continuing source of controversy which only increases as parks have become more crowded. Notable conflicts have arisen over the use of motorized vehicles in parks (snowmobiles in Yellowstone, motorized rafts in and aircraft flights over the Grand Canyon) and wildlife management (invasive species control, reintroduction of wolves, interactions between park animals and agriculture). Adjacent landowners can affect parks through their land uses outside the park border.[13]

Congress is vested with plenary power over land owned by the federal government by the Property Clause of the U.S. Constitution.[14] This provision provides a significant source of power because the federal government owns roughly 640 million acres, about 28 percent of the land in the United States, and the percentages of federal land ownership are even higher in many of the states west of the Mississippi River.[15] Congress delegated to the President the power to designate

---

11 Sturgeon v. Frost, 139 S. Ct. 1066 (2019) (finding the Alaska National Interest Lands Conservation Act (ANILCA) limits the regulatory power of the National Park Service in Alaska to only public lands (lands to which the United States holds title) and not to hovercraft operation on the state-owned Nation River), https://casetext.com/case/sturgeon-v-frost-4.

12 Defenders of Wildlife v. Everson, 984 F.3d 918 (10th Cir. 2020) (upholding an exemption from federal hunting regulations over private lands within the park on the grounds that Wyoming retained jurisdiction over them), https://casetext.com/case/defenders-of-wildlife-v-everson.

13 See, e.g., Adjacent Land Use, NPS, https://www.nps.gov/im/guln/adjacent-landuse.htm. Another example is fertilizer use by farmers in the Everglades Agricultural Area resulting in high phosphorus concentration water flowing into Everglades National Park and changing the vegetation.

14 U.S. Const. art. IV, sec. 3, cl. 2 ("The Congress shall have Power to dispose of and make all needful Rules and Regulations respecting the Territory or other Property belonging to the United States; . . . "), https://constitution.congress.gov/browse/essay/artIV_S3_C2_1_1/ALDE_ 00001172/#:~:text=The%20Congress%20shall%20have%20Power,or%20of%20any%20partic ular%20State.

15 Carol H. Vincent et. al., Cong. Rsch. Serv., R42346, Federal Land Ownership: Overview and Data (2020), https://fas.org/sgp/crs/misc/R42346.pdf.

"historic landmarks, historic and prehistoric structures, or other objects of historic or scientific interest" as national monuments.[16] Thus, the President can act quickly to preserve land that could be irreparably altered by currently permissible activities. Proclamation of national monuments can be controversial due to their size, inclusion of non-federal lands, and the restrictions on commercial development imposed on areas designated as national monuments. Congress can modify national monuments, but it is unsettled whether the President is authorized to reduce the size of a national monument designated by a previous President.[17]

Preserving wilderness

Aldo Leopold, an influential conservationist and author, was instrumental in persuading the Forest Service to establish the Gila wilderness area in New Mexico, the nation's first land dedicated to preserving wilderness.[18] Shortly thereafter, the Forest Service began designating areas where transportation, subsistence, and habitation were of primitive means as wilderness areas.[19] The Wilderness Act of 1964[20] replaced decades of piecemeal wilderness preservation accomplished using agency regulations with a congressionally-mandated wilderness standard. The Act defines a wilderness as "an area where the earth and its community of life are untrammeled by man, where man himself is a visitor who does not remain."[21] It is an area of undeveloped federal

---

16 For an excellent review of Presidential powers to establish national monuments, see CAROL H. VINCENT, CONG. RSCH. SERV., R41330, NATIONAL MONUMENTS AND THE ANTIQUITIES ACT (2018). https://fas.org/sgp/crs/misc/R41330.pdf.

17 For example, in 2017 President Trump purported to reduce the size of two national monuments in Utah by two million acres. Julie Turkewitz, *Trump Slashes Size of Bears Ears and Grand Staircase Monuments*, N.Y TIMES (Dec. 24, 2017), https://www.nytimes.com/2017/12/04/us/trump-bears-ears.html. His action was challenged in court and on his first day in office, President Biden promised to revisit the issue. Brian Maffly et al., *President Joe Biden starts process to restore Utah's national monuments*, SALT LAKE TRIB. (Jan. 20, 2021), https://www.sltrib.com/news/environment/2021/01/20/biden-starts-process/.

18 Gila Wilderness Area was established in 1924 and became the wilderness area included in the National Wilderness Preserve System created by the Wilderness Act of 1964.

19 For a brief history of wilderness preservation history of the Forest Service, see Tom Tidwell, Chief, Forest Service, Speech at the 31st Annual Frank Church Conference on Public Affairs: "Wilderness: America's Heritage" (Oct. 20, 2014), https://www.fs.usda.gov/speeches/americas-wilderness-proud-heritage.

20 The Wilderness Act of 1964, 16 U.S.C. §§ 1131 *et seq*, https://www.law.cornell.edu/uscode/text/16/chapter-23.

21 16 U.S.C. § 1131(c).

land where commercial enterprise, permanent roads, mechanized transportation, and structures are prohibited, but the wilderness is not necessarily pristine and totally unaffected by humans.[22]

The Act immediately designated 9.1 million acres as wilderness areas in a new National Wilderness Preserve System. Wilderness areas are managed by the four federal land management agencies—National Park Service, Bureau of Land Management, Fish and Wildlife Service, and the Forest Service—in accordance with the unique agency purpose. These agencies inventoried their lands to identify wilderness candidates that Congress could later designate.

Commercial enterprises are prohibited in wilderness areas.[23] The degree to which humans should leave these wilderness areas alone, even if the lack of intervention results in drastic changes to the plants and animals living there, is increasingly important as climate change threatens to shift vegetation and animal ranges.

The Roadless Rule

Treatment of federal lands that are not yet protected as wilderness areas but might be so designated in the future is a perennial source of controversy because it pits federal versus state control over local land uses.[24] The 1976 Federal Land Policy and Management Act (FLPMA)[25] requires the Bureau of Land Management to manage its candidate wilderness areas so as not to impair their suitability for preservation as wilderness. The Forest Service took a different approach with the candidate wilderness areas under its jurisdiction, *inventoried roadless areas*. Historically new roads were allowed to be built in 2.8 million acres of inventoried roadless areas which made them less desirable to preserve as wilderness. That stopped in 2001 when the Clinton Administration issued the *Roadless Rule*[26] prohibiting new roads and timber harvesting

---

22 For example, the use of aircraft or motorboats is allowed where those uses were already established and existing mining claims and grazing established prior to the Wilderness Act are also permitted.

23 Wilderness Society Alaska Center v. U.S. Fish & Wildlife Service, 316 F.3d 913 (9th Cir. 2003) (finding that stocking a wilderness lake with millions of salmon fry is a commercial enterprise prohibited by the Wilderness Act).

24 Peter A. Appel, *Wilderness and the Court*, 29 STAN. ENVTL. L.J. 62 (2010), https://digitalcom mons.law.uga.edu/fac_artchop/798/.

25 Federal Land Policy and Management Act of 1976, 43 U.S.C. § 1701 *et seq.*

26 Special Areas; Roadless Area Conservation, 66 Fed. Reg. 3244 (Jan. 12, 2011) (to be codified at 36 C.F.R. pt. 294), https://www.law.cornell.edu/cfr/text/36/part-294.

using mechanized vehicles on an estimated 58.5 million acres of undeveloped federal lands.[27] As a concession to local interests in land management, however, the Roadless Rule allowed states to petition the Secretary of the Department of Agriculture (USDA) to remove the roadless designation and permit uses that would otherwise be prohibited. A number of states filed such petitions, which has resulted in litigation with varying outcomes.[28]

In 2018, Alaska filed a petition requesting an exemption to allow logging in the Tongass National Forest, our largest national forest covering approximately 17 million acres. The Tongass serves as an enormous carbon sink as well as home to approximately 70 000 people, including the state capital Juneau.[29] Following the preparation of an EIS concluding that there would be no significant effect on the human environment from granting the petition,[30] on October 28, 2020 the USDA under President Trump granted Alaska's request to exempt the Tongass National Forest from the Roadless Rule.[31] However, a lawsuit challenging the exemption was filed soon thereafter[32] and on his first day in office, President Biden directed the USDA to reconsider exempting the Tongass from the Roadless Rule.[33]

---

27 *2001 Roadless Rule*, U.S. Forest Service, https://www.fs.usda.gov/roadmain/roadless/2001road lessrule#:~:text=The%202001%20Roadless%20Rule%20establishes,on%20National%20Forest%20 System%20lands.

28 Organized Vill. of Kake v. United States Dep't of Agric., 795 F.3d 956 (9th Cir. 2015) (holding the USDA failed to provide a reasoned explanation for exempting the Tongass National Forest from the Roadless Rule), https://casetext.com/case/organized-vill-of-kake-v-us-dept-of-agric-3; Jayne v. Rey, 780 F. Supp. 2d 1099 (D. Idaho 2011) (holding the Idaho Roadless Rule, "which opened over 5,000 acres of roadless areas to road construction for phosphate mining," was not arbitrary and capricious), https://casetext.com/case/jayne-v-rey; High Country Conservation Advocates v. U.S. Forest Serv., 951 F.3d 1217 (10th Cir. 2020) (finding the Forest Service's promulgation of an exemption to the roadless rule of a coal mining area violated NEPA and the APA), https://casetext.com/case/high-country-conservation-advocates-v-us-forest-serv-5.

29 *Tracking Deregulation in the Trump Era – Alaska Roadless Rule*, Brookings (Feb. 1, 2020), https://www.brookings.edu/interactives/tracking-deregulation-in-the-trump-era/.

30 *Id*. For an explanation of EISs and findings of no significant impact (FONSIs), see Chapter 14.

31 *USDA Exempts Tongass National Forest from the 2001 Roadless Rule*, USDA (Oct. 28, 2020), https://www.usda.gov/media/press-releases/2020/10/28/usda-exempts-tongass-national-forest-2001-roadless-rule.

32 Yereth Rosen, *Lawsuit challenges Trump's lifting of roadless rule in Alaska's Tongass forest*, Reuters (Dec. 23, 2020), https://www.reuters.com/article/us-environment-alaska-forest/law suit-challenges-trumps-lifting-of-roadless-rule-in-alaskas-tongass-forest-idUSKBN28Y06L.

33 Dana Zigmund, *Conservationists welcome Biden's Roadless Rule review order Local conservation group reacts to news, looks to the future*, Juneau Empire (Jan. 22, 2021), https://www.juneauem pire.com/news/conservationists-welcome-bidens-roadless-rule-review/.

Private preservation

In addition to these efforts by government to preserve wilderness, private organizations called *land trusts* promote conservation goals by buying and preserving private lands, primarily through a legal device called a *conservation easement*, "a voluntary, legal agreement that permanently limits uses of the land in order to protect its conservation values."[34] Land trusts can be found in all fifty states, some operating in a single community, others on a regional basis, and some nationally. A recent census by the Land Trust Alliance, an umbrella organization serving as the "voice of the land trust community,"[35] identified 1363 land trusts across the nation.[36]

One such organization, The Nature Conservancy (TNC), has over one million members and funds conservation efforts in all fifty states. With billions of dollars spent in recent decades, TNC has protected more than 119 million acres (48 million hectares) of land and thousands of miles of rivers.[37] Because of their voluntary nature, some see efforts by TNC and other private organizations to preserve land as less controversial than mandatory actions by the federal government that override the authority of state and local governments to regulate land uses but others criticize its efforts because they do not necessarily require maintaining the land as wilderness.

But without question, private conservation efforts now supplement federal and state government parks, forests, monuments, and wilderness areas all across the nation in important ways. As Larry Selzer, President and CEO of the Conservation Fund, another major land trust, recently observed: "if we are to conserve the vast important landscapes needed to protect biodiversity and water quality and become more resilient to climate change, land conservation is likely to focus

---

34 *What is a Conservation Easement?* NATIONAL CONSERVATION EASEMENT DATABASE, https://www.conservationeasement.us/what-is-a-conservation-easement/#:~:text=A%20conserva tion%20easement%20is%20a,a%20property%20for%20future%20generations.

35 *What We Do*, LAND TRUST ALLIANCE, https://www.landtrustalliance.org/what-we-do.

36 LAND TRUST ALLIANCE, https://www.landtrustalliance.org/number-accredited-land-trusts-reaches-milestone#:~:text=There%20are%201%2C363%20land%20trusts,by%20the%20Land%20Trust%20Alliance.

37 *Accountability*, THE NATURE CONSERVANCY, https://www.nature.org/en-us/about-us/who-we-are/accountability/#:~:text=The%20Nature%20Conservancy%20is%20one,100%20marine%20conservation%20projects%20globally.

less on fee ownership by public agencies and more on conservation easements on . . . private lands."[38]

Wild and scenic rivers

The Wild and Scenic Rivers Act[39] created the Wild and Scenic Rivers System to preserve certain rivers with outstanding natural, cultural, or recreational values in a free-flowing condition. The Act is a reaction to a series of water management projects and impoundments. Rivers are protected from impoundments. Congressional designation, or state nomination with the approval of the Secretary of the Interior, adds rivers to the system. Candidate rivers are studied by the Secretary of Interior or Secretary of Agriculture to determine suitability for designation. The four federal land management agencies, states, tribes, and NGOs may be designated as managers of rivers. Rivers can be designated as wild, scenic, or recreational. Protection is afforded to congressionally-designated rivers while they are being studied.

The Act requires the appropriate federal land manager to create a comprehensive management plan for protected river segments and requires boundary setting. Legal challenges involve whether a comprehensive management plan was sufficient or existed and whether boundary setting was adequate.

In a little over 150 years, the United States created a system of laws to preserve a portion of Aldo Leopold's "blank spots on the map" and John Muir's natural cathedrals of spiritual renewal, as well as the National Forests and rangelands that are subject to multiple uses and sustainable yield. The legacy of the early preservation and conservation movement remains for the public to enjoy in over 109 million acres of National Wilderness Preserves, 84 million acres of national parks and monuments, 193 million acres of National Forests and Grasslands, 245 million Bureau of Land Management acres, 94 million acres of wildlife refuges, and 12,700 miles of wild and scenic rivers.[40] Stressors

---

38 Larry Selzer, *The Future of Conservation in America*, in A BETTER PLANET: 40 BIG IDEAS FOR A SUSTAINABLE FUTURE (Daniel C. Esty ed., 2019).

39 For an excellent summary of the Act, see SANDRA L. JOHNSON AND LAURA B. COMAY, CONG. RSCH. SERV., R42614, THE NATIONAL WILD AND SCENIC RIVERS SYSTEM: A BRIEF OVERVIEW (2015), https://nationalaglawcenter.org/wp-content/uploads//assets/crs/R42614.pdf.

40 *Wilderness*, U.S. FOREST SERVICE, http://bit.ly/3aZ81AZ; *How Many National Parks are There?*, NATIONAL PARK FOUNDATION, http://bit.ly/3bI1ryo; *National Forests on the Edge:*

originating outside the park or wilderness borders will stimulate debate
on what elements of place define a wilderness and whether the concept of wilderness requires preservation of specific plants and animals.
Under current management strategies, dramatic changes in species
composition may occur as climates change and habitats become more
fragmented.

Additional resources

Leopold, Aldo (1949). *A Sand County Almanac: And Sketches Here and There.* Oxford:
     Oxford University Press.
National Park Service (n.d.). https://www.nps.gov/index.htm.
Sax, Joseph L. (1980). *Mountains Without Handrails: Reflections on the National Parks.*
     Ann Arbor, Michigan: University of Michigan Press, https://www.nps.gov/parkhis
     tory/online_books/sax/.
Selzer, Larry (2019). The Future of Conservation in America. In Daniel Esty (Ed.), *A
     Better Planet: 40 Big Ideas for a Sustainable Future* (pp. 38–45). New Haven,
     Connecticut: Yale University Press.
The Wilderness Society (n.d.). The Wilderness Act. https://www.wilderness.org/arti
     cles/article/wilderness-act.

Development Pressures on America's National Forests and Grasslands, U.S. FOREST SERVICE,
http://bit.ly/30oLuok; *8 Things You Didn't Know About the Bureau of Land Management*, U.S.
DEPARTMENT OF THE INTERIOR (July 13, 2017), https://on.doi.gov/3r2YHlm; *America's National
Wildlife Refuge System*, U.S. FISH & WILDLIFE SERVICE, https://www.fws.gov/refuges100/facts/
Wilderness%20FACT%20SHEET.pdf; *Wild & Scenic Rivers*, U.S. FOREST SERVICE, http://bit.
ly/2ZWiUxa.

14 NEPA and information disclosure: techniques copied around the world

Success of a statute can be measured in different ways, but one is whether the basic idea—the *meme*[1]—is copied elsewhere. By that standard, the first U.S. environmental law of the modern era, the *National Environmental Policy Act of 1969* (NEPA),[2] has been a rousing success; it has been copied by over 100 other countries, international organizations, and development banks around the world.[3]

NEPA: National Policy and Environmental Impact Assessment

NEPA did several things:

(1) Declared a national policy that all government departments and agencies should take the environment into account "to the fullest extent possible" in making all decisions and in administering all statutes and regulations;[4]
(2) Proclaimed that "[t]he Congress recognizes that each person should enjoy a healthful environment and that each person has a responsibility to contribute to the preservation and enhancement of the environment."[5]

---

1 *Meme*, MERRIAM-WEBSTER, https://www.merriam-webster.com/dictionary/meme.
2 National Environmental Policy Act of 1969, 42 U.S.C. §§ 4331–4370. Although its official title is the National Environmental Policy Act of *1969*, President Nixon actually signed NEPA into law 1 January 1970.
3 *International Environmental Impact Assessment*, COUNCIL ON ENVIRONMENTAL QUALITY, https://ceq.doe.gov/get-involved/international_impact_assessment.html.
4 NEPA § 102, 42 U.S.C § 4332, https://www.law.cornell.edu/uscode/text/42/4332.
5 NEPA § 101(c), 42 U.S.C. § 4331(c), https://www.law.cornell.edu/uscode/text/42/4331. For an exploration of how a system of environmental law based on the right to a healthful environment would be different, see Daniel C. Esty and *Law*, NYU ENVTL. L.J. (forthcoming 2021), https://ssrn.com/abstract=3762022.

(3) Established a White House office for the environment, the Council on Environmental Quality (CEQ);[6]
(4) Provided, almost as an after-thought, that all recommendations for "major Federal actions significantly affecting the quality of the human environment . . . [shall be accompanied by] a detailed statement[7] by the responsible official on—

  (i)   the environmental impact of the proposed action,
  (ii)   any adverse environmental effects which cannot be avoided should the proposal be implemented,
  (iii) alternatives to the proposed action,
  (iv)   the relationship between local short-term uses of man's environment and the maintenance and enhancement of long-term productivity, and
  (v)   any irreversible and irretrievable commitments of resources which would be involved in the proposed action should it be implemented."[8]

Interestingly, both (1) above, the declaration of national policy, a legal device which is sometimes called a "super-mandate,"[9] and (2) the recognition of a right to a *healthful environment* have become virtual *dead letters*. Today these declarations of national policy have little or no effect on most agencies of government, which are often not even aware of their existence, probably because a strong enforcement mechanism did not back them up.

---

6 NEPA §§ 111–117, 42 U.S.C. §§ 4341–4347, https://www.law.cornell.edu/uscode/text/42/chapter-55/subchapter-II.

7 Note that the meaning and scope of almost every word in this sentence—"major," "federal," "significantly," and "human"—has been litigated. *See, e.g.*, NORML v. Dep't of State, 452 F. Supp. 1226 (D.D.C. 1978), https://law.justia.com/cases/federal/district-courts/FSupp/452/1226/2302948/ (finding the United States' participation in herbicide spraying of marijuana and poppy plants in Mexico is a "major" federal action); Silva v. Romney, 473 F.2d 287 (1st Cir. 1973), https://law.justia.com/cases/federal/appellate-courts/F2/473/287/226057/ (holding a private developer's HUD mortgage guarantee established sufficient "contact" with a federal agency to create a "federal action"); Save Our Ten Acres v. Kreger, 472 F.2d 463 (5th Cir. 1973), https://law.justia.com/cases/federal/appellate-courts/F2/472/463/368283/ (analyzing whether the impact of a proposed building would "significantly" affect the environment); Metro. Edison Co. v. People Against Nuclear Energy, 460 U.S. 766, 772 (1983), https://supreme.justia.com/cases/federal/us/460/766/ (concluding Congress's intent in using the term "human environment" referred only to the "physical environment").

8 NEPA § 102, 42 U.S.C. § 4332(C), https://www.law.cornell.edu/uscode/text/42/4332.

9 *See* Cass R. Sunstein, Congress, *Constitutional Moments, and the Cost-Benefit State Legislative Foreword*, 48 STAN. L. REV. 247 (1996), https://doi.org/10.2307/1229364 (suggesting a "substantive super-mandate" requiring benefit-cost analysis by agencies).

On the other hand, (4) above, the requirement for what has come to be called an *environmental impact statement* (EIS), has been revolutionary. The courts picked it up and ran with it by allowing persons challenging proposed federal actions to obtain injunctions against projects for failing to produce an adequate EIS.[10] Private projects that require federal regulatory approvals also require environmental assessments under NEPA. Often challenges are brought for failing to consider alternatives to the project, such as conservation or renewables, as opposed to building a new powerplant or pipeline. For many years, injunctions were essentially automatic if a court found an EIS was required but had not been prepared, or the EIS failed to consider an issue or alternative adequately. In recent years, however, the Supreme Court has tightened up by applying traditional balancing of the equities principles to NEPA injunction, which includes weighing private harm against the public interest.[11] The extraordinary development of EIS by the courts is somewhat ironic in that, unlike the other environmental statutes of the 1970s, NEPA does not contain an explicit judicial review provision providing for citizen suits.

Nonetheless, today an EIS for a major project can require thousands of pages and take four to ten years to compile. To avoid the costs and delays attendant upon preparing a full-scale EIS, two shortcuts through the process have been developed. First, if an initial *environmental assessment* (EA), which is a shorter environmental study typically running about thirty to fifty pages, supports a *finding of no significant impact* (FONSI), which is a conclusion by the agency that the proposed project will *not* have a significant effect on the human environment, then NEPA does not require a full-blown EIS. Second, agencies may offer a *categorical exclusion* (CE), which is a generic finding that certain types of actions do not typically have a significant effect on the environment and thus are presumptively exempt from preparing an EIS unless someone shows otherwise.[12]

---

10 *See, e.g.,* Calvert Cliffs' Coordinating Comm., Inc. v. U.S. Atomic Energy Comm'n, 449 F.2d 1109 (D.C. Cir. 1971), https://law.justia.com/cases/federal/appellate-courts/F2/449/1109/240994/. *Calvert Cliffs* is often considered "the first important court interpretation . . . of NEPA." Calvert Cliffs' Coordinating Committee, Inc. v. Atomic Energy Commission, Wikipedia, https://en.wikipedia.org/wiki/Calvert_Cliffs'_Coordinating_Committee,_Inc._v._Atomic_Energy_Commission.

11 Winter v. Natural Resources Defense Council, 555 U.S. 7 (2008), https://supreme.justia.com/cases/federal/us/555/7/.

12 40 C.F.R. § 1508.1 (2020), https://www.law.cornell.edu/cfr/text/40/1508.1. For a good explanation of EA's, CEs and EISs, see Council on Environmental Quality, A Citizen's Guide

Unlike some analogous state statutes that provide for *de novo* court review of the substance of decisions on projects affecting the environment,[13] the Supreme Court has declared federal NEPA to be "essentially procedural,"[14] meaning that the federal courts cannot enjoin an agency's proposed action on the merits for failing to pick the least environmentally harmful alternative. However, agencies will often modify projects along the way to reduce their environmental impacts so that they can qualify for a FONSI, simplify the task of preparing an EIS, or provide a basis for settlement of NEPA litigation.

The courts did not develop this system of lesser environmental reviews on their own. As the White House environmental coordinator across government agencies, CEQ has issued detailed regulations implementing NEPA that have been very influential with the courts. CEQ not only spelled out the process for EAs and CEs but has also provided detailed guidance on what should be considered.[15] In addition, a 1977 amendment to the Clean Air Act empowered an office at EPA to review and comment on all draft EISs.[16] This review of EISs by environmental experts within the executive branch has led some to wonder whether a second review by generalist judges really adds value commensurate with its costs in terms of expense and delay.[17]

"Every reform, however necessary, will by weak minds be carried to an excess, that itself will need reforming," wrote the poet and philosopher

---

TO THE NEPA: HAVING YOUR VOICE HEARD (2007), https://ceq.doe.gov/docs/get-involved/Citizens_Guide_Dec07.pdf.

13 Sierra Club v. County of Fresno, 431 P.3d 1151 (Cal. 2018), https://law.justia.com/cases/california/supreme-court/2018/s219783a.html (demonstrating that the California Environmental Quality Act (CEQA) provides for judicial review of the substance of an Environmental Impact Report (EIR)).

14 Vermont Yankee Nuclear Power Corp. v. NRDC, 435 U.S. 519, 558 (1978) ("NEPA does set forth significant substantive goals for the Nation, but its mandate to the agencies is essentially procedural."), https://supreme.justia.com/cases/federal/us/435/519/.

15 NEPA Implementing Regulations, 40 C.F.R. §§ 1500–1508, https://www.law.cornell.edu/cfr/text/40/chapter-V/subchapter-A.

16 Clean Air Act § 309, 42 U.S.C. § 7609, https://www.law.cornell.edu/uscode/text/42/7609; *See also EPA Review Process under Section 309 of the Clean Air Act,* EPA, https://www.epa.gov/nepa/epa-review-process-under-section-309-clean-air-act.

17 *See, e.g.,* Mark C. Rutzick, *A Long and Winding Road: How the National Environmental Policy Act Has Become the Most Expensive and Least Effective Environmental Law in the History of the United States, and How to Fix It,* REGULATOR TRANSPARENCY PROJECT (Oct. 16, 2018), https://regproject.org/wp-content/uploads/RTP-Energy-Environment-Working-Group-Paper-National-Environmental-Policy-Act.pdf.

Samuel Taylor Coleridge.[18] In recent years, some have argued that the EIS requirement under NEPA has gradually become too burdensome. For example, best-selling author Philip K. Howard argues that NEPA has too often become a mechanism for stopping projects that people oppose for reasons unrelated to protecting the environment.[19] Common Good, the non-partisan NGO that Howard chairs, produced an influential report, *Two Years, Not Ten Years: Redesigning Infrastructure Approvals*,[20] which argued that the United States should emulate other countries such as Canada and Germany that are able to conduct environmental reviews in one to two years versus the four to ten years that it sometimes takes in the United States by using techniques such as setting deadlines and page limits.[21]

After three years of public notice and comment, the Trump Administration CEQ adopted in 2020 a controversial rule to *modernize* the EIS process. The rule includes deadlines and page limits a well as a number of other *reforms* including restricting consideration of cumulative and indirect effects such as climate change.[22] Many national environmental groups sued, calling the changes "harmful."[23] Moving forward, the Biden Administration is reconsidering the rule, announcing in 2021 a two-year delay on the Trump Administration's proposed reforms.[24] But while the Trump package of NEPA reforms may not stand, the need for a faster EIS process now has broad support. Indeed, a number of environmental advocates seek a more streamlined

---

18 SAMUEL TAYLOR COLERIDGE, BIOGRAPHICA LITERARIA 13 (Ernest Rhys ed., 1906), http://www. archive.org/details/biographialitera027747mbp.

19 PHILIP K. HOWARD, THE RULE OF NOBODY: SAVING AMERICAN FROM DEAD LAWS AND BROKEN GOVERNMENT 62 (2014) (NEPA "was turned into a weapon to stop or delay any project. Instead of a tool for balancing the common good, environmental review became a weapon against democratic choice").

20 PHILIP K. HOWARD, COMMON GOOD, TWO YEARS, NOT TEN YEARS: REDESIGNING INFRASTRUCTURE APPROVALS (2015), https://bit.ly/3bI7CCd.

21 For an argument that countries that are not the first to adopt an approach to an environmental problem are often able to learn from the experiences of other countries and do it better, see E. Donald Elliott, E. D, *U.S. Environmental Law in Global Perspective: Five Do's and Five Don'ts from Our Experience*, 5 NAT'L TAIWAN U. L. REV. 144 (2010), http://digitalcommons.law.yale.edu/fss_papers/2717/.

22 Update to the Regulations Implementing the Procedural Provisions of the National Environmental Policy Act, 85 Fed. Reg. 43,304 (July 16, 2020), http://bit.ly/3b1T4yi.

23 Press Release, NRDC, Groups Sue Trump Administration Over Harmful NEPA Rules (Aug. 6, 2020), https://www.nrdc.org/media/2020/200806.

24 Clark Mindock, *Agencies Get More Time to Weigh in on NEPA Overhaul*, LAW360 (June 28, 2021), https://www.law360.com/articles/1398188/agencies-get-more-time-to-weigh-in-on-nepa-overhaul.

review process for clean energy infrastructure projects, fearing that the traditional slow pace will delay America's efforts to combat climate change.[25]

Toxic Release Inventory

Laws mandating information disclosure have become a core element of the structure of environmental protection in America. Most notably, the Toxic Release Inventory (TRI)—a provision of the 1986 Superfund Amendments and Reauthorization Act (SARA)[26]—requires companies (with annual toxic releases above 25,000 pounds) to report on their emissions of 770 listed toxic chemicals to the land, air, and water.[27] Where an entity does not have a precise measure of its toxic releases, it can provide an estimate based on a mass balance calculation.[28]

While the TRI rules do not limit the amount of pollution that a company can emit, the fact that the scale of the toxic releases must be calculated and made public has created a powerful incentive for entities to rethink their use of chemicals with an eye toward minimizing their emissions. The availability of TRI data has resulted in

---

25 *See* Trevor Salter, *NEPA and Renewable Energy: Realizing the Most Environmental Benefit in the Quickest Time*, 34 U.C. DAVIS ENVTL L. & POL'Y J. 173 (2011), https://environs.law.ucdavis. edu/volumes/34/2/salter.pdf; Kelsey Brugger, *NEPA Rewrite Reveals Tensions between Greens, Renewables*, E&E NEWS (Jan. 13, 2020), https://www.eenews.net/stories/1062071569. In a similar vein, the Aspen Institute, a Washington D.C. think tank, convened a bipartisan expert group to analyze how to ensure that NEPA reviews and unnecessary permitting delays would not obstruct the build-out of the clean energy projects required to respond to climate change. *See* Aspen Institute, *Building Cleaner, Faster* (2021).

26 Title III of SARA is known as the "Emergency Planning and Community Right-to-Know Act." Superfund Amendments & Reauthorization Act of 1986, codified at 42 U.S.C. § 9601.

27 TRI, Emergency Planning and Community Right-to-Know Act § 313(f)(1)(B)(iii), 42 U.S.C. § 11023(f)(1)(B)(iii), https://www.epa.gov/toxics-release-inventory-tri-program/tri-listed-chemicals.

28 Mass balance means:

> an accumulation of the annual quantities of chemicals transported to a facility, produced at a facility, consumed at a facility, used at a facility, accumulated at a facility, released from a facility, and transported from a facility as a waste or as a commercial product or byproduct or component of a commercial product or byproduct.

> Emergency Planning and Community Right-to-Know Act § 313(l)(4), 42 U.S.C. § 11023(l) (4), https://www.law.cornell.edu/uscode/text/42/11023; *Guidance: Estimating Releases and Other Waste Management Quantities*, EPA, https://ofmpub.epa.gov/apex/guideme_ext/ f?p=guideme:gd:::::gd:chemical_distribution_4.

numerous newspaper stories about the biggest polluters in a particu-lar state or region.[29] For example, the National Wildlife Federation used the TRI numbers to create a *Toxic 500* list of the largest emitters across America.[30] All this negative publicity added momentum to the push in the corporate world for reduced chemical use and *pollution prevention*.[31] As a result, thousands of companies have undertaken initiatives to reduce their toxic releases, and the emissions reported under the TRI have fallen significantly even though the number of chemicals on the list for which reporting is required has expanded.[32]

TRI's success in delivering emissions' reductions without a specific government pollution control mandate has spawned great interest in information disclosure as a policy tool.[33] Seen by many as less intrusive and more cost-effective than command-and-control mandates, infor-mation disclosure requirements can now be found across the envi-ronmental policy landscape including in provisions that call out water pollution permit violations (through mandatory *discharge monitoring reports*),[34] reduce the harms of pesticide misuse (with product labels indicating proper application levels and protective gear required),[35] and encourage consumers to consider the sustainability of food and

---

29 *Special Report: Tracking Toxics*, USA TODAY (July 3, 1989–Aug. 2, 1989).

30 DEAN L. NORMAN AND RANDALL J. BURKE, THE TOXIC 500: THE 500 LARGEST RELEASES OF TOXIC CHEMICALS IN THE U.S. NATIONAL WILDLIFE FEDERATION (1989).

31 *See, e.g.*, Hiroko Tabuchi et al., *Floods Are Getting Worse, and 2,500 Chemical Sites Lie in the Water's Path*. N.Y. TIMES (Feb. 6, 2018), https://www.nytimes.com/interactive/2018/02/06/cli mate/flood-toxic-chemicals.html.

32 According to the TRI National Analysis dataset, between 2007 and 2019 emissions of TRI chemi-cals to the air decreased by 57 percent. *TRI National Analysis: Air Releases*, EPA (Jan. 2021), https://www.epa.gov/trinationalanalysis/air-releases.

33 Daniel C. Esty and Quentin Karpilow, *Harnessing Investor Interest in Sustainability: The Next Frontier in Environmental Information Regulation*, 26 YALE J. REG. 625 (2019), https:// digitalcommons.law.yale.edu/yjreg/vol36/iss2/3; Cass R. Sunstein, *Informational Regulation and Informational Standing*, 47 U. PENN. L. REV. 613 (1999), https://scholarship.law.upenn.edu/ penn_law_review/vol147/iss3/2; Paul R. Kleindorfer and Eric W. Orts, *Informational Regulation of Environmental Risks*, 18 RISK ANALYSIS 155 (1998), https://doi.org/10.1111/j.1539-6924.1998. tb00927.x.

34 Clean Water Act § 402, 33 U.S.C. §1318, https://www.law.cornell.edu/uscode/text/33/1318; 40 C.F.R. § 122.2, https://www.law.cornell.edu/cfr/text/40/122.2.

35 Federal Insecticide, Fungicide, and Rodenticide Act § 12(a)(1)(b), 7 U.S.C. § 136(j)(a)(1)(B)); 40 C.F.R § 156, https://www.law.cornell.edu/cfr/text/40/part-156; *See also Introduction to Pesticide Labels*, EPA, https://www.epa.gov/pesticide-labels/introduction-pesticide-labels ("Unlike most other types of product labels, pesticide labels are legally enforceable, and all of them carry the statement: 'It is a violation of Federal law to use this product in a manner inconsistent with its labeling.'").

other goods they purchase (through eco-labels)[36]—which an expanding number of *green consumers* are eager to do.[37]

In some of these cases (e.g., pesticide use or organic food), the government prescribes the disclosure requirements.[38] In other circumstances,
corporate disclosure has been driven by public expectations or private
data services gathering and distributing sustainability metrics that
someone (including consumers, investors, or other companies) wants
and will pay for. Pressure has recently mounted for more complete and
rigorous disclosure concerning the *environmental, social, and governance* (ESG) performance of public companies as a growing number of
investors and investment advisors now want to factor sustainability
considerations into their portfolio choices[39]—a topic that will be taken
up more fully in Chapter 15.

California's Proposition 65

Another important example of the use of information disclosure
to achieve environmental goals is California Proposition 65, a 1986
ballot initiative adopted by an overwhelming 63 percent to 37 percent
vote in a state-wide referendum rather than by the state legislature.[40]

---

36 *Introduction to Ecolabels and Standards for Greener Products, Sustainable Marketplace: Greener Products and Services*, EPA, https://www.epa.gov/greenerproducts/introduction-ecolabels-and-standards-greener-products; *see also* James Salzman, *Informing the Green Consumer: The Debate Over the Use and Abuse of Environmental Labels*, 1 J. INDUS. ECOLOGY 11 (1997), https://onlineli brary.wiley.com/doi/epdf/10.1162/jiec.1997.1.2.11.

37 Diana Bekmagambetova, *Two-Thirds of North Americans Prefer Eco-Friendly Brands*, BARRON'S (Jan. 10, 2020 8:08 AM), https://www.barrons.com/articles/two-thirds-of-north-americans-pre fer-eco-friendly-brands-study-finds-51578661728; DANIEL C. ESTY AND P.J. SIMMONS, THE GREEN TO GOLD BUSINESS PLAYBOOK: HOW TO IMPLEMENT SUSTAINABILITY PRACTICES FOR BOTTOM-LINE RESULTS IN EVERY BUSINESS FUNCTION 268–275 (2011).

38 40 C.F.R § 156, https://www.law.cornell.edu/cfr/text/40/part-156 (outlining pesticide labelling requirements); 7 C.F.R. § 205, https://www.law.cornell.edu/cfr/text/7/part-205 (establishing the National Organic Program's regulations on labelling); *Organic Labelling Standards*, USDA, https://www.ams.usda.gov/grades-standards/organic-labeling-standards.

39 Daniel C. Esty, D.C, *Creating Investment-Grade Corporate Sustainability Metrics*, in VALUES AT WORK: SUSTAINABLE INVESTING AND ESG REPORTING 51–66 (Daniel C. Esty and Todd Cort eds., 2020). YALE INITIATIVE ON SUSTAINABLE FINANCE, TOWARD ENHANCED SUSTAINABILITY DISCLOSURE: IDENTIFYING OBSTACLES TO BROADER AND MORE ACTIONABLE ESG REPORTING (2020), https://envirocenter.yale.edu/toward-enhanced-sustainability-disclosure-identifying-obst acles-broader-and-more-actionable-esg.

40 The official name is the Safe Drinking Water and Toxic Enforcement Act of 1986 but it is typically referred to as Proposition 65. CAL. HEALTH & SAFETY CODE §§ 25249.5–25249.14 (West 1989).

> "⚠ **WARNING**: This product can expose you to chemicals including arsenic, which is known to the State of California to cause cancer. For more information, go to www.P65Warnings.ca.gov."

Source: https://www.p65warnings.ca.gov/new-proposition-65-warnings.

Figure 14.1   Proposition 65 sample warning label

Proposition 65 requires a state agency, the *California Office of Health Hazard Assessment* (OEHHA), to maintain and annually update a list of chemicals known to cause cancer or reproductive toxicity. This list includes chemicals[41] identified by two independent committees of scientific and health experts convened by OEHHA, known as the *State's Qualified Experts*, as causing cancer, birth defects, or other reproductive harm. In addition, the list also includes chemicals classified as carcinogens or reproductive toxicants by organizations deemed *authoritative bodies*, which include both U.S. agencies and the World Health Organization's International Agency for Research on Cancer (IARC).[42] In turn, Proposition 65 requires businesses to inform Californians about exposures to such chemicals in their products and locations, usually through a warning label (see Figure 14.1).

Although OEHHA has developed *de minimis* exposure levels below which warnings are not required, today roughly 900 substances and thousands of products and locations must contain such warnings. Critics argue this results in *disclosure fatigue*: "the more ubiquitous disclosures become, the less effective they are."[43] On the other hand, supporters, including the principal author, David Roe, cite many accomplishments that they attribute to Proposition 65's innovative approach to making products safer, which unlike TSCA,[44] clearly

---

41 OEHHA, *How Chemicals are Added to the Proposition 65 List*, CA.GOV, https://oehha.ca.gov/proposition-65/how-chemicals-are-added-proposition-65-list.

42 *International Agency for Research on Cancer*, WORLD HEALTH ORGANIZATION, https://www.iarc.fr/.

43 Daniel J. Herling, *A Federal Court Gets Opportunity to Weigh In on Prop 65 With a Little Help from Some Friends*, MINTZ (Jan. 11, 2018), https://www.mintz.com/insights-center/viewpoints/2171/2018-01-federal-court-gets-opportunity-weigh-prop-65-little-help.

44 *See* Chapter 8 on the Toxic Substances Control Act (TSCA).

puts the burden to prove safety on the manufacturer rather than the government.[45] According to Roe:

> Proposition 65 has quietly driven cancer- and birth defect-causing chemicals out of thousands of everyday consumer products; created and enforced new safety standards for hundreds of such chemicals; sliced through a Gordian knot of complex science that multiple federal agencies have been struggling to untie since the 1970s; and found and filled gaping holes in the federal safety net.[46]

Unlike NEPA's declaration of national policies,[47] Proposition 65 is vigorously enforced by a combination of citizens suits, which, if successful, can be lucrative to the plaintiffs, private attorneys bringing them, and the California Attorney General's office.[48]

Disclosure strategies for the information age

With ever more performance data on products, production processes, and corporate activities available online in forms that are easily accessible and low cost, we anticipate that reporting rules (and informal pressure on companies for more disclosure from other sources—including consumers, investors, and NGOs) will play an ever-larger role in environmental protection in the years ahead.[49] Indeed, we have elsewhere called for a reframing of environmental law around a commitment to *end externalities*. By this we mean that polluters should stop any emissions causing harm to the fullest extent feasible and pay compensation for any harms arising from activities that offer net benefits to society but entail emissions that are technologically unavoidable. We further propose that emitters be obligated to disclose emissions that might

---

45 David Roe, *Barking Up the Right Tree: Recent Progress in Focusing the Toxics Issue*, 13 COLUM. J. ENVTL. L. 275 (1988), https://journals.library.columbia.edu/index.php/cjel/article/download/5744/2805.

46 David Roe, *Little Labs Lost: An Invisible Success Story*, 15 GREEN BAG 2D 275 (2012), http://www.greenbag.org/v15n3/v15n3_articles_roe.pdf; *see also* Clifford Rechtschaffen, *How to Reduce Lead Exposures with One Simple Statute: the Experience of Proposition 65*, 29 ENVTL. L. REP. 10581 (1999), https://digitalcommons.law.ggu.edu/cgi/viewcontent.cgi?article=1038&context=pubs (contrasting reductions in lead exposure at the federal level with more substantial reductions in California).

47 *See* text accompanying note 4.

48 For a detailed summary of enforcement provisions, see *Proposition 65 Information and Enforcement Reporting*, State of California Department of Justice, http://bit.ly/3sDuPfL.

49 *See* notes 28–30 and accompanying text.

cause harm but where the science is not yet clear—and that this disclosure include their scientific basis for concluding that whatever releases are occurring are not harmful.[50]

More broadly, governments may increasingly define reporting metrics and methodologies in some circumstances rather than prescribe specific pollution controls or other regulatory standards. In creating a distinctly lighter and less intrusive environmental protection framework, information disclosure strategies empower those buying from or investing in companies to make their own judgments about whether a particular enterprise meets their environmental needs or sustainability expectations.

This flexible disclosure-based approach makes sense in the context of business interactions where *buyers* get to choose the level of environmental commitment that best matches their own risk tolerances, cost tradeoffs, and other desires—and they get the benefit (or burden) of their choices. For example, some consumers with the means and opportunity to do so will choose to buy organic fruits or vegetables. These products are more expensive—and in purchasing them, customers pay a premium for the perceived environmental benefits. But these products are neither universally available nor affordable, and so cheaper, non-organic alternatives often remain consumers' dominant choices in the market. More readily available and validated environmental information could make individual *choice* a bigger part of society's environmental protection toolkit in the years ahead.

Additional resources

Conant, James K. and& Balint, Peter J. (2016). *The Life Cycles of the Council on Environmental Quality and the Environmental Protection Agency: 1970–2035*. Oxford University Press.

Esty, Daniel C. and Cort, Todd (2020). *Values at Work: Sustainable Investing and ESG Reporting*. London: Palgrave Macmillan.

Ghio, Alessandro and Verona, Roberto (2020). *The Evolution of Corporate Disclosure: Insights on Traditional and Modern Corporate Disclosure*. New York: Springer International Publishing.

---

50 Daniel C. Esty & E. Donald Elliott, *The End Environmental Externalities Manifesto: A Rights-Based Foundation for Environmental Law*, NYU ENVTL. L.J. (forthcoming 2021), https://ssrn.com/abstract=3762022.

Kraft, Michael E., Stephan, Mark and Abel, Troy D. (2011). *Coming Clean: Information Disclosure and Environmental Performance.* Cambridge, Massachusetts: MIT Press.

Mandelker, Daniel R. (2020). *NEPA Law and Litigation* (2nd ed.). Toronto: Thompson Reuters.

Mareddy, Anji R. (2018). *Environmental Impact Assessment: Theory and Practice.* Oxford: Butterworth-Heinemann.

15 Beyond traditional environmental governance: corporate sustainability, performance benchmarking, private standard setting, and public–private partnerships

While federal statutes and regulations shape pollution control and ecosystem vitality across America in important ways, environmental decisionmakers face other incentives for change in addition to those emanating from Washington—and beyond legal mandates. State law has become ever more important in addressing some issues including climate change. Moreover, companies may choose in some circumstances to invest in environmental protection beyond the requirements of the law based on softer incentives such as EPA guidance, policy *challenges*, or other signals about best practices regarding issues such as energy conservation. In addition, business leaders in recent years have ramped up their environmental efforts in response to various corporate stakeholders including their customers, industry peers, communities, and employees.

Drivers of private environmental initiatives

The 1992 Presidential election produced a fundamental realignment of environmental politics in the United States. Up until that time, our two main political parties competed for the votes of environmentalists.[1] In 1988, the Republican nominee for president, George Herbert Walker Bush ("Bush 41"), made his opponent's failure to clean up

---

1 For a description of the competition between Republicans and Democrats that led to the formation of EPA and strong legislation including the 1970 Clean Air Act and the 1972 Clean Water Act, see E. Donald Elliott, Bruce A. Ackerman and John C. Millian, *Toward a Theory of Statutory Evolution: The Federalization of Environmental Law*, 1 J. Law, Econ. & Org. 313 (1985), http://digitalcommons. law.yale.edu/fss_papers/147/.

Boston Harbor one of the main election issues and promised to be "the environmental president" while in office. He backed that up by appointing a career environmentalist, William K. Reilly, to head EPA and proposing and supporting the Clean Air Act Amendments of 1990, the most sweeping environmental legislation in our history. However, when Bush 41 ran for re-election in 1992, virtually all of the national environmental groups supported his opponent, Arkansas Governor Bill Clinton, who had a controversial record on the environment in Arkansas, in part because he relied heavily on voluntary agreements with industry.[2] Rightly or wrongly, this broad-scale shift of the environmental community into the Democratic camp convinced many Republicans—including the then-president's son, George W. Bush ("Bush 43"), who later became president himself—that whatever Republicans did, they could not win the support of environmentalists. As a result, the Republican party gave up and stopped supporting ambitious new legislation. Environmental policy thus became a *wedge* issue in American politics—and has continued to be so through the 2020 election.

This partisan divide has brought environmental progress delivered through the Congress nearly to a halt. Without some degree of Republican support, it has proven impossible to pass significant new legislation addressing emerging issues such as climate change.[3] Indeed, nearly three decades have now passed without any new major environmental statutes clearing the Congress—and environmental policy has become a zone of bitter partisan battles.[4]

Environmental agencies such as EPA have continued to expand regulation in certain areas via additional rulemaking and aggressive

---

2   Keith Schneider, *THE 1992 CAMPAIGN: Candidate's Record; Clinton Relies on Voluntary Guidelines to Protect Environment in Arkansas*, N.Y. TIMES (Apr. 4, 1992), https://www.nytimes.com/1992/04/04/us/1992-campaign-candidate-s-record-clinton-relies-voluntary-guidelines-protect.html.

3   The two exceptions, the 1996 Food Quality Protection Act and the 2016 amendment to TSCA, discussed in Chapter 8, were both bipartisan and non-controversial compromises to fix a badly broken statute. *See also* E. Donald Elliott, Bruce A. Ackerman and John C. Millian, *Toward a Theory of Statutory Evolution: The Federalization of Environmental Law*, 1 J. LAW, ECON. & ORG. 313 (1985), http://digitalcommons.law.yale.edu/fss_papers/147/ (predicting that it would be possible to legislate to fix TSCA, a prophecy that came true five years later).

4   For an analysis of the origins of this partisan divide, see Daniel C. Esty, *Red Lights to Green Lights: From 20th Century Environmental Regulation to 21st Century Sustainability*, 47 ENVTL L. REV. 1, 3–9 (2017); E. Donald Elliott, *Politics Failed, Not Ideas*, 28 ENVTL F. 42 (Sept./Oct. 2011), https://digitalcommons.law.yale.edu/fss_papers/5110/.

interpretations of existing law and regulation, but in the U.S. system, there are significant limits to what can be done by the executive branch alone without new statutory authority.[5] As a result of the *logjam* in Congress[6] since 1992, much of the innovation and accomplishments in the United States in protecting the environment have shifted away from *hard law* regulation by the federal government to environmental efforts by states and private actors. For example, one U.S. company, Walmart, has pledged to achieve a reduction in greenhouse gases from its own operations and those of its suppliers by a *billion* tons by 2030, an 18 percent reduction that dwarfs the commitments of many countries.[7] These private initiatives to reduce adverse environmental impacts are sometimes called *voluntary* actions, but as we detail below, they are generally a response to incentives, sometimes from public entities but often from private ones, so we prefer to call them *private environmental initiatives* rather than voluntary.[8]

Incentives created by government

Private environmental initiatives can result from incentives created by government as well as private stakeholders. Many companies learned from the market-based approaches to regulation during the 1990s that the *flexibility* to address environmental issues in ways of their own choosing rather than having the government dictate solutions served them well by reducing adverse publicity as well as allowing them to develop cost-effective approaches to achieving environmental goals. As a result, a number of far-sighted industries have decided to come together to address environmental issues themselves and thereby stave off the need for the government to mandate command and control

---

5   E. Donald Elliott, *Portage Strategies for Adapting Environmental Law and Policy During a Logjam Era*, 17 NYU ENVTL L.J. 24 (2008), http://digitalcommons.law.yale.edu/fss_papers/2221/.

6   DAVID SCHOENBROD, RICHARD B. STEWART AND KATRINA M. WYMAN, BREAKING THE LOGJAM: ENVIRONMENTAL PROTECTION THAT WILL WORK (2010).

7   *Walmart Launches Project Gigaton to Reduce Emissions in Company's Supply Chain*, WALMART (Apr. 19, 2017), https://corporate.walmart.com/newsroom/2017/04/19/walmart-launches-proj ect-gigaton-to-reduce-emissions-in-companys-supply-chain; MICHAEL P. VANDENBERGH AND JONATHAN M. GILLIGAN, BEYOND POLITICS: THE PRIVATE GOVERNANCE RESPONSE TO CLIMATE CHANGE (2017).

8   *See* E. Donald Elliott, *Environmental TQM: A Pollution Control Program that Works!*, 92 MICH. L. REV. 1840 (1994) (review of QUALITY ENVIRONMENTAL MANAGEMENT SUBCOMMITTEE PRESIDENT'S COMMISSION ON ENVIRONMENTAL QUALITY, TOTAL QUALITY MANAGEMENT; A FRAMEWORK FOR POLLUTION PREVENTION (1993)), https://repository.law.umich.edu/cgi/view content.cgi?article=3273&context=mlr.

RESPONSIBLE CARE®
OUR COMMITMENT TO SUSTAINABILITY

Source: https://responsiblecare.americanchemistry.com/.

Figure 15.1   Responsible Care logo

solutions. An early prototype for this strategy is the *Responsible Care* program sponsored by the American Chemistry Council (ACC), the leading trade association for the chemical industry in the United States. The program was founded in Canada in 1984 and adopted in the United States in 1988, and is now practiced in sixty-eight economies around the world. The CEOs of companies that join the Responsible Care program pledge personally that their companies will abide by certain general principles[9] and in return are allowed to use the Responsible Care logo on their products and advertising (see Figure 15.1).

According to its sponsors, the program has achieved the following moderately impressive results. Responsible Care companies:

- Have an employee safety record nearly five times better than the U.S. manufacturing sector, and almost three times better than the business of chemistry overall.
- Voluntarily track process safety incidents and have reduced their occurrence by 6 percent since 2010 and 48 percent since 2000.
- Reduced their recordable injury and illness incidence rates by 22 percent since 2010, making significant progress toward the overall industry goal of no accidents, injuries or harm to human health.
- Reduced hazardous pollutant releases by more than 24 percent since 2010.

---

9 Responsible Care, *Guiding Principles*, AM. CHEMISTRY COUNCIL, https://responsiblecare.ameri canchemistry.com/ResponsibleCare/Responsible-Care-Program-Elements/Guiding-Principles/.

- Invested approximately $25.7 billion to further enhance security at facilities since September 11, 2001.
- Improved their energy efficiency by 19 percent since 1992.[10]

Critics note, however, the absence of strong enforcement mechanisms other than peer pressure and wonder aloud whether progress would have been even greater if government had regulated.

Other examples of private initiatives to address environmental problems, which are sometimes called *self-regulation,* are the American Petroleum Institute's standards of recommended best practices for drilling wells discussed in Chapter 11; the work of The Nature Conservancy and other privately-funded land trusts to buy and preserve millions of acres of undeveloped land described in Chapter 13; the Sage Grouse Initiative also discussed in Chapter 13; an initiative by the pharmaceutical industry to address pharmaceuticals in the environment without regulation;[11] and the program by the oil industry to reduce methane releases from natural gas wells.[12]

In addition to industry self-regulation, private standard-setting organizations such as the American National Standards Institute (ANSI) and the International Standards Organization (ISO) also develop voluntary consensus standards. For example, ISO 14001 is a recommended standard for environmental management systems and ISO also has a standard for *sustainable development goals.*[13]

EPA has adapted to the *competition* from private initiatives and standard-setting by developing its own suite of *partnership programs* by which the agency encourages private parties to comply with EPA policies that are not backed up by punitive enforcement, but rather by positive incentives such as certifications, awards, or other favorable publicity. A good example is EPA's *Safer Choice* program, which authorizes consumer product companies to use an EPA logo on their

---

10 Responsible Care, *Responsible Care Fast Facts,* AM. CHEMISTRY COUNCIL, https://responsi blecare.americanchemistry.com/default.aspx?gclid=CjoKCQiAvbiBBhD-ARIsAGM48bzH7f HKxbmBiX9JpXtvwMxAKZEAJwFV-Bjg14UNJojlzSZqBzFL4BAaAny4EALw_wcB.

11 Natasha Gilbert, *Industry says Voluntary Plan to Curb Antibiotic Pollution is Working, but Critics want Regulation,* SCIENCE (Jan. 24, 2020, 12:40 PM), https://www.sciencemag.org/news/2020/01/ industry-says-voluntary-plan-curb-antibiotic-pollution-working-critics-want-regulation.

12 *See EPA's Voluntary Methane Programs for the Oil and Natural Gas Industry,* EPA, https://www. epa.gov/natural-gas-star-program.

13 Both ISO standards are described briefly at https://www.iso.org/standard/60857.html.

Source: https://www.epa.gov/saferchoice.

Figure 15.2   Safer Choice logo

products if they use ingredients deemed by EPA's experts to be safer than the alternatives (see Figure 15.2).[14]

In this way, EPA can exert substantial influence over the ingredients in products without going through the arduous public procedures, including judicial review, that would be necessary if EPA tried to ban the ingredients that it considers less safe through traditional regulatory approaches. But critics denounce these efforts which they call *regulation by press release* without appropriate administrative due process.[15] In other cases, EPA has offered *guidance* or *challenges* that engage companies without mandating specific standards or outcomes and thus represent a *soft law* approach to environmental improvement.[16]

---

14 *Safer Choice*, EPA, https://www.epa.gov/saferchoice.

15 Karen de Witt, *Aide Says Cut Would Hobble Product Safety Agency*, N.Y. TIMES (Mar. 14, 1981):

> 'The agency [CPSC, not EPA] has used the tactic of *regulation by press release* rather than valid scientific data, which deprives the regulated industry of the appropriate due process under the Administrative Procedure Act,' said James M. Ramey, chairman of the Formaldehyde Institute, a national association of 70 companies and trade associations involved in the manufacture or use of formaldehyde and formaldehyde-based products (*emphasis added*).

> https://www.nytimes.com/1981/03/14/us/aide-says-cut-would-hobble-product-safety-agency.html.

16 EPA's 33/50 toxic materials challenge and *Greenlights* energy efficiency program targeting CEOs with information on costs savings from relighting of facilities offer prime examples of such efforts. Robert Innes and Abdoul G. Sam, *Voluntary Pollution Reductions and the Enforcement of Environmental Law: An Empirical Study of the 33/50 Program*, 51 J. L. & ECON. 271 (2008). On the *Greenlights* program, see EPA, *Introducing . . . The Green Lights Program* (1993), https://tinyurl.com/b4648pzv.

Business strategy logic for corporate sustainability

Environmental progress can sometimes be driven by incentives entirely outside government. In fact, in recent decades, many companies adopted a *beyond compliance* approach to pollution control and other legal obligations spurred on by a commitment to corporate sustainability—and the business logic for improved environmental performance that exists in some circumstances.[17]

Risk reduction and cost savings

Companies may voluntarily adopt environmental standards that exceed regulatory requirements when they see a business benefit in doing so. Some corporate sustainability initiatives help companies to reduce their operating costs or to minimize marketplace risks. For example, an initiative to improve energy efficiency (perhaps by shifting to LED lighting or undertaking other energy conservation investments) will cut costs—and reduce the emissions associated with the power generation of the electricity that is no longer required. Such investments may have high returns on investment and short payback times—thereby improving corporate competitiveness and profitability while delivering environmental gains.

Likewise, companies may work to reduce the toxicity of the materials in their products to avoid regulatory compliance costs and potential exposure risk for their employees during production or for customers during use of the product. For instance, S.C. Johnson, a major producer of home care products, subjects all of the chemicals and other raw materials it uses to an internal review process it calls *Greenlist*, which scores each ingredient based on its biodegradability, toxicity, and other environmental attributes. The company's product designers are asked to steer away from ingredients that the Greenlist analysis suggests have notable negative impacts and thus pose significant environmental risks.

---

17 For a complete review of how companies use a sustainability focus to reduce risks, cut costs (and improve resource productivity), drive growth, and build brand identity and intangible value, see Daniel C. Esty and Andrew Winston, Green to Gold: How Smart Companies Use Environmental Strategy to Innovate, Create Value, and Build Competitive Advantage (2009).

Other corporate sustainability initiatives aim to foster innovation and generate product breakthroughs that attract new buyers or increase the *value* a sustainability-minded customer perceives in the product, thus enabling the company to charge higher prices and increase profit margins. In this regard, Patagonia offers the quintessential sustainability growth story, having converted its brand identity as a maker of eco-friendly outdoor clothing and gear into an $800 million per year business.

Stakeholder engagement

Other companies work to reduce their emissions or commit to environmental standards beyond the requirements of the law to capture the intangible benefits of better relations with critical *stakeholders*, including customers, employees, communities, and investors. And in our Information Age and era of heightened transparency, many non-governmental organizations (NGOs), business associations, media companies, and governments at various levels produce environmental scorecards of various kinds that provide a mechanism for tracking sustainability performance across a range of dimensions.[18] The metrics tracked, best practices identified, and top-tier results honored can provide a powerful inducement to better performance.[19] Indeed, in some settings, these efforts constitute a structure of *private governance* that creates incentives as important as government laws and regulations.[20]

Green consumers

Every company seeks to be customer-oriented, but particularly those lower down the value chain and closer to the retail consumer, as opposed to those that are producing basic raw materials or serving a business-to-business (B2B) market. As more consumers demand

---

18 Daniel C. Esty, *Environmental Protection in the Information Age*, 79 NYU L. Rev. 115 (2004), https://digitalcommons.law.yale.edu/cgi/viewcontent.cgi?article=1430&context=fss_papers. One example of this sort of sustainability scorecard is the Environmental Performance Index (EPI), available at: epi.yale.edu.

19 Daniel C. Esty, *Measurement Matters: Toward Data-Driven Environmental Policymaking*, in Routledge Handbook of Sustainability Indicators 494 (Simon Bell and Stephen Morse eds., 2020).

20 Michael P. Vandenbergh, *Private Environmental Governance*, 99 Cornell L. Rev. 129 (2013), https://scholarship.law.cornell.edu/cgi/viewcontent.cgi?article=4615&context=clr.

environmentally less-damaging products, business leaders have responded with sustainability strategies that seek to capture the *green consumer* segment of the marketplace. Examples of customer-driven corporate sustainability efforts and marketing abound from brown (unbleached) Melitta coffee filters that promise a chlorine-free morning cup of coffee to Stop & Shop's booming *Nature's Promise* line of organic products.[21] Note that some product claims, such as *organic*, have specific government-defined criteria, while others, such as *natural*, are not defined by government.[22]

Some marketplace indicators of environmental virtue derive directly from government standards. For instance, the yellow *EnergyGuide* labels on major appliances are supervised by the Federal Trade Commission using standards set by the Department of Energy. Similarly, computers and other products bearing the *Energy Star* label must meet high-efficiency guidelines set by EPA.[23] At the same time, the ever-expanding use of privately-established eco-labels to signal specific environmental attributes highlights the extent of corporate efforts to appeal to sustainability-minded customers. Examples of such labels include the Marine Stewardship Council's *sustainable seafood* logo, the Forest Stewardship Council's *sustainable wood* certification, and the Green Seal offered on a variety of consumer products.[24]

Sustainability-based competition for customers in the B2B marketplace can be even more intense. For example, jet engine makers GE and Pratt & Whitney compete intensely to produce more energy efficient engines knowing that for their customers (airlines) fuel consumption represents both a major cost and a source of environmental concern as the pressure to reduce greenhouse gas emissions mounts. Perhaps even more dramatically, Walmart requires its 70,000

---

21 DANIEL C. ESTY AND P.J. SIMMONS, GREEN TO GOLD BUSINESS PLAYBOOK: HOW TO IMPLEMENT SUSTAINABILITY PRACTICES FOR BOTTOM-LINE RESULTS IN EVERY BUSINESS FUNCTION 127, 275–76 (2011) [hereinafter GREEN TO GOLD BUSINESS PLAYBOOK].

22 The U.S. Department of Agriculture sets standards for what can be labelled as "organic," but the use of terms such as "natural" are limited only by the Federal Trade Commission's disciplines on fraudulent claims. Lesley Fair, *Are your "all natural" claims all accurate?*, FED. TRADE COMM'N (Apr. 12, 2016), https://www.ftc.gov/news-events/blogs/business-blog/2016/04/are-your-all-natu ral-claims-all-accurate.

23 Details for these programs can be found on the websites of the government agencies. See, e.g., the Federal Trade Commission's Consumer Information. *Shopping for Home Appliances? Use the EnergyGuide Label*, FED. TRADE COMM'N., https://www.consumer.ftc.gov/articles/0072-shopping-home-appliances-use-energyguide-label.

24 GREEN TO GOLD BUSINESS PLAYBOOK at 210–11.

suppliers to fill out a sustainability scorecard—creating not just an incentive for elevated environmental results across its supply chain but a mandatory set of standards that have (most notably) lifted the performance of tens of thousands of Chinese companies above the requirements of Chinese law.[25]

Employee recruitment and retention

Corporate success in the twenty-first century depends ever more directly on attracting and retaining the best employees—especially high-end knowledge workers. As companies compete for these prized employees, corporate culture and values have become significant factors in recruiting. Companies thus tout their sustainability leadership as a differentiating factor in the battle for top-tier workers, and face consequences for less-than-stellar environmental reputations. For example, while GE's famously hard-charging CEO Jack Welch battled EPA for years over the Agency's demand for extensive clean-up of the PCBs that the company had spilled into the Hudson and Housatonic Rivers, he pulled back when his human resources team told him that executive recruitment was suffering as a result of the perception that GE was anti-environmental.[26]

Communities

Most business leaders want their companies to be seen as good corporate citizens and themselves to be seen as upstanding members of the communities in which they live and work—creating another incentive for environmental care. Companies that fall short of these expectations may well put at risk their *social license to operate*, which is not an actual license and nor does it reflect any specific legal obligations, but rather relates to community and societal expectations for corporate behavior.[27] What precisely is expected will evolve over time, but environmental care and fair treatment of workers are central to the ethical standards embedded in this concept.

25 *Id.* at 212–15.
26 DANIEL C. ESTY AND ANDREW WINSTON, GREEN TO GOLD: HOW SMART COMPANIES USE ENVIRONMENTAL STRATEGY TO INNOVATE, CREATE VALUE, AND BUILD COMPETITIVE ADVANTAGE 90–91 (2009).
27 LEEORA BLACK, THE SOCIAL LICENSE: YOUR MANAGEMENT FRAMEWORK FOR COMPLEX TIMES (2013).

We further note that companies are increasingly being held to a standard that demands that they not privately profit at the expense of their community or society more generally. In this regard, we see challenges ahead for companies whose business model and profitability depends on sending pollution up a smokestack or effluent out a pipeline into nearby rivers or streams. With expectations for corporate legitimacy moving toward a *do no harm* or *no externalities* standard, the baseline for sustainability performance continues to rise.[28] We believe that this shift will render outdated the idea of *corporate social responsibility*, a framework that credited companies for good deeds (such as contributions to the hospitals, ballet, museums, or local youth sports teams in their communities) as a way to make up for the pollution or other harms for which they might otherwise be held responsible.

Sustainability-minded investors

Alongside their customers, companies care a great deal about how investors perceive them. For decades a small segment of *socially responsible investors* factored corporate environmental performance into their investment decisions. But in recent years, a growing number of mainstream investors have indicated a desire for better alignment between their values and their portfolios.[29] These sustainability-minded investors have begun to insist that their investment advisors provide more data and information on the sustainability performance of the companies in which they hold shares or bonds, driving growth in environmental, social, and governance (ESG) reporting.

More methodologically consistent and easily available ESG metrics facilitate the benchmarking of sustainability results across companies—thus motivating corporate leaders to pay more attention to their air and water pollution, greenhouse gas emissions, chemicals and waste management, and land and resource use.[30] With increased

---

28 David Lubin and Daniel C. Esty, *The Sustainability Imperative*, HARV. BUS. REV. (May 2010); Tensie Whelan and Carly Fink, *The Comprehensive Business Case for Sustainability*, HARV. BUS. REV. (Oct. 21, 2016), https://hbr.org/2016/10/the-comprehensive-business-case-for-sustainabil ity; Andrew J. Hoffman, *The Next Phase of Business Sustainability*, STAN SOC. INNOVATION REV. (2018), https://ssir.org/articles/entry/the_next_phase_of_business_sustainability#.

29 Daniel C. Esty and Todd Cort, *Sustainable Investing at a Turning Point*, in VALUES AT WORK: SUSTAINABLE INVESTING AND ESG REPORTING 3, 4–5 (Daniel C. Esty and Todd Cort eds., 2020).

30 Daniel C. Esty, *Environmental Protection in the Information Age*, 79 NYU L. REV. 115 (2004), https://digitalcommons.law.yale.edu/cgi/viewcontent.cgi?article=1430&context=fss_papers; Daniel C. Esty and Todd Cort, *Corporate Sustainability Metrics: What Investors Want and*

transparency the norm and ever more metrics available, companies have begun to track and compare their environmental performance across their own facilities, against their industry competitors, and in contrast to global sustainability leaders.[31] For companies with extensive operations, these comparative sustainability analyses now extend beyond their own production facilities to their supply chains[32]—again creating a benchmark from which to drive improved environmental conduct.[33]

To ensure that ESG benchmarking will accurately separate sustainability leaders from laggards and unmask *greenwashing* (where company environmental claims are revealed to be more spin than substance), calls have mounted for government-defined ESG reporting. In this regard, the European Union has introduced mandatory ESG disclosure.[34] In the United States, many observers expect the Biden Administration to advance a new framework of ESG metrics under expanded Securities and Exchange Commission (SEC) reporting rules.[35] A first step in this direction was taken in 2021 when President Biden signed an executive order directing government agencies and departments to develop climate-related financial risk policies,[36] which the SEC has signaled it considers a mandate to expanding its reporting framework.[37]

Don't Get, 8 J. ENVTL INV. 11 (2017), https://corporate-sustainability.org/wp-content/uploads/Corporate-Sustainability-Metrics.pdf.

31 Bradley C. Karkkainen, *Information as Environmental Regulation: TRI and Performance Benchmarking, Precursor to a New Paradigm?*, 89 GEORGETOWN L.J. 257 (2001).

32 Verónica H. Villena and Dennis A. Gioia, *A More Sustainable Supply Chain*, HARV. BUS. REV. (Mar./Apr., 2020), https://hbr.org/2020/03/a-more-sustainable-supply-chain; *see also* GREEN TO GOLD BUSINESS PLAYBOOK at 205–20.

33 Tannis Thorlakson, Joann de Zegher & Eric F. Lambin, *Companies' Contribution to Sustainability Through Global Supply Chains*, 115 PROC. NAT'L ACAD. SCI. 2072 (2018), https://www.pnas.org/content/115/9/2072.

34 Regulation (EU) 2019/2088 of the European Parliament and of the Council of 27 November 2019 on sustainability-related disclosures in the financial services sector, O.J. (L 317), https://eur-lex.europa.eu/eli/reg/2019/2088/oj.

35 Aaron Nicodemus, *Biden's SEC Set to Require Disclosure of ESG, Climate Change Risk*, COMPLIANCE WEEK (Dec. 3, 2020, 4:12 PM), https://www.complianceweek.com/regulatory-policy/bidens-sec-set-to-require-disclosure-of-esg-climate-change-risk/29788.article.

36 Amanda Iacone & Andrew Ramonas, *Biden Presses for Climate Disclosures: Executive Order Explained*, BLOOMBERG LAW (May 24, 2021), https://news.bloomberglaw.com/financial-accounting/biden-presses-for-climate-disclosures-executive-order-explained.

37 *See* Andrew Ramonas, *SEC's Gensler Eyes ESG Reporting Rules After Public Input*, BLOOMBERG LAW (May 6, 2021), https://news.bloomberglaw.com/securities-law/secs-gensler-eyes-esg-reporting-rules-after-public-input.

Non-governmental organizations

Environmental advocacy groups and other NGOs have become another important driver of corporate sustainability, often spurring companies toward improved results through their role as watchdogs calling out sub-par performance. Greenpeace, for instance, notoriously undertakes *direct action* against companies it deems environmental bad actors—scaling corporate offices to unfurl giant protest banners, spilling fake blood on company executives, or chasing fishing boats.[38]

In other cases, NGOs form partnerships with companies and work to help them identify environmental best practices, and sometimes even provide external validation of a company's environmental strategy and supply chain practices. Chiquita Brands International, for example, asked the Rainforest Alliance to help to establish the sustainability standards at its banana plantations in Central America.[39] Similarly, the Environmental Defense Fund (EDF), a New York-based environmental group, opened an office in Bentonville, Arkansas to work day-to-day with Walmart (headquartered in Bentonville) on its sustainability initiatives.[40] And many of the nation's leading environmental groups including EDF, the Natural Resource Defense Council, the World Wildlife Fund, The Nature Conservancy, and others have created corporate councils to work systematically with companies on sustainability issues.

In recent years, corporate sustainability alliances have sprung up across the nation and around the world, providing business executives opportunities for sustainability collaboration and platforms for the exchange of ideas on environmental best practices. In this regard, the Corporate Eco-Forum, the World Business Council for Sustainable Development, the Global Environmental Management Initiative, The Climate Group, and Ceres bring corporate leaders together on a regular basis to compare notes on a wide range of sustainability challenges, with subgroups often working to define best practices on topics such as supply chain auditing, greenhouse gas emissions reporting, and waste management practices.

---

38 Rex Weyler, Greenpeace: How a Group of Ecologists, Journalists, and Visionaries Changed the World (2015).

39 J. Gary Taylor and Patricia J. Scharlin, Smart Alliance: How a Global Corporation and Environmental Activists Transformed a Tarnished Brand (2004).

40 *See Walmart*, EDF + Business, https://business.edf.org/partnerships/walmart/.

Beyond hard law and regulation

While laws and regulations remain critical to the promise of environmental progress, green consumers, sustainability-minded investors, ESG data providers, and environmental activists can also drive change. These alternative points of leverage will often be seen as particularly critical in circumstances where political processes are at loggerheads— as many would say Washington has been over the past several decades. In addition, these private initiatives often prove to be less adversarial[41] and can sometimes lead to creative approaches that traditional regulation might overlook.[42]

Additional resources

Allan, Jen Iris (2021). *The New Climate Activism: NGO Authority and Participation in Climate Change Governance*. Toronto: University of Toronto Press.

Esty, Daniel C. and Cort, Todd (eds.) (2020). *Values at Work: Sustainable Investing and ESG Reporting*. New York: Palgrave Macmillan.

Esty, Daniel C. and Simmons, P.J. (2011). *The Green to Gold Business Playbook: How to Implement Sustainability Practices for Bottom-Line Results in Every Business Function*. Hoboken, N.J.: John Wiley Publishing.

---

41 EPA experimented briefly with *regulatory negotiation* in the 1990s. Phillip J. Harter, *Negotiating Regulations: A Cure for Malaise*, 71 GEO. L.J. 1 (1982), https://bit.ly/3uByNHi. *See* Negotiated Rulemaking Act of 1990, Pub. L. No. 101-648, 104 Stat. 4969 (codified as amended by Pub. L. No. 104-320, 110 Stat. 3870 (1996) at 5 U.S.C. §§ 561–70); Exec. Order 12,866 § 6(a)(1), 58 Fed. Reg. 51,735 (Oct. 4, 1993). However, recent scholarship has generally been negative about this approach. Susan Rose-Ackerman, *Consensus Versus Incentives: A Skeptical Look at Regulatory Negotiation*, 43 DUKE L.J. 1206 (1994), https://digitalcommons.law.yale.edu/cgi/viewcontent. cgi?article=1597&context=fss_papers; Cary Coglianese, *Assessing Consensus: The Promise and Performance of Negotiated Rulemaking*, 46 DUKE L.J. 1255 (1997), https://scholarship.law.duke. edu/dlj/vol46/iss6/1/. The Administrative Conference of the United States has made numerous recommendations regarding negotiated rulemaking, but the most recent one in 2017 is less enthusiastic about its potential than the earlier ones and recommends other devices are better for securing public engagement in most instances. *Negotiated Rulemaking and Other Options for Public Engagement*, ADMIN. CONF. U.S., https://www.acus.gov/recommendation/negotiated-rulemaking-and-other-options-public-engagement.

42 For an example, see E. Donald Elliott, *The Last Great Clean Air Act Book?*, 5 ENVTL L. 321, 325 (1998) (reviewing THE CLEAN AIR ACT HANDBOOK (Robert J. Martineau and David P. Novello, eds., 1998)) (describing a regulatory negotiation led by Vickie Patton, then an EPA attorney but later General Counsel of the Environmental Defense Fund, to develop emission limits on a powerplant that was adversely affecting visibility in the Grand Canyon that "led to identification of a new win-win alternative that had been previously overlooked by EPA."), https://digitalcommons. law.yale.edu/fss_papers/5100/; *see also* D. Michael Rappoport and John F. Cooney, *Visibility at the Grand Canyon: Regulatory Negotiations Under the Clean Air Act*, 24 ARIZ. ST. L.J. 627 (1992).

Esty, Daniel C. and Winston, Andrew S. (2009). *Green to Gold: How Smart Companies Use Environmental Strategy to Innovate, Create Value, and Build Competitive Advantage*. Hoboken, N.J.: John Wiley Publishing.

Lyon, Thomas P. (2010). *Good Cop/Bad Cop: Environmental NGOs and their Strategies Toward Business*. Washington, D.C.: RFF Press.

Vandenbergh, Michael P. and Gilligan, Jonathan M. (2017) *Beyond Politics: The Private Governance Response to Climate Change*. Cambridge: Cambridge University Press.

16 Conclusion: the best and the worst

"It was the best of times. It was the worst of times," begins Charles Dickens's novel about the French Revolution, *A Tale of Two Cities*. One could say something similar about U.S. environmental law: it illustrates both the best and the worst aspects of U.S. approaches to regulation.[1]

Regulating the effects of human beings on the environment stands out as one of the most ambitious projects humanity has ever undertaken. In many areas, U.S. environmental law has been a leader in that effort. On the positive side, America's environmental rules and programs have helped to clean up the air, water, and land, as well as manage waste and limit exposures to unsafe chemicals. But more work still remains to be done. On the negative side, progress has been slow and expensive.[2] In addition, the framework of environmental law and policy has failed to keep pace with scientific progress, new pollution control strategies made possible by information technologies, and the emergence of new environmental pressures and issues. Moreover, many of the *command-and-control* regulations promulgated by the Environmental Protection Agency (EPA) are very complex and difficult for anyone but an expert to understand. As we have explained in a number of the preceding chapters, the existing legal framework provides too little in the way of incentives for innovation on which improved performance in government as well as business and other domains depends.[3]

Nevertheless, scholars and other observers see EPA as one of the U.S. government's most innovative agencies. Indeed, over recent decades,

---

1 E. Donald Elliott, *U.S. Environmental Law in Global Perspective: Five Do's and Five Don'ts from Our Experience*, 5 Nat'l Taiwan Univ. L. Rev. 144 (2011), http://digitalcommons.law.yale.edu/fss_papers/2717.

2 *See generally* E. Donald Elliott, *A Critical Assessment of the EPA's Air Program at Fifty and a Suggestion for How It Might Do Even Better*, 70 Case W. Rsrv. L. Rev. 895 (2020), https://scholarlycommons.law.case.edu/caselrev/vol70/iss4/6.

3 Daniel C. Esty, *Red Lights to Green Lights: Toward an Innovation-Oriented Sustainability Strategy*, in A Better Planet: 40 Big Ideas for a Sustainable Future (Daniel C. Esty ed., 2019).

the Agency pioneered a wide range of new pollution control strategies, devices, and regulatory techniques such as market-based trading
of pollution allotments, information disclosure systems, and positive
incentives to encourage safer products. We see many opportunities
for further creativity and advances in environmental results through
enhanced commitments to *federalism* (and a more carefully structured
division of regulatory leadership across the federal, state, and local
governments), better use of data and performance metrics (including expanded corporate environmental, social, and governance (ESG)
reporting), and implementation of international agreements (including the 2015 Paris Climate Change Agreement and Sustainable
Development Goals), which spur attention to global best environmental practices.

Some have criticized EPA for not using economic incentives as fully as it
might have and relying instead on legalistic rules and enforcement, which
are often expensive, inflexible, and inefficient.[4] Others critique the legal
framework for its media-by-media approach (derived from the separate
statutes discussed in this volume) and the *silos* this structure introduces,
which prevent a more integrated and *systems-oriented* environmental
protection regime.[5] Yet other observers decry the fact that policymakers
pay too little attention to incentives for behavioral change or the funding
required to move society toward a sustainable future.

Perhaps the greatest failing of the U.S. environmental law system has
been its inability to date to address climate change at the national
level, although it should be noted that about half of the states do
regulate greenhouse gases (GHGs) in some form.[6] Federal action to

---

4 *Id. See generally* Daniel C. Esty, *Red Lights to Green Lights: From 20th Century Environmental
Regulation to 21st Century Sustainability*, 47 ENVTL. L. 1 (2017), https://digitalcommons.law.yale.
edu/fss_papers/5186; E. Donald Elliott, *A Critical Assessment of the EPA's Air Program at Fifty
and a Suggestion for How It Might Do Even Better*, 70 CASE W. RSRV. L. REV. 895 (2020), https://
scholarlycommons.law.case.edu/caselrev/vol70/iss4/6.

5 Perhaps the most important contribution of ecologists to environmental policy centers on the
logic of integrated approaches to environmental protection that recognize the interconnections
across habitats and species. *See, e.g.*, Oswald Schmitz, *Sustaining Humans and Nature as One*, in
A BETTER PLANET: 40 BIG IDEAS FOR A SUSTAINABLE FUTURE 11–20 (Daniel C. Esty ed., 2019).
On the value of "systems thinking" and integrated policy approaches, see Paul Anastas and Julie
Zimmerman, *Environmental Protection through Systems Design, Decision-Making, and Thinking*,
in A BETTER PLANET: 40 BIG IDEAS FOR A SUSTAINABLE FUTURE 97–104 (Daniel C. Esty ed.,
2019).

6 *See generally* E. Donald Elliott, *Why the United States Does Not Have a Renewable Energy Policy*, 43
ENVTL. L. REP. 10095 (Feb. 2013), http://dx.doi.org/10.2139/ssrn.1878616.

control GHG emissions may ramp up under the Biden Administration, which has promised an aggressive new national effort to address the issue. We have, however, heard this promise before, and the Biden Administration faces the challenge of pushing reforms through a Congress that remains deeply divided on the subject. Despite a historically weak federal approach to mitigating climate change, U.S. GHGs have declined substantially over the last two decades.[7] Of course, those reductions derive largely from the replacement of coal in electricity generation with natural gas as well as renewables such as solar and wind, changes attributable to market pricing and efforts at the state and local levels to reduce GHGs.[8] We do, however, see a rising interest in deep decarbonization strategies and associated legal reforms for shifting society toward a clean energy future.[9]

To date the U.S. framework of environmental law has delivered the low-hanging fruit—pollution reductions that were relatively easy to address cost-effectively with existing regulatory techniques. While the chapters in this volume—and many other analyses from policymakers, academics, NGO leaders, think tank researchers, and business executives—spell out opportunities to refine America's structure of environmental law, fix the shortcomings of today's pollution control programs, and set a course toward a sustainable future,[10] the Congress

---

7 See 2020 *Environmental Performance Index*, YALE CENTER FOR ENVIRONMENTAL LAW AND POLICY, https://epi.yale.edu/; *see also Climate Change Indicators: Greenhouse Gases*, EPA, https://www.epa.gov/climate-indicators/greenhouse-gases:

> In the United States, greenhouse gas emissions caused by human activities increased by 7 percent from 1990 to 2014. Since 2005, however, total U.S. greenhouse gas emissions have decreased by 7 percent. . . . Worldwide, net emissions of greenhouse gases from human activities increased by 35 percent from 1990 to 2010.

8 Roughly half of the U.S. states have adopted GHG reduction targets and others have a variety of programs to address climate change. *See Policy Hub State Climate Policy Maps*, CENTER FOR CLIMATE AND ENERGY SOLUTIONS, https://www.c2es.org/content/state-climate-policy ("Twenty-four states plus the District of Columbia have adopted specific greenhouse gas reduction targets to address climate change.").

9 *Accelerating Decarbonization in the United States: Technology, Policy, and Societal Dimensions*, NATIONAL ACADEMIES OF SCIENCES (Feb. 2021), https://www.nationalacademies.org/our-work/accelerating-decarbonization-in-the-united-states-technology-policy-and-societal-dimensions; *America's Zero Carbon Action Plan*, SUSTAINABLE DEVELOPMENT SOLUTIONS NETWORK (2020), https://www.unsdsn.org/Zero-Carbon-Action-Plan.

10 *See, e.g.,* NORMAN J. VIG AND MICHAEL E. KRAFT, ENVIRONMENTAL POLICY: NEW DIRECTIONS FOR THE TWENTY-FIRST CENTURY (2018); Daniel C. Esty, *Red Lights to Green Lights: From 20th Century Environmental Regulation to 21st Century Sustainability*, 47 ENVTL. LAW 1 (2017); RICHARD L. REVESZ AND MICHAEL A. LIVERMORE, REVIVING RATIONALITY: SAVING

has failed to act. Throughout this book, we have identified pathways forward beyond new statutes and in settings that do not require Congressional action. But the combination of pollution problems that remain unaddressed and the emergence of new issues and threats makes legal reform an urgent priority in the environmental domain.

We thus conclude with a simple thought: the future challenges us to develop new strategies and techniques to fulfill the promise of our first modern environmental statute, the National Environmental Policy Act, to guarantee everyone the right to a healthy environment.[11]

Additional resources

Esty, Daniel C. (ed.) (2019). *A Better Planet: 40 Big Ideas for a Sustainable Future.* New Haven, Connecticut: Yale University Press.

Esty, Daniel C. (2017). Red Lights to Green Lights: From 20th Century Environmental Regulation to 21st Century Sustainability. *Environmental Law 47*(1), 1–80. https://digitalcommons.law.yale.edu/cgi/viewcontent.cgi?article=6186&context=fss_papers.

Esty, Daniel C. and Cort, Todd (eds.) (2020). *Values at Work: Sustainable Investing and ESG Reporting.* London: Palgrave Macmillan.

Elliott, E. Donald (2010). U.S. Environmental Law in Global Perspective: Five Do's and Five Don'ts from Our Experience. *National Taiwan University Law Review 5*(2), 144–186. http://digitalcommons.law.yale.edu/fss_papers/2717.

Hawken, Paul (ed.). (2017). *Drawdown: The Most Comprehensive Plan Ever Proposed to Reverse Global Warming.* London: Penguin Books.

Rahm, Dianne (2019). *U.S. Environmental Policy: Domestic and Global Perspectives.* St. Paul, Minnesota: West Academic.

Revesz, Richard L. and Livermore, Michael A. (2011). *Retaking Rationality: How Cost-Benefit Analysis Can Better Protect the Environment and our Health.* Oxford: Oxford University Press.

Revesz, Richard L. and Livermore, Michael A. (2020). *Reviving Rationality: Saving Cost-Benefit Analysis for the Sake of the Environment and Our Health.* Oxford: Oxford University Press.

COST-BENEFIT ANALYSIS FOR THE SAKE OF THE ENVIRONMENT AND OUR HEALTH (2020); MARK TERCEK AND JONATHAN S. ADAMS, NATURE'S FORTUNE: HOW BUSINESS AND SOCIETY THRIVE BY INVESTING IN NATURE (2015); Richard Stewart, *A New Generation of Environmental Regulation?*, 29 CAP. U. L. REV. 1 (2001); *An OECD Framework for Effective and Efficient Environmental Policies*, OECD (2008), http://www.oecd.org/greengrowth/tools-evaluation/41644480.pdf; STEPHAN SCHMIDHEINY, CHANGING COURSE: A GLOBAL BUSINESS PERSPECTIVE ON DEVELOPMENT AND THE ENVIRONMENT (1992).

11 For a proposal by the present authors for the future of environmental law, see E. Donald Elliott and Daniel C. Esty, *The End Environmental Externalities Manifesto: A Rights-Based Foundation for Environmental Law*, NYU ENVTL. L.J. (forthcoming 2021), https://ssrn.com/abstract=3762022.

Smith, Zachary A. (2017). *The Environmental Policy Paradox* (7th ed.). Milton, Oxfordshire, United Kingdom: Routledge.

Vig, Norman J. and Kraft, Michael E. (2018). *Environmental Policy: New Directions for the Twenty-First Century.* Washington, D.C.: CQ Press.

Appendix: key Supreme Court environmental cases

Chapter 1

Auer v. Robbins, 519 U.S. 452 (1997) (deference to agency interpretations of their own regulations unless inconsistent with their language)

Kisor v. Wilkie, 139 S. Ct. 2400 (2019) (limiting deference to agency interpretations of their own regulations to instances in which the court has exhausted "traditional tools of interpretation" and competing interpretations are "in equipoise.")

Printz v. United States, 521 U.S. 898 (1997) (requiring states to implement background checks under the Brady Handgun Violence Prevention Act violated the Tenth Amendment to the United States Constitution)

New York v. United States, 505 U.S. 144 (1992) (federal government may not require states to pass laws managing nuclear waste because under the 10th Amendment, federal legislation may not "commandeer state governments into the service of federal regulatory purposes")

South Dakota v. Dole, 483 U.S. 203 (1987) (uphold cutting off federal highway funds to states that do not implement a drinking age of 21 because it has a logical nexus to the purpose of the federal funding)

United States v. Mead Corp., 533 U.S. 218 (2001) (agency interpretations of statutes by officials other than the head of an agency are entitled to lesser Skidmore deference based on their "power to persuade" rather than *Chevron* deference)

Motor Vehicle Mfrs. Ass'n v. State Farm Mut. Auto Ins. Co., 463 U.S. 29 (1983) (revocation or amendment of rules made via notice and comment requires another of notice and comment subject to judicial review to determine whether there is a rational basis for the changes)

Chevron v. NRDC, 467 U.S. 837 (1984) (courts must defer to agency interpretations of statutes over which an agency has been given interpretive authority if Congress did not decide the question and the agency's interpretation is reasonable)

Chapter 2

Michigan v. EPA, 576 U.S. 743 (2015) (consideration of cost and benefit was required under Clean Act provision requiring a "finding" that regulation was "necessary and appropriate")

Friends of the Earth, Inc. v. Laidlaw Environmental Services, Inc., 528 U.S. 167 (2000) (persons having a reasonable "concern" that a violation of Clean Water Act permit limits may harm their health have standing to sue to enforce the regulations)

American Electric Power Corp. v. Connecticut, 564 U.S. 410 (2011) (common law remedies for climate change are preempted by the comprehensive regulatory scheme under the Clean Air Act)

Monongahela Navigation Co. v. U.S., 148 U.S. 312 (1893) (*just compensation* requirement of the Constitution's Fifth Amendment Takings Clause is designed to prevent "the public from loading upon one individual more than his just share of the burdens of government")

Nollan v. California Coastal Comm'n, 483 U.S. 825 (1987) (Commission was required to demonstrate an "essential nexus" between its permit condition and a legitimate state interest)

Pennsylvania Coal Co. v. Mahon, 260 U.S. 393 (1922) (regulatory action constitutes a Fifth Amendment *taking* if the regulation "goes too far" by imposing disproportionate economic costs)

Loretto v. Teleprompter Manhattan CATV Corp., 458 U.S. 419 (1982) (installation of wires on private property by government mandate constituted a regulatory taking because it created a permanent physical occupation of the property regardless of public interest or only small economic impact)

Lucas v. South Carolina Coastal Council, 505 U.S. 1003 (1992) (regulations that deprive a property owner of all economically beneficial use of property constitute a regulatory taking)

Dolan v. City of Tigard, 512 U.S. 374 (1994) (permit condition must be "reasonably proportional" to the regulatory goal)

Penn Central Transportation Co. v. New York City, 438 U.S. 104 (1978) (upholding historic preservation of building façade against a regulatory taking claim based on weighing the economic impact on the property owner and the character of government action where other beneficial uses of the property continued to be allowed)

Palazzolo v. Rhode Island, 533 U.S. 606 (2001) (purchase of property after the enactment of a challenged regulation does not prevent a claim by the owner that the regulation constitutes an uncompensated taking)

Babbitt, Secretary of the Interior v. Sweet Home Chapter of Communities for a Great Oregon, 515 U.S. 687 (1995) (Secretary of the Interior reasonably defined "harm" as "significant habitat modification or degradation that actually kills or injures wildlife" within the definition of "take" under the Endangered Species Act)

Andrus v. Allard, 444 U.S. 51 (1979) (prohibition on sale of eagle feathers did not constitute an unconstitutional "taking" of private property without just compensation because other uses of the feathers were still permissible)

Chapter 3

Union Elec. Co. v. EPA, 427 U.S. 246 (1976) (EPA is not required to consider economic and technical infeasibility in setting National Ambient Air Quality Standards but states may do so in developing their State Implementation Plans)

Envt'l. Def. v. Duke Energy Corp., 549 U.S. 561 (2007) (term "modification" in the Clean Air Act may be interpreted differently in two of its programs, Prevention of Significant Deterioration and New Source Performance Standards)

EPA v. EME Homer City Generation, L.P., 572 U.S. 489 (2014) (upholding EPA's Cross State Air Pollution rule which permitted trading rather than setting facility-specific limits)

West Virginia v. EPA, 136 S.Ct. 1000 (2016) (granting a stay of the Clean Power Plan on grounds that challengers had likelihood of success on the merits)

Chapter 4

Massachusetts v. EPA, 549 U.S. 497 (2007) (states have standing to sue EPA and EPA's stated reasons for deciding that greenhouse gases were not a "pollutant" subject to regulation under the Clean Air Act were invalid)

American Electric Power v. Connecticut, 564 U.S. 410 (2011) (states may not sue corporations for their emission of greenhouse gases because the Clean Air Act delegates the decision to regulate to EPA)

Lujan v. Defenders of Wildlife, 504 U.S. 555 (1992) (plaintiffs failed to establish standing to sue under the Endangered Species Act because their alleged injury that they intended to observe endangered species in the future was too speculative and not individualized)

Friends of the Earth, Inc. v. Laidlaw Environmental Services, Inc., 528 U.S. 167 (2000) (persons "concerned" that a violation of Clean Water Act permit limits may harm their health have standing to sue to enforce the regulations)

Chapter 5

United States v. Riverside Bayview, 474 U.S. 121 (1985) (wetlands adjacent to navigable waters are subject to federal regulation)

Solid Waste Agency of Northern Cook County v. United States Army Corps of Engineers, 531 U.S. 159 (2001) (migratory birds nesting in wetlands provide an insufficient basis to subject wetlands to federal regulatory jurisdiction)

Rapanos v. United States, 547 U.S. 715 (2006) (divided 4-1-4 decision, holding EPA may regulate wetlands if they have a "significant nexus" to navigable waters)

Chapter 6

(None)

Chapter 7

Sackett v. EPA, 566 U.S. 120 (2012) (EPA's orders under the Clean Water Act not to build on property EPA considers a wetland are "final agency actions" subject to judicial review under the Administrative Procedure Act)

Burlington Northern & S. F. R. Co. v. United States, 556 U.S. 599 (2009) (liability as an "arranger for disposal" under CERCLA § 107(a)(3) requires an intentional act to dispose of waste and was not satisfied by incidental leaking of pesticide spills that were "a peripheral result of the legitimate sale of an unused, useful product")

Cooper Indus., Inc. v. Aviall Servs., Inc., 543 U.S. 157 (2004) (potentially responsible parties (PRPs) may sue for other PRPs contribution under § 107 of CERCLA only during or following a civil action)

United States v. Atl. Research Corp., 551 U.S. 128 (2007) (potentially responsible parties under CERCLA may sue other potentially responsible parties under § 113 of CERCLA for contribution toward the cost of cleaning up contaminated property)

Chapter 8

(None)

Chapter 9

Ruckelshaus v. Monsanto Co., 467 U.S. 986 (1984) (analysis of whether a taking has occurred is an "ad hoc" inquiry into the character of the government action, economic impact, and interference with investor-backed expectations)

Chapter 10

Indus. Union Dept., AFL-CIO v. Am. Petrol. Inst., 448 U.S. 607 (1980) (remanding the OSHA benzene standard for failure to find a "significant" risk to health)

Chapter 11

Exxon Shipping Co. v. Baker, 554 U.S. 471 (2008) (reducing punitive damage award from the *Exxon Valdez* oil spill)

Robbins Dry Dock & Repair Co. v. Flint, 275 U.S. 303 (1927) (no recovery for purely economic losses unless the plaintiff sustained physical damage to property in which she had a proprietary interest)

Chapter 12

TVA v. Hill, 437 U.S. 153 (1978) (halting construction of Tellico dam due to an endangered species, the snail darter)

Chapter 13

Sturgeon v. Frost, 139 S. Ct. 1066 (2019) (navigable waters in the Alaska are exempt from the National Park Service's regulations because the Alaska National Interest Lands Conservation Act defines them as "non-public")

Chapter 14

Metro. Edison Co. v. People Against Nuclear Energy, 460 U.S. 766 (1983) (Nuclear Regulatory Commission violated NEPA when it failed to consider in the environmental impact statement the possible psychological trauma to nearby residents of restarting the nuclear reactor at Three Mile Island following a previous accident than had emitted radioactive material)

Vermont Yankee Nuclear Power Corp. v. NRDC, 435 U.S. 519 (1978) ("NEPA does set forth significant substantive goals for the Nation, but its mandate to the agencies is essentially procedural")

Chapter 15

(None)

Chapter 16

(None)

Index

"This is an important contribution from two of our leading thinkers that lifts from the ponderous body of environmental law the key features that have animated progress in reducing the human toll on the environment. A go-to resource for anyone involved in building our environmental future."

Scott Fulton, President, Environmental Law Institute and former General Counsel, U.S. Environmental Protection Agency

"This book is an extraordinary resource for anyone wanting a sophisticated overview of a field that is both enormously complex and extremely important. Yale Professors E. Donald Elliott and Daniel C. Esty bring to this project their extraordinary experiences as leading academics and former high-ranking government officials. The book is both highly sophisticated and easily readable and should be of interest to broad audiences, ranging from graduate and professional students to practitioners."

Richard L. Revesz, AnBryce Professor of Law and Dean Emeritus, New York University School of Law, USA

"Advanced Introduction to U.S. Environmental Law lives up to its title. This sophisticated analysis will satisfy advanced readers and the detailed explanations regarding how regulation actually works will be useful to beginners and experts alike."

Seth D. Jaffe, Partner, Foley Hoag LLP and Past President, American College of Environmental Lawyers

"Don Elliott and Dan Esty seamlessly weave legal, political, scientific, and economic insights together as they highlight the successes and the failures of the U.S. environmental regulatory system. The book brings readers up to speed on decades of regulation under important statutes and identifies the challenges that future regulation must overcome. The treatment is comprehensive, nuanced, and pragmatic; written in a way that's accessible to anyone interested in environmental law. I look forward to using the book in my environmental law course as supplemental reading and to introducing students to key issues in statutes that we don't cover in detail."

Caroline Cecot, Professor, Antonin Scalia Law School, George Mason University, USA

Titles in the **Elgar Advanced Introductions** series include:

International Political Economy
Benjamin J. Cohen

The Austrian School of Economics
Randall G. Holcombe

Cultural Economics
Ruth Towse

Law and Development
Michael J. Trebilcock and Mariana Mota Prado

International Humanitarian Law
Robert Kolb

International Trade Law
Michael J. Trebilcock

Post Keynesian Economics
J.E. King

International Intellectual Property
Susy Frankel and Daniel J. Gervais

Public Management and Administration
Christopher Pollitt

Organised Crime
Leslie Holmes

Nationalism
Liah Greenfeld

Social Policy
Daniel Béland and Rianne Mahon

Globalisation
Jonathan Michie

Entrepreneurial Finance
Hans Landström

International Conflict and Security Law
Nigel D. White

Comparative Constitutional Law
Mark Tushnet

International Human Rights Law
Dinah L. Shelton

Entrepreneurship
Robert D. Hisrich

International Tax Law
Reuven S. Avi-Yonah

Public Policy
B. Guy Peters

The Law of International Organizations
Jan Klabbers

International Environmental Law
Ellen Hey

International Sales Law
Clayton P. Gillette

Corporate Venturing
Robert D. Hisrich

Public Choice
Randall G. Holcombe

Private Law
Jan M. Smits

Consumer Behavior Analysis
Gordon Foxall

Behavioral Economics
John F. Tomer

Cost-Benefit Analysis
Robert J. Brent

Environmental Impact Assessment
Angus Morrison-Saunders

Migration Studies
Ronald Skeldon

Landmark Criminal Cases
George P. Fletcher

Comparative Legal Methods
Pier Giuseppe Monateri

U.S. Environmental Law
E. Donald Elliott and Daniel C. Esty